Investec provides a diverse rang
services to a niche client base in
South Africa and Australia.

We focus on delivering distinctive profitable solutic
namely Asset Management, Wealth & Investment a

Our strategic goals and objectives are based on the ⸻ a distinctive
specialist bank and asset manager. This distinction ⸻ uur entrepreneurial spirit which
is balanced by a strong risk management discipline, client centric approach and an ability to be
nimble, flexible and innovative. We do not seek to be all things to all people and aim to build well-
defined, value added businesses focused on serving the needs of select market niches where we
can compete effectively.

Our core offering comprises:

- Asset Management, which provides investment management services to third party institutions, clients and intermediated savers.

- Wealth & Investment, which provides investment management services and independent financial planning advice.

- Specialised Banking, which offers a broad range of services from advisory structuring, lending, transactional banking, treasury and trading and investment activities. These services are aimed at government, institutional, corporate and high net worth and high income clients.

Our Manchester office is in an ideal, central location to provide an entrepreneurial, diverse and an
innovative service to customers and local residents. It is a vibrant city full of culture and heritage.

We are delighted to sponsor this guide and hope you use it to take pleasure from your experience
of the city with increased knowledge, insight and involvement in the great amount of activities and
attractions which it has to offer.

Enjoy Manchester

Out of the Ordinary®

Investec
Private Bank

Editor and writer:
Jonathan Schofield

Designed by: inkYolk Creative
Media Solutions (enquiries@inkYolk.
com)

Publisher: Margaret Hope,
Manchester Books Limited

Thanks to: Jacob McCarthy
Schofield, Oliver McCarthy
Schofield, Ralph McCarthy
Schofield; ManchesterConfidential.
co.uk writing team for help with
the food and drink section; Mark
Eaton for help in compiling the
quotes; Mike Sheehy for serving
much needed hot chocolate to
the grouchy designer, and Thomas
Sheehy for being very grown-up
about missing his bedtime story;
Matthew Frost for Matthewing;
Emma Golpys for photo sourcing.
For the gentleman who tweeted
me the picture on pages 80-81 and
whose name I lost, lunch for two on
us. Also R Haworth, D Humphreys,
Nadine Mansfield, Emma Mansfield,
B Schofield, D Liff for Wikimedia
images. And Manchester City
Council for Manchester Day images,
Manchester Cathedral for Cathedral
images and Manchester Central for
their images.

Special thanks to: Sharon McCarthy
for being a guiding light.

Cover images clockwise from top:
Chetham's, Spinningfields, Town
Hall, Whitworth Park, Manchester
House, Central Library.

Backcover images from top:
Deansgate, Timber Wharf, Dig the
City, City view, Adrift by Cassidy,
Town Hall Extension, Northern
Quarter.

For Doreen McCarthy and John
Schofield for their strong character
and wonderful influence.

CONTENTS

Welcome to this guide to Manchester. It covers all the main aspects of Manchester life and we hope it surprises and delights in equal measure while delivering a faithful reflection of this dynamic, eccentric, fascinating city.

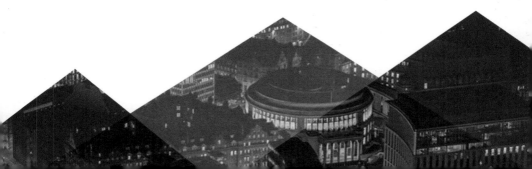

A Month of Activity in MANCHESTER

This list of 31 activities isn't in priority order, some people may prefer visiting a museum to sipping a local beer or watching City or United to either. But certainly take one of the City Walks on p80 and get to know the soul of the city through the soles of your shoes.

1. Take a tour around **Manchester Town Hall** to view the Great Hall Murals of Ford Madox Brown or take in a Pre-Raphaelite picture at **Manchester Art Gallery.**

2. Visit **Cloud 23** for a view round the 2.7m strong metropolis of Greater Manchester.

3. Listen to some live music in **Band on the Wall** or **Night and Day.**

4. Root around shopping bazaar **Afflecks Palace.**

5. Go all haute couture at **Harvey Nichols.**

6. Buy some hand-made shoes at **Edwards**, the oldest retailer in Manchester from 1830.

7. Take a bus down **Oxford Road**, through the biggest university campus in the UK, to Curry Mile and Rusholme.

8. Dream to the **Manchester Cathedral** choir in the best medieval chancel in the North of England.

9. View the table in the fifteenth century building of **Chetham's Library** where Benjamin Disraeli (and Karl Marx) studied.

10. Catch a gig at the beautiful **Albert Hall** on Peter Street.

11. Drink a pint of local ale in the **Marble Arch Pub** or **The Briton's Protection.**

12. Be Blue or Red at the **Etihad** or **Old Trafford**, go dog-racing at **Belle Vue** or watch cricket at **Old Trafford** or rugby at the **AJ Bell Stadium.**

13. Take a taster cycling session around

the Olympic Track at the **National Cycling Centre.**

14. Join a debate or a reading at the **Portico Library.**

15. Indulge in a glass of wine at **Salut.**

16. Take in a classical concert at **The Bridgewater Hall** or the **RNCM.**

17. Scale the heights at **Manchester Climbing Centre** or fly downhill at **Chill Factore** indoor ski slope.

18. Take the spectacular circular walk across the Ship Canal at Salford Quays past **MediaCityUK**, **The Lowry** and **The Imperial War Museum North.**

19. Take in some jazz at **Matt and Phreds** or have a laugh at the **Comedy Store** or the **Frog and Bucket.**

20. Buy something unique at **Manchester Craft and Design Centre.**

21. Drink with the trendies till the early hours in **Fitzgeralds.**

22. Fine dine at **The French** or **Manchester House** or stuff a burger in your face at **Almost Famous** or **Solita.**

23. Glam up and show off in **Australasia** or spot a footballer in **San Carlo Restaurant.**

24. Take an afternoon tea at **Propertea.**

25. Take an excursion to **Dunham Massey Deer Park** for a country stroll or take a walk on the moors above **Ramsbottom**

26. Stroll along boho **Beech Road** in Chorlton or equally boho **Burton Road** and **Lapwing Lane** in West Didsbury.

27. Be blown away by one of the top ten collections of books and manuscripts in the world in **John Rylands Library**

28. Stroke a huge steam engine in the **Museum of Science and Industry**

29. Cheekily tap the table for the weird acoustics in the **Wolfson Reading Room** at Central Library, or just relax and read.

30. Join a **guided tour** of the city centre and learn the inside story, maybe be even scream along to the **Haunted Underworld** tour

31. Dance the night away with tickets for the **Warehouse Party** crew in some dark undercroft somewhere.

MANCHESTER TODAY
City politics

Politics in Manchester has never been so meaningless and so important.

In May 2014 council election results gave the Labour Party in Manchester all the seats in the council chamber, all 96. It seems, as the expression goes, if you put a red rosette on a monkey in the city it'll be elected. So if a Labour victory is inevitable why bother voting? Surely politics has become meaningless in the city?

Then, in November 2014, the Conservative Chancellor of the Exchequer, George Osborne, announced he was going to devolve powers to Greater Manchester Combined Authority (p11). So in 2017 elections will be held for a regional mayor on the London model taking in the whole metropolitan area of 2.7m people. Decisions will soon be taken at a macro level on transport, planning, housing, skills, training and policing rather than piecemeal within the jigsaw of local authorities.

Politics is reborn, but at a more rational regional level. This is the biggest political news regionally since before WWII. As Sir Richard Leese, the Manchester council leader, said: "Greater Manchester has been in the vanguard of the national devolution debate. It was clear that an over-centralised national system was not delivering the best results for our people or our economy. We are extremely pleased that we can now demonstrate what a city region with greater freedoms can achieve and contribute further to the growth of the UK."

Greater Manchester has been singled out for this treatment ahead of other cities because it has demonstrated a willingness to pull together and show vision. This is partly down to that one party security of tenure in the main administration of the region. With an overwhelming council majority and now a complete redwash of seats, the administration of the city of Manchester can make long term strategic decisions without fear of them being overturned because no other party will replace Labour.

Economics, the good and the ugly

There was more good news from the government in 2014 with again the Chancellor referring to Manchester as the centre of a 'Northern Powerhouse' and grand talk of HS2 and HS3. These are the proposed high speed rail links between, respectively, Manchester and London, and across the north through Manchester.

Private enterprise has joined the mood of post-recession buoyancy with major city centre schemes such as Allied London's St John's Quarter and the Cooperative's NOMA. In the south of the city the proposed Airport City was given a boost when during a trade mission to China a partnership worth £800m was announced with Beijing Construction Engineering Group set to create 16,000 jobs.

Meanwhile local developer Peel Group has delivered schemes such as MediaCityUK bringing more than 2,000 BBC jobs to Greater Manchester. Conventions and exhibitions at Manchester Central have performed well.

One element of investment has surprised everybody; that of a football club. Not only has Manchester City, through the Anglo Arabic holding company, Abu Dhabi United Group, set about winning trophies and extending the stadium to more than 62,000 seats but also built a 'campus' linked to the main Etihad stadium worth more than £200m with its own 7,000 capacity reserve ground, 16 pitches, an accommodation block and a sixth-form college for the local community.

Abu Dhabi United then announced a £1bn partnership with Manchester City Council to build 6,000 homes for rent between the city centre and the Etihad Stadium. Never has a football club moved so far from its core activity.

Manchester Central

Higher education has pumped millions of pounds into the economy too. In 2014/15 the so-called 'knowledge corridor' along Oxford Road made up of the University of Manchester, Manchester Metropolitan University and other institutions, is set to bring in £400m of investment, providing scientific, health, educational and cultural facilities. These will include the National Graphene Institute worth £61m. The world's thinnest material is bringing fat material gains.

All good news - resulting in Manchester's ranking in the top sixteen of European cities in which to start a business and to live, one of the few non-capital cities.

But the positives have to be viewed with the negatives. The evident progress and wealth can mask the desperate conditions, particularly in the north and east. There are tens of thousands of people, established and recent immigrants, who feel excluded from any upswing, trapped in areas with some of the worst indices of health, well-being and employment in the country.

By some measures the city of Manchester is the 4th most deprived local council in England – a situation not helped by the city falling victim to some of the harshest funding cuts as the government attempts to balance the UK books. It's typical of this contrary region, that while unemployment rates in the city are stuck around 11% (regionally 8%), Greater Manchester is said to be home to more multi-mil-

lionaires than anywhere outside London. Occasionally it seems the divide between rich, comfortable and poor is as wide as it was in the 19th century, although the experience of poverty might be very different. A few kilometres south west of the city of Manchester is the Tatton constituency which records the highest average UK income outside the south-east.

Kenneth Branagh's Macbeth production, at MIF 2013

Regained Confidence

Still Manchester has changed hugely, especially in its central areas, especially in its confidence. Clever initiatives such as Manchester International Festival (MIF) have helped, a biennial showpiece of new ideas in art and culture reflecting the pioneering heritage of the city demonstrated on pages 74-77.

Certainly a walk across the city centre today reveals a city more open and accessible and enlivened with new buildings and squares yet with easy access to countryside and outer districts. The central area has become more and more popular as a place to live reversing a hundred years of English suburban sensibility: some city centre apartments, despite the downturn of 2007/8, are being sold for well-over £1m.

A recent report stated, 'Manchester has been at the cutting edge of innovation over the last years. It is a model for a city with a great past, combining traditional and revolutionary architecture, giving its citizens a fine and stimulating environment for work and leisure.'

These words need to apply to many more of its citizens before Manchester can take things for granted, but the underlying confidence is welcome. It's rewarding the parochial attitude of previous decades, during years of industrial decline, has been thrown aside in favour of thinking big. Manchester has once more begun to conceive on a grand scale: it is beginning to live up to the expansionist liberal tradition that made it one of the global players.

People are now waiting to see what the new elected mayor and a more holistic approach to local governance can deliver.

Christmas Markets

Greater Manchester

Greater Manchester covers 1,277 km2 (493 sq miles). It lies mainly to the north of the River Mersey and mainly in the south east corner of what was formerly part of the county of Lancashire although it contains chunks of Cheshire and Yorkshire as well. It was created in 1974.

Manchester is the largest borough of the ten boroughs of Greater Manchester. It has a population of just over half a million. These figures are misleading though. Many of the areas just over the border from the city in places such as Prestwich, Stretford, Failsworth, Denton and Middleton have much more in common with the city than with the administrative boroughs they find themselves within and consider them-selves Mancunian.

Salford's a special case. It's an irrational quirk of history that the two cities, sepa-rated by less than 20m (65ft) of the River Irwell, have never formally merged. For Salfordians 'going into Town' means going into Manchester. As far back as the early 19th century Manchester writer Thomas de Quincy (author of *Confessions of an English Opium Eater*) said of Salford, it is 'a quarter of Manchester as regards inter-course and reciprocal influence'. Not much has changed.

For the further towns such as Bolton, Wigan, Oldham, Rochdale and Stockport their relationship with Manchester has often been uneasy. They are fiercely inde-pendent, and to many of their populations, the city can seem alien. Indeed, the harder, quicker, more ethnically influenced Manchester accent is very different from the slower, deeper accents on each side.

Still the situation is fluid. The smaller Greater Manchester towns have had much of the life of their centres hollowed out as the city centre has grown back to its pre-WWII pre-eminence and shopping and leisure patterns have shifted. Now it appears under the Greater Manchester

The River Irwell dividing Salford on the left and Manchester on the right

Combined Authority, for the first time for more than a century the smaller towns are prepared to accept Manchester's dominance. How far that will change when Greater Manchester gains an elected mayor in 2017 remains to be seen.

Manchester Population

Greater Manchester boroughs at the census, 2011, with population variance since 2001.

Manchester	503,100	+19%
Salford	233,900	+7.8%
Bolton	276,800	+5.9%
Bury	185,100	+2.4%
Rochdale	211,700	+2.6%
Oldham	224,900	+2.9%
Tameside	219,300	+2.6%
Stockport	283,300	-0.5%
Trafford	226,600	+7.8%
Wigan	317,800	+5.4%

Total GM population at 2011 census: 2,682,500 (2001: 2,516,200) +6.6%

Melting Pot Manchester

Manchester is defined by immigration. Perhaps more than any other UK city, apart from the capital, it is composed of layers of incomers some generations old and some first generation.

The first wave came during the early part of the 19th century when Manchester attracted people from all across the United Kingdom and Ireland for work in the rapidly expanding industries. This period also marks out Manchester (and London and Liverpool) as different from other cities. The two Lancashire metropolises looked across the world to do business, the port of Liverpool - and later the Port of Manchester - the point of access to a global trade. Through this many immigrants to the city were wealthy drawn by the potential of increasing their fortunes. It was largely businessmen of German origin, for instance, who bank-rolled the Hallé Orchestra in its developing years.

The second period in the later nineteenth century is made up of overseas working class immigration into Manchester. The main elements in this were Irish again plus Jewish East Europeans escaping the pogroms and Italians escaping poverty.

The third main period is post World War Two, first of refugees from Europe particularly Polish, Ukrainian and Yugoslavian fleeing the Soviets, then of peoples from the ex-colonies of the British Empire. From the fifties onwards Manchester began to receive significant populations of Afro-Carribbean, Pakistani (and subsequently Bangladeshi) and Indian people. There was also a significant increase in first generation Irish escaping a lack of opportunity. A little later a Cantonese population arrived plus Somalian refugees. In the last decade large numbers of East Europeans, particularly Polish, have formed city communities as European Union regulations have relaxed. There has been a notable increase in peoples from China and especially Afghanistan, Iraq and Iran. Immigration has accounted in large measure to recent rises in population.

This gives intelligent Mancunians an open world view. Manchester has never had anything approaching the class-defined establishment often recruited from the public schools of the nation as London has. Manchester has been an immigrant city but those immigrants have helped build the place from the top down as much from the bottom up. It's the mix of local and incomer that makes it tick – the current population is over 30% non-white. Manchester is still, of course, very British, even Lancastrian, but it's also a city forced by the way it developed to look out to the greater world.

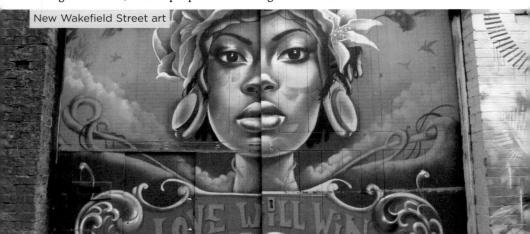

New Wakefield Street art

Places to Visit

The mighty gable of the Town Hall Extension
viewed through the portico of Central Library.

Manchester Town Hall

Albert Square, City centre, 0161 234 1892. Free. Walk One, Page 81.

Opening times are generally Mon-Fri 9am-4.30pm but the Town Hall is a working building so hours are unpredicatable, ring ahead or try your luck. It's best to join a tour. Call 07505 685942 or check out the Manchester Guided Tours website.

Completed in 1877, this Alfred Waterhouse building is also Manchester's greatest monument. For many, it is a candidate for the Victorian building *par excellence* – the whole age summed up in one: the extravagance, the energy, the self-belief and the achievement. At the opening banquet, MP John Bright described the way the city felt about the new building: 'With regard to this edifice, it is truly a municipal palace. Whether you look at the proportions outside or the internal decorations... there is nothing like it... in any part of Europe.'

The first-time visitor coming into Albert Square from Cross Street or Lloyd Street might well agree. A cliff of ornate Gothic stonework drags the eyes upward to the giant clock tower above – the minute hand is 3m (10ft) in length and the spire 85m (288m) above ground level.

Architect Alfred Waterhouse's favourite view of the Town Hall

On the top of the spire is a golden ball with spikes symbolising a cotton bud about to burst, but also the sun, for wherever the sun shone Manchester had business. The roofline is a wonderland of pinnacles, gables, chimneys and metalwork.

The city is in some ways lucky to have the building. In the competition judged on St Valentine's Day 1868, Alfred Waterhouse's design ranked only fourth in terms of appearance, but was superior to the others in its practical use of the awkward triangular site and the best in its handling of light, access and ventilation. The biggest problem was the tower. Waterhouse redesigned it several times until he hit upon a solution. He still wasn't happy and six years into construction as the Town Hall neared completion, he suspended work. He called the building committee together and explained that the proportions were still wrong and the tower needed to be 5m (16ft) higher. They agreed. On three sides over the clocks picked out in gold are words taken from the Bible, 'Teach us to number our days'. In other words don't waste your time on this earth.

The style chosen for the Town Hall was Gothic from the 13th century – a style called Early English and seen as patriotic. Gothic was also intended to form a link with the medieval trader cities of the Hanseatic League and of the Low Countries, from where legend said

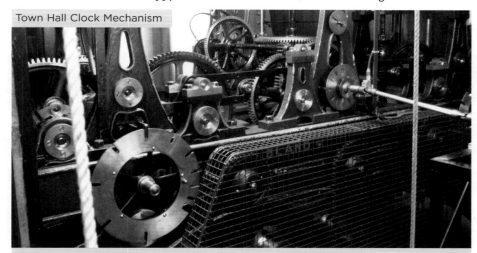

Town Hall Clock Mechanism

Town Hall Clock

If the clock tower tours are running get on one. There are many joys to experience including the clock mechanism: a phantasmagoria of immense brass wheels with clunky levers and gears clicking and whirring. Higher again is the chamber behind the clock faces, with the hour and minute hands silhouetted against the sky. On the balcony above, despite all the fancy detail, the gargoyles, the curlicues and finials, there's no more solid space in Manchester. This was one of the key qualities of Alfred Waterhouse. He could do fancy when required but his talent lay in solidity, making buildings that feel as though they will never fall down. When you're 200ft up, that's a valuable quality. You access the hour bell chamber from the balcony. Great Abel is inside. The hour bell is named after businessmen, political radical and the Mayor of Manchester at the time of opening. It's bigger than a generous three-man tent. Cast round the top are lines from Alfred Lord Tennyson's poem *In Memoriam*. They read 'Ring out the false, ring in the true.'

Manchester's textile roots had sprung. Manchester was being fashionable too, adopting the in-vogue Gothic style in conscious contrast with the Classical style favoured by Liverpool.

The celebrations for the opening in September 1877 extended over several days, and included a procession of cavalry and infantry, police force and fire brigades, a banquet, a ball and a gathering of over 40,000 local working men with examples of their crafts. The United Flint Glass Cutters created glass swords, a surviving example of which was returned to the Town Hall in November 2014. The outpouring of feeling was reinforced by the fact the city was desperate for a new Town Hall. Manchester by 1877 had become a city state. It controlled the local administration, the gas, the water, the police, the education, the parks and roads, and it was rich. The full construction cost of over £1m was met by the rate-payers.

If you feel the Town Hall looks familiar, it may be because it's the TV and movie body double for the Palace of Westminster (Houses of Parliament) in London. It's featured in the original *House of Cards* in the 1990s, in *Sherlock Holmes* the movie in 2008 and in the film about Margaret Thatcher, *The Iron Lady*. The place also helped a well-known architect develop his career. During lunchtime breaks from work in the City Treasurer's department, Norman Foster, now Sir Norman, would tramp the corridors sketching the building. The Town Hall is still the focus for civic events and remains the political and administrative centre of the city. See pages 10-12 for more on the political picture.

Town Hall, The Great Hall

A Self-Guided Town Hall Tour

Before entering, take a walk around the building to get a full idea of its size and its ingenuity. All four sides are different, each with varied treatments of stonework and statuary.

❶ Statues of key characters

On the corner of Princess Street and Albert Square, statues of key characters from the city's history stare down at passers-by.

Waterhouse cleverly placed a statue of General Agricola, the Roman who founded Manchester in 79AD, over the main doorway. Enter here and you find yourself walking directly under the great tower and a ceiling decorated with the Royal Coat of Arms. This is a disguised trapdoor through which the bells of the Town Hall can be raised or lowered.

❷ Manchester's Scientists

On each side is a statue commemorating two of the city's most important scientists: John Dalton, atomic theory, colour blindness and meteorology, and James Prescott Joule, physics. The main entrance chamber lies to the right and is now the Sculpture Hall with works commemorating famous people or events.

❸ Stylised Constellations

Take the staircase to the right of the reception desk. As you climb the stairs, notice the stylised constellations above.

❹ Symbolism

Aside from the practical aspect of providing a focus for the city administration, the Town Hall was intended to be a unified piece of

art. Architecture, fine arts, sculpture and music were brought together amidst a mass of symbolism. Throughout, the visitor will spot cotton flowers and bees the latter a symbol of Manchester's industrious hardworking personality. For instance, on the landing at the top of the stairs, there is a simple pattern in mosaic of bees and cotton flowers.

❺ The Great Hall

Push open the wooden doors to your right here and enter the Great Hall (for picture see page 16), which John Ruskin called 'the most truly magnificent Gothic apartment in Europe'.

Above, in the panels of the great hammerbeam roof, there are richly gilded coats of arms of the nations with which Manchester traded, including the USA, Russia, India and China.

❻ Murals by Ford Madox Brown

On the walls are the famous 12 murals (1879-1893) by Ford Madox Brown, the celebrated Pre-Raphaelite artist, illustrating episodes in Manchester's history. The last to be finished was 'Bradshaw's Defence of Manchester AD 1642' in the English Civil War. This was painted with the artist's left hand after Brown had suffered a stroke. Not that the viewer can tell. The most entertaining is the picture that depicts the opening of the Bridgewater Canal with two chunky infants sat on a canal barge.

Banqueting Room

Reception Room

❶

❼

Entrance

❸

❽

❹

Inner Courtyards

❷

❺❻ Great Hall

Organ Chamber

❽

ALBERT SQUARE

❽

PRINCESS STREET

COOPER STREET

Mayor's Parlour

LLOYD STREET

Council Chamber

Bridge to Town Hall Extension

Commitee Rooms

● Ground Floor
● First Floor
● External

❼State Rooms

Opposite the Great Hall are the elaborate main staterooms. These are saturated with all the decoration and detail the High Victorians adored. They are all worth visiting, but perhaps the two most impressive are at either end. The present Conference Hall was originally the Council Chamber. It contains a vast Gothic chimney piece, the Lord Mayor's chair, an oak screen and carefully wrought-iron galleries for the press and public. The Banqueting Hall has a fine minstrels' gallery and original curtains from the Royal School of Art Needlework, South Kensington.

❽Inner Courtyards

If, on a visit, you pause to look into the inner courtyards (8), you will also gain

a vision of Manchester in its industrial glory and grime. The stonework has never been cleaned and is black – coated in soot spewed from numberless chimneys.

Town Hall Extension

Lloyd Street, City centre. Free. Walk One page 81.

Rates Hall open most days, enquire about access to the Council Chamber and Ante Room at the desk.

Manchester in the Depression-hit 1930s was clear of one thing: it is a council's duty to make citizens proud. You can see this in the Town Hall Extension and the Central Library. Emmanuel Vincent Harris, the architect of both, was given enough funds to not only complete the buildings but also to create assertive, exciting, civic spaces. The project to build the Town Hall Extension (completed in 1938) and Central Library (completed in 1934) was tagged 'the really big thing' in UK architectural circles and the results were called 'a good deed in a depressing world'.

The Rates Hall in the Town Hall Extension is one of best chambers in the country from the 1930s. The curve of the space as it enfolds Central Library, the use of polychromatic marbles, the lofty doors, the exceptional light fittings, the splendid

The Rates Hall

coats of arms (see page 207), the light casting shadows from tall windows, the repeated pattern of arches on each side impresses the viewer with its power but also its feeling of 'rightness'. If you are designing a space to reflect civic authority, dignity and duty you can't do better than this: a room full of symbolism, a representation of the bigger idea, of shared identity for rich and poor, a common purpose.

The same goes for the Council Chamber higher in the building with its great walnut desks for the councillors. More intriguing is the Ante Room where councillors gather before entering the chamber. This has a dramatic Art Deco interior. Note the studded leather doors like a 1930s Hollywood set of the Alhambra.

Externally the Town Hall Extension links with the Town Hall with a series of elegant bridges over Lloyd Street. On Mount Street, the building has an Elizabethan feel, facing St Peter's Square the only ornament on the towering and sheer wall is provided by simple window apertures and an elegant arcade. The immense gable ends carved with a grille of shields and vast crawling designs of roses, thistles and shamrocks - the symbols of Great Britain's component parts (see page 13) are very dramatic.

Council Chamber

Ante Room Door

The Royal Exchange

St Ann's Square, City centre, M2 7DH, 0161 833 9833. Free. Walk one p93.

Mon-Sun but theatrical performances may limit entry.

This is the city's emblematic building, the first of which was erected in 1729. Manchester was created not through royal favour, church patronage nor military significance but through trade. Cotton, and the businesses surrounding the production of cotton, made it important. Its ability to build upon cotton dominance and diversify kept it important for decades.

The Exchange cemented the influence of cotton and other textiles by becoming the industry's head office complete with trading floor. It was just as effective as a talking shop, for merchants to discuss what was happening in cotton across the world and at home, what the trends were, who was up and who was down. By the late nineteenth century it controlled 80% of the world's finished cotton trade.

The fourth rebuilding of 1874 was extended during WW I in the neo-classical style. Round the inside of the main dome are the words, 'Who would find eternal treasure, must use no guile in weight or measure'. Around the doubled hall were ten

1961 Royal Exchange Membership card

Royal Exchange from the bottom up

floors which included 250 offices, 38 shops, six restaurants and a Post Office. It was, by far, the largest place of assembly for traders of any kind in the world. The architects were Bradshaw, Gass and Hope.

During boom times the whole room would be filled with an international gathering on the 'Change days of Tuesday and Friday. Members would occupy a position indicated by the intersection of letters and numbers, like a map reference. Thus the textile machinery company of J&H Schofield Limited would meet at J2. Business would spill out onto the streets

🏛 Royal Exchange

On the 'Change

This picture shows a packed day at the Royal Exchange in the 1920s. During the same period, HV Morton, in the Daily Express, followed a trader as he moved through the crowd.

As I look down with a feint Olympic feeling from the Strangers' Gallery I try to follow one little man through his adventures on the floor. I see him moving through the monster, a part of it, yet to me the most important part of it because I am thinking of him as an individual and I watch him stop at various groups, edge his way, say his little bit and move on, watching, searching, trying to make money, and the whole thing so casual, so removed from roll-top desks and all the paraphernalia of the business.

He stops to make a joke. Someone tells him a joke that makes him laugh just a little bit too much. He is anxious to please. Now he looks grave, and rubs his chin with his little hand and shakes his little head. Did someone try to sell him a pup? Sometimes a man comes to him or rather seems swept up against him in the chaos, and they bring out notebooks and look solemn. They have booked an order. He is, I am sure, having a good day. He is a cheerful little man. I watch him tell the same story time after time in different groups. Often I see him standing politely waiting until a conversation ends before he introduces himself. 'Change is the only place in Manchester where a man will not butt into a conversation, no matter how much he wants to. It is not done.

And the little man, just as I am beginning to like him, just as I begin to hope that he is kind to his wife and always takes her home presents, when his pencil has been busy on 'Change, goes and loses himself in the rather grim impersonality of the monster. And the voice of cotton goes on and on and on...'

and into the neighbouring cafés and pubs. The hotels were filled with merchants from across the globe. It was exciting and with a worldwide membership of 11,000, must have seemed indestructible.

But the clouds were gathering over the Lancashire cotton industry, other countries were catching up particularly Japan. Trade fell and during WWII the bombs fell. The Royal Exchange was severely damaged. Rebuilding took 13 years, and the hall size was reduced by almost half. But the fatal blow was delivered by the growth of the industry in countries that produced the raw material, frequently with cheaper labour costs. It soon became clear that the Exchange was no longer viable, and when the doors closed on 31 December 1968, 249 years of history closed with them.

The city was faced with the dilemma of what to do with the building. The shops and offices around the shell produced good rents, but the central hall had lost its function. But then a theatre group occupied the hall. Campaigns were launched and, after a long battle, Sir Laurence Olivier on 15 September 1976 announced "I declare this theatre... open!" It has been a success ever since, acclaimed for its range of productions, its talented actors, and for the excellence and immediacy of its in-the-round auditorium. The design is a bold response to the potentially overwhelmingly classical space around it. High tech and powerful, like a Pompidou Centre or a lunar module, it nestles under the great dome. The design was the work of Richard Negri with Levitt Bernstein Associates, the steel elements made by foundries building Britain's North Sea oil rigs.

The bombs returned with the IRA attack in June 1996. Two years and £30m later, the building reopened after repairs and improvements. The theatre was enlarged to take over 750 people and a studio theatre for 150 was created. The eating and drinking facilities were also extended, and purpose-built space pro-

vided for the bookshop and the crafts centre. Meanwhile, the upper reaches of the hall, which had been obscured under decades of dust and dirt, were lightened and revealed. Of particular note are the columns with their golden capitals and the glass panels by Amber Hiscott, representing textiles in a variety of shades. Look out for the former trading board close to the ceiling on the west side of the room.

The best way to view the hall is by taking the stairs on the south side of either entrance and strolling the post-1996 balcony.

Royal Exchange, theatre and domes

Manchester Cathedral

Victoria Street, City centre, M3 1SX, 0161 833 2220. Free. Walk one, p103.

Open daily from 8.30am, but services may mean some parts of the Cathedral can't be visited. There are tour guides always available. There's a suggested donation at the entrance to help with building mainte-nance.

Manchester Cathedral has been at the centre of Manchester life for over a thousand years. It remains so today and while daily religious life continues has added a further element by hosting gigs from artists such as Alicia Keys, Elbow and Fun Lovin' Criminals. This is a return to tradition rather than a break with it, as in earlier times the nave of the building being the largest stone built structure in the town would have hosted much of the public life of Manchester. Look out for regular shows from visiting artists as well as readings, theatrical performances and classical concerts. For an atmospheric and beautiful break from city life try and catch Evensong.

The present Cathedral is mostly the product of the last 600 years. It has a very complicated dedication to St Mary the Virgin, St Denys and St George. This dates from 1421 when the parish church was raised in status to that of Collegiate Church - one with greater rights and a college of one warden and eight priests. St Denys is the patron saint of France and is included because, according to one story, the King wanted his claim to the French throne recognised. In 1421 the monarch was Henry V and he'd beaten the French at Agincourt.

The expanded building was to be a chantry college where masses were said to speed the souls of the rich to Paradise. In other words, it would earn good cash and attract patronage as well as being the spiritual fountain for a 100 sq km, (60 sq mile) parish. This is why Manchester Cathedral can now claim to have the widest nave of any cathedral in the UK. The chantry chapels for various families were built against the walls. These have been removed, leaving an uninterrupted space from wall to wall wider than any other: indeed the nave width is two thirds the length of the building. Joseph Crowther, the 19th century architect who restored the church, described the nave as "arch behind arch, pier behind pier... posess-ing one of those features which so fascinate the visitors to the Arabian Mosques."

In the early 1500s, the quire was erected, which with the ceilings, reveal some of the finest late medi-eval wood carving in the north of England. The style of architecture in the church is called Perpendicular, which is unique to England and is notable for its strong vertical lines in windows and piers.

The dragon is the devil in the quire

The Quire

The West Front was massively reconstructed for Queen Victoria's Diamond Jubilee in 1897 by architect Basil Champneys who also designed John Rylands Library in the city. The Collegiate Church had been formally recognised as Manchester Cathedral in 1847.

The 19th century stained glass which had darkened the interior was blasted out on Sunday 22 December 1940 when the Cathedral received direct hits from German bombs. The windows acted as a safety valve and as they shattered, helped release the pressure of the blast. Partly because of this, most of the main structure of the Cathedral and miraculously, the woodwork, were preserved. The post-WWII stained glass represents the best of the new decoration in the Cathedral.

The bomb landed in the Regimental Chapel of the Manchester Regiment. In the Books of Remembrance lining the walls is the name of one of the last casualties of WWI: the poet Wilfred Owen, who is also commemorated by a brass plaque in the Chapel.

Looking around

Start a tour of the Cathedral by standing in the nave and looking up. The ceiling is oak and beautiful. The beams supporting the ceilings terminate in a consort of angels – a heavenly choir with, amongst others, dulcimer, harp, bagpipes and lute. These date from the late 1400s when it was thought music divine as it lifted the soul to heaven. The existence of guardian angels was also taken for granted. The angels play wind instruments on the north side and strings on the south – aside from where, close to the quire, the 19th century restorers returned two instruments to the wrong places.

At the western end of the Cathedral is the tower and at the top of the pillars where the arch adjoining the nave springs are Green Men. These mysterious faces surrounded by leaves, or with leaves sprouting from noses and mouths are found across Northern Europe. They are possibly pre-Christian in origin but tie in well with Christ's resurrection as a symbol of rebirth. Manchester's, from the 1300s, are unusual, often the faces are twisted as though rebirth is painful. These Green Men look almost tranquil.

Behind the nave altar lies the quire screen, a gloriously ornate introduction to the joys beyond. Most of the carving here was completed in the years around 1500. On entry you are surrounded by the exquisite stalls, or seats, of the choir. These are surmounted by a myriad of superbly carved canopies: each an elegant mass of spires and crochets resembling a series of perfect

Nave Angel

churches, like a late medieval imagining of a new Jerusalem. There is symbolism everywhere – on the benches in front of the choir seats a lion represents Christ and a dragon represents the Devil.

Under the main seats are the misericords – brackets to help support occupants during long periods of standing. The carvings under these carry an impish sense of humour not often associated with the times. Here you'll find men playing backgammon in a tavern, a woman scolding a man who's broken her cooking pots and rabbits cooking the hunter. All have meanings beside the obvious imagery. One shows a sleeping pedlar being robbed by monkeys. On one side there is a monkey with a baby and on the other is one with a bottle. This is a urine sample. Doctors said that with a urine sample they could diagnose illness – this satire says you might as well trust your sample or your baby to a monkey and all doctors want to do is rob you.

Also in the choir is the brass of John Huntingdon, the first warden of the Collegiate church who died in 1458. Straight ahead to the east over this brass is the Lady Chapel. This has an arch with a scene of hunting at one end and of beer or wine barrels, formerly called tuns, at the other end. Here we have a rebus, or architectural pun, on the surname of the first warden.

To the left of the screen is the Fire Window by Margaret Traherne, marking where a German bomb fell in 1940. This appears to flicker and burn. Close by is the statue of Humphrey Chetham, pock-marked with

Quire stalls detail

bomb damage. On the other side of this end of the church is the Fraser Chapel with the very entertaining reredos by Mark Cazelet of St Denys wandering the modern city with his head tucked under his arm, it features a black St George.

On the west side of the church are five modern windows by Tony Holloway. In order, from the entrance porch, these represent Genesis, St George, St Mary, St Denys and Revelations. On the exterior walls look out for the Eric Gill sculpture of the Christ Child with St Mary, St Denys and St George from 1933 and George Wheeler's *Mother and Child*, or the Lancashire Madonna, Mary sporting a typical Lancashire shawl.

There are several memorials in the Cathedral worth noting but the most moving is Robert Lever's 17th century elergy to his six dead children – perhaps victims of the plague.

Here dy'd their Parents hopes and feares,
Once all their Ioy, now all their tearres,
They'r now past hope, past feare, or paine,
It were a sinne to wish them here againe.
Had they liv'd to th'age of Man,
This Inch had growne but to a span.
But now they take the lesser roomes.
Rock't from their cradles to their Toombes,
View but the way from whence wee come,
You'le say He's blest that soon'st at Home.
You see their Age and years of Grace,
I hope that Heaven's their dwelling place.

Cathedral in 1889

St Ann's Church

St Ann's Square, City centre, M2 7LF, 0161 834 0239. Free. Walk one, p97.

Open every day although services and weddings may prevent access to the church. There are regular concerts and events.

This church was the first in Manchester to use the Classical style of architecture. The designer was probably John Barker, it cost £5,300 and was consecrated in 1712. The dedication refers to the saint, of course, but also to the lady who provided the money, Lady Ann Bland and the Queen at the time, Queen Anne. It was the society church when it was built and pew rents for the best seats were more than £1,000 – an astronomical sum. The poor were left to stand or find a cramped seat in the gallery. Some of the parish registers record the odd first names based on abstract qualities of the 18th century: Abstinence, Desire, Experience, Lamentation and Silence. In 1793 John Ghost had married Mary Sexton, and thus become Mr and Mrs Ghost. In May 1805, 'River, son of River and Rebecca Jordan' was baptized.

The interior is as cool as the exterior is elegant, with galleries squatting on chubby Tuscan columns. A restrained restoration was carried out by the Town Hall architect Alfred Waterhouse in 1887-89. The church is built from the local purple-red sandstone, a material that crumbled badly under the pollution of the early industrial age, hence its rarity in the buildings of the city centre, and the attractive piebald nature of the stone here marking where St Ann's was repaired with different varieties of stone.

The church tower is the traditional centre of the city, splendidly restored in 2012. On the left near the tower door is the arrow-like surveyors' mark showing how the tower was used as a platform from which to measure distances. In Manchester all roads lead to St Ann's.

Of particular note are the windows especially the three east windows by Frederick Shields, a Manchester-based artist, from 1887-89. The centre one is best. In his own words: 'The design depicts Jesus Christ as the Good Shepherd, with Moses and St Paul on either side. Jesus is portrayed leading his sheep through the valley of the Shadow of Death. One lamb reposes in his left arm; with the crook in his right hand he restrains another on the verge of a steep abyss. A lamb looks at his wounded foot, and the flock passes through the black gorge safe from the wolf peering down from above'. The wolf is Satan of course.

East Window, St Ann's

St Mary's Roman Catholic Church

St Mary's interior

Mulberry Street, City centre, M2 6LN, 0161 834 3547. Free. Walk one p96.

Open every day although services and weddings may prevent access to the church.

The earlier church on this site from 1794 was the first purpose-built Catholic church in England since the Reformation. The present building dates from 1848 by Weightman and Hadfield. This is sign-posted all around the city as The Hidden Gem – christened thus by a visiting bishop. Not all have agreed. The noted architect Pugin, in petulant mood, said the building 'shows to what depth of error even good men fall when they go whoring after strange styles'. The ornate marble interior with the Caen stone statuary has become even more eye-opening with the addition of Norman Adams' Stations of the Cross. These are graphic, full of energy and contrast violently with the 19th century interior.

Sacred Trinity

Chapel Street, Salford, M3 5DW, 0161 839 1180. Free.

Ring ahead for opening times as they may vary. Check out local listings for gig nights.

The tower of Sacred Trinity is Gothic in style and dates from 1634-35, the rest of the church was rebuilt in 1752-3 in the fashionable Classical style. The money in the 1600s was given by Humphrey Booth, a textile manufacturer. There are no other Anglican churches which are called 'sacred', traditionally a Roman Catholic term. The name stems from the religious conflicts of the mid-1600s when the Church of England was under pressure from austere puritans. Salford's first place of worship was named as a deliberate snub to these hardliners. The most remarkable element of the interior is the memorial to local men killed on one day in WWI. It commemorates 'the four hundred officers and men of the Salford Battalions of the Lancashire Fusiliers who were killed on the first of July 1916', the first day of the Battle of the Somme – a similar number to service personnel killed in action in the UK's 13 year, 2001-2014, involvement in Afghanistan. The church puts on exhibitions and was one of the first in the country to introduce rock gigs complete with a bar. "How long have people been putting on gigs here," the Rev Andy Salmon's been asked. "Since 1635," he replies. A former vicar of Sacred Trinity was Peter Green from 1902-1911. In a troubled area he published a book called: *How to deal with Lads*. This was followed by *How to deal with Men*.

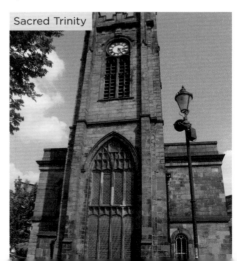

Sacred Trinity

Chetham's Library and coat of arms, one of Manchester's superb collection of libraries.

Central Library, Wolfson Reading Room and *Reading Girl* by Ciniselli

Central Library

St Peter's Square, City centre, M2 5PD, 0161 234 1983. Free. Walk one p85

Mon-Thu 9am–8pm, Fri-Sat 9am–5pm.

"The portico of the magnificent edifice quickly became a popular rendezvous and 'Meet you at the Ref (Central Library)' became a familiar phrase on the lips of students, lovers and unemployed youths," said Salford songwriter Ewan MacColl *(Dirty Old Town, The First Time Ever I Saw Your Face)*. MacColl was at the 1934 opening of Central Library, attended by King George V.

Manchester school children before the event had been given handkerchiefs printed with the brave words 'Knowledge is power'. That remains true today, as does the Library's popularity, following refurbishment and reopening in 2014. Of course in the Digital Age the place has wifi and endless plug sockets to charge up devices, but the enduring appeal of this grand and very public building shows no sign of dwindling. The flirting between lovers goes on as well.

Central Library was designed by Vincent Harris along with the Town Hall extension next door as part of a civic rebuilding scheme in Manchester. The circular design is said to have been inspired by the Pantheon in Rome. The two grandest spaces are the entrance hall, called the Shakespeare Hall, and the Wolfson Reading Room.

The former has a fine stained-glass window dedicated to William Shakespeare by Robert Anning-Bell and grand plaster shields and coats of arms in the ceiling. On the left landing as you enter is a sweet little statue called *Reading Girl* by Italian sculptor Giovanni Ciniselli.

The Wolfson Reading Room on the first floor is circular with at the centre a clock balanced on ornate supports like a particularly elaborate piece of garden furniture.

The original desks, with eighty years of graffiti, have been retained and a special sound dampening paint applied to the dome that has dulled, but not eradicated, the startling echo. Tap a table and see what happens.

Round the dome there are words from the Old Testament's *Book of Proverbs:* 'Wisdom is the principal thing; therefore get wisdom, and with all thy getting get understanding. Exalt her and she shall promote thee; she shall bring thee to honour when thou dost embrace her, she shall give of thine head an ornament of grace, a crown of glory she shall deliver to thee.'

Certainly Harris's library is 'an ornament of grace' to Manchester. Walking the corridors and through the various departments is to glide through arch after elegant arch. The Library's design was exhaustively researched by Harris and the Chief Librarian of the time, Stanley Jast, a polymath and playwright, as well as bookworm. Their research took them to America to study the latest techniques. Jast seems to have been inspired by more than just libraries, memorably stating: "Perhaps the two most valuable and satisfactory products of American civilization are the librarian on the one hand and the cocktail in the other."

Ryder Architecture in their refurbishment has greatly increased the amount of public space in the building. The committee rooms, for instance, even the Chief Librarian's Office with its false door, can now be hired for weddings and events. But the main challenge was to insert a new stairwell and lifts and to open up the area under the Wolfson Reading Room to house the Local Studies, Archive and Family History sections.

The library hosts exhibitions and events, there's a performance space and a media lounge plus specialist business, music and children's libraries. The libraries special collections are very strong with a hand-

Chetham's Library, clockwise from top, the stacks, medieval cat flap, Johnson's Dictionary of English, doorbell, exterior, the Engels and Marx table

written, 13th century copy of the Codex Justinianus, a code of law compiled for the Roman Emperor Justinian. The Henry Watson Music Library has an important collection of early and original music scores, including Vivaldi's Manchester Violin Sonatas, signed by the composer, which only came to light after they arrived in Manchester.

"I want this to be Manchester's Living Room," says Neil MacInnes, head of Manchester's library service. On target for two million visitors a year, his wish seems to be coming true.

Chetham's Library and School of Music

Long Millgate, City centre, M3 1SB, 0161 834 7961. Free. Walk one p103. Mon-Fri 9am-4.30pm

'Please Ring', says the sign on the door. It's the best invitation in the city. If tourism is about discovery and if the best discoveries are surprises then Chetham's Library works every time.

The atmosphere of antiquity is palpable, the buildings are alive with the ghosts of passing generations. Some say one still walks. Dr Dee (1527-1609) is one of the most fascinating figures in British history. He's known as a scientist, mathematician and philosopher but also as an astrologer, alchemist and occultist. Dee lived for several years in Manchester and his official residence and offices still exist at Chetham's School and Library. In the Audit Room under the Library there is a burn mark on a table where Dee is said to have raised the devil.

Chetham's Library and School is the oldest complete structure in the city, dating from 1421, erected as a single building to house the clergy from the Collegiate church.

After the Reformation, starting 1537,

the premises were variously abused. They were reborn when local merchant Humphrey Chetham founded a charity school in 1653 for 40 poor boys and a free public library for the 'use of scholars and others well-affected'. His will insisted the librarian 'require nothing of any man that cometh into the library'. The present librarian remains true to those 350 year old instructions.

Only the library has daily public access and only during the week, but this is set to change in the next few years. The school security guard at the Long Millgate entrance will direct you through the ancient gatehouse and across the courtyard to a doorway with the 'Please Ring' instruction.

Ring it. The Library is on the first floor. Most of the fixtures and fittings are original and date from the mid-1600s. The books are contemporary from that date and some are older. They are all shielded behind 18th century gates and were formerly chained to the shelves, as they could be worth the equivalent of a man's salary each. In a peculiar reversal of today's values, the buildings cost the trustees of Chetham's will £500, the books £1,000.

The library still collects new books on local matters, but the original collection is more diverse and includes the Matthew Paris' 13th century *Flores Historiacum*. An edition of Plato's *Complete Works* was poet and playwright Ben Jonson's own copy and is signed by him.

There's a first edition of the *Dictionary of English* by Samuel Johnson from 1755, a ground-breaking, nine year work. The famous wit had fun compiling it. 'Oats' is defined as 'a grain which in England is generally given to horses, but in Scotland appears to support the people'. A 'patron' is 'a wretch who supports with insolence and is paid with flattery'.

On the east is the main Reading Room with a wooden relief displaying the coat of arms of the benefactor, Humphrey Chetham.

John Rylands Library, clockwise from top, unexpected sleepers, the haunted ladies toilet, library life, the Reading Room

The elements are balanced on books. On one side is a pelican feeding its young with its own blood – a symbol of charity – and on the other a crowing cock: a symbol of awareness, of education.

On the square table in the bay window, Friedrich Engels, who spent 22 years in Manchester, would study with Karl Marx, the man he supported with money and ideas. Other library visitors have included Daniel Defoe, Benjamin Franklin, Benjamin Disraeli, Winston Churchill and Damon Albarn – who was here to prepare for writing his Manchester International Festival opera, *Dr Dee: An English Opera*.

To the left, as you leave the library, is a doorway that leads into the lovely court-yard of the former cloisters. Behind is the magnificent Baronial Hall with its sweet inglenook and original screens. These are part of Chetham's School of Music, which takes children from 8 to 18 years-of-age of special musical ability. There are around 300 pupils. On Wednesdays during term time, there are free concerts and tours. To check times, call 0161 834 9644.

John Rylands Library

150 Deansgate, City centre, M3 3EH, 0161 306 0555. Free. Walk one p95.

Tues-Sat 10am-5pm; Sun-Mon noon-5pm

Enriqueta Rylands wanted to commemo-rate her late husband with a fitting memo-rial. A library was perfect. The building opened on New Year's Day 1900. It is not only one of the city's most beautiful build-ings, but also contains one of the top ten collections of manuscripts and printed materials on the planet.

John Rylands was a successful cotton mer-chant and manufacturer. He was also a noted philanthropist at home and abroad. He died in 1888 leaving an estate of more than £2.5m (the largest estate ever left by a non-aristocrat), his second wife, Enriqueta,

resolved to convert his private theologi-cal book collection into a public one. Basil Champneys, the architect, couldn't believe his luck and while designing a building combining the atmosphere of a medieval college with modern amenities, he played with space as no-one else has in the city.

The main frontage on Deansgate includes the sumptuous entrance with two octago-nal towers placed beneath the larger towers. In the centre is the large east window of the reading room with its mass of sensuous window tracery.

Inside, the place is one 'reveal' after another and this starts with the modern work by Austin-Smith: Lord from 2007, where the new extension with study areas, shop, café and disabled access is brilliant white leading to a bridge that dramatically thrusts you into Victorian Gothic mystery. The his-torical Reading Room includes stained glass and sculptures illustrating literary, religious and philosophical greats. At one end there is a marble statue of Enriqueta Rylands and at the other, one of John Rylands. The ladies toilet in the original building is said to be haunted so beware.

The collections go back to the third millen-nium BC, and are written on most kinds of materials used by man including clay, papyrus, linen, parchment, paper, wood, bone, bark, bamboo and palm-leaf. The works include the oldest fragment of the *New Testament*, the oldest printed material from Europe, first editions of Shakespeare's *Sonnets*, Newton's *Principia*, Joyce's *Ulysses*, most of the Caxtons ever printed, Guttenberg Bibles and medieval illumi-nated manuscripts. In the Oriental section alone, there are 20,000 manuscripts in 40 different languages. Similarly the Aramaic section is one of the most acclaimed in Europe.

There's also the *Wicked Bible* from 1631. The name comes from a terrible typo-graphical error. The vital little word 'not' was omitted from the seventh command-ment: it read 'Thou Shalt Commit Adultery'.

The Library also has letters from Sigmund Freud to his Manchester relatives in particular Sam Freud, the son of Emanuel Freud who'd emigrated to Manchester in 1861. Emanuel died before his time falling from a train between Manchester and Stockport – an unfortunate and literal Freudian slip. The letters paint a personal picture of a Freud, gossipy almost, cranky occasionally. He adored the *Manchester Guardian* newspaper and said he'd like 'to become an Englishman, in spite of the fog, rain, drunkenness and conservatism'. After WWI his modest Manchester relations sent packages to Vienna because of the awful conditions there. With the rise of the Nazis, politically it was far worse for Jews and the last letter in the collection, from June 1938, says: 'Leaving Vienna for good today. Any chance of our meeting after so many years?' Freud fled to London but died a year later.

The Library has a lively programme of events and a rolling series of art exhibitions. Of recent works, the 11m *Totem* in glass by Derek Hunt is the most impressive.

Portico Library and Gallery

57 Mosley Street (entrance on Charlotte Street), City centre, M2 3HY, 0161 236 6785. Free. Walk two, p36.

Mon & Fri 9.30am-4.30pm; Tues-Thurs 9.30am-5.30pm; Sat 11am-3pm

The Portico Library is the oldest subscription library in the UK. Your visit will be attended by the spirits of John Dalton, Elizabeth Gaskell, Richard Cobden, John Edward Taylor, Sir Robert Peel, Charlotte Bronte, Charles Dickens, Sir Ernest Rutherford and many more. Recent members have included novelists Val McDermid, Emma Jane Unsworth and musician Guy Garvey. In the nineties footballer Eric Cantona attended lectures.

If Chetham's Library and John Rylands

Portico Library

library are about the mystery of books, the Portico and Central Library are about their revelation, the clarity they bring life. The style of architecture gives it all away. The Portico is bathed in the afterglow of the Age of Enlightenment. It was completed in 1806 in the Grecian style to the designs of Thomas Harrison. The first secretary was Peter Mark Roget, the man who would come up with the eponymous Thesaurus. Built and stocked through private subscription, the ground floor was sold off in the 1920s for use first as a bank and now as a pub.

The reading room is a lovely space with a sweet saucer dome and an original wind dial by Thwaites, later manufacturers of Big Ben's clock. Only the main reading room can be accessed by the public. For access to the inner sanctum of the members' room you have to be signed in or join. Go on a Saturday though and it's different. Between 11am-3pm you can enjoy cakes, scones, tea, coffee, wine and beer in the members' room. Throughout the week there are refreshments available from the kitchen all day and light lunches from noon-2pm including an afternoon tea. The reading room holds art exhibitions for local and national artists, book-related exhibitions and talks.

Manchester Art Gallery

Mosley Street, City centre, M2 3JL, 0161 235 8888. Free. Walk two, p123.
Mon-Sun 10am-5pm, until 9pm on Thurs.

Architect Charles Barry's 1820s' motto for this building was 'Nihil Pulchrum Nisi Utile' or 'Nothing Beautiful Unless Useful'. A very Manchester sentiment, Charles Dickens, the author of *Hard Times* might have thought in 1843 as he lectured in the city. After all Manchester was the town of Thomas Gradgrind, who would say, "You are never to fancy. I want facts."

But that would have been a misinterpretation. Barry, meant that beauty, when achieved, is useful in and of itself, magnifying mere function into moral and aesthetic utility. Manchester gained architectural beauty with this building and its dignified neo-Greek design, fashionable at the time as foreigners including Barry began to travel to Greece.

The building was completed in 1835, first as a private Royal Institution, then from 1882 as the public art gallery. The entrance hall is a real show-off. High on the colourful walls are George Westmacott's plaster casts of the Elgin Marbles from The Parthenon, a gift from George IV. The first floor galleries are equally vivid with Victorian colour schemes featuring in the Pre-Raphaelite Room, a golden Manchester bee.

There are two other major parts of the gallery: a tasteful and elegant new block by Hopkins Architects and the former Athenaeum club, also by Charles Barry from 1837 and an influential Manchester building (p120, 123). The Athenaeum is where Dickens delivered his 1843 lecture.

The collection includes works from the 18th and 19th centuries by Stubbs, Gainsborough, Claude Lorrain, Canaletto, Turner, Constable, Pisarro, Gaugin, Rodin.

The Pre-Raphaelite collections are outstanding including works by Holman Hunt, John Everett Millais, Dante Gabriel Rossetti and Ford Madox Brown. Usually there's an example of French artist Adolphe Valette's remarkable series of Impressionist paintings of Manchester from the early 20th century. Stanley Spencer, Lucien Freud, Francis Bacon, David Hockney, Bridget Riley and Antony Gormley are represented. From the pre-1700s there are interesting Flemish and Renaissance works. The craft and design section includes objects by Lalique, Faberge, Picasso, Conran.

The programme of special exhibitions is always innovative, often placing objects from different decades next to each other to show how influence spreads. There's an award-winning children's gallery, an extensive shop and a cafe.

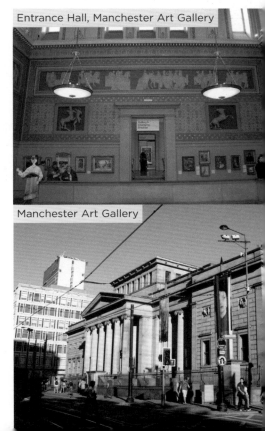

Entrance Hall, Manchester Art Gallery

Manchester Art Gallery

Work (1852-1865), Ford Madox Brown

Ford Madox Brown (1852-1865)

Ford Madox Brown was always an outsider, a Pre-Raphaelite by nature but never a paid up member. Tutored abroad, often in financial trouble, anti-art establishment, prickly, resentful, an innovator, amusing, handsome (known as 'the King of Hearts'), he is one of the UK's more interesting artists. While in Manchester working on the Town Hall murals he lived in a *ménage a trois* with his wife Emma Hill and German writer Mathilde Blind. Politically a radical he helped found a labour exchange to help unemployed workers.

Work, the painting above, from Manchester Art Gallery, is Pre-Raphaelite painter Ford Madox Brown's masterpiece. It was bought in 1885 and is, typical of High Victorian ethos. Here in one picture Brown is attempting to capture all society, rich and poor, in relation to the benefits of honest physical or intellectual toil, set against the malign effects of lack of work, either through choice or circumstance. The picture was inspired by a scene witnessed on Heath Street, Hampstead.

The quotes in this description are all Brown's. The central figure is physical work made heroic. The young navvy is a model of virile health and beauty – a celebration of physical labour. Nearby is the older navvy 'who does his work and loves his beer'. Brown admired the 'British...navvy in the full swing of his activity' and found him just as worthy of artistic depiction as 'a fisherman of the Adriatic.'

To the left foreground is the herb and flower seller who has never been taught to work and who 'with his restless gleaming eyes, he doubts and despairs of every one.' On the right looking on are two intellectuals: Thomas Carlyle, whose book *Past and Present* was greatly admired by Brown, and the Rev. FD Maurice, a pioneer of working class education.

The aristocratic gent on horseback is 'true-hearted'. Brown is saying: If only he could get to our two 'brainworkers' he would be converted to their enlightened thinking. In the foreground there's a ragged group of children, 'the mother dead, note the baby's black ribbons, and the father a drinker'. The ten year old daughter is looking after her siblings and making the best of it in counterpoint to the flower seller.

Behind the flower seller is a lady whose 'only business

in life, is to look beautiful for our benefit.' Modelled on Brown's wife, this lady might be reminded of the fleeting nature of beauty if she paid attention to her lap dog in the red coat who 'will run through that lime' and burn its paws.

Behind beautiful is the busybody. Again with no need to work she carries her pamphlets called 'The Bread of Life' – attempting to reform the working class and poor without any desire to learn about them.

Along the road are sleeping tramps revealing the necessity of work in human life. 'The man with the beer tray is a specimen of town pluck and energy contrasted with country thews and sinews.' This man is another hero for Brown. Despite being 'starved, stunted with gin', as a child, he has found the energy and resourcefulness to become a much respected beer-man.

Clockwise from top: fossilised tree, Ancient Worlds, Vivarium, Roman altar found in Manchester

Manchester Museum

University of Manchester, Oxford Road, University, M13 9PL, 0161 275 2634. Free. Daily: 10am-5pm

This is a charming building full of picturesque views across halls and stairways, complete with internal bridges and quirky nooks and crannies housing one of the great provincial museum collections.

The oldest elements are by Manchester Town Hall architect, Alfred Waterhouse, from 1888. It was extended by his son Paul in 1912 and 1927 and has undergone extensive refurbishment over the last decade with a particularly handsome entrance by Manchester-based Ian Simpson Architects.

Waterhouse was asked to produce a building in line with Charles Darwin's theory of evolution, with a progression of galleries. Ironically Waterhouse in his Natural History Museum in London, opened in 1881, had been asked to produce a building in line with Richard Owen's more creationist ideas. Architects need to be flexible.

Administered by the University of Manchester there are galleries dedicated to Archaeology, Egyptology, Geology, Zoology, Archery, Medicine and much else including live beasts in the Vivarium.

Ancient Worlds includes a renowned Egyptology section with everyday items and sacred artefacts, along with an array of 'mummies' in various stages of preservation, from the completely wrapped via the exposed and leathery to skeletons. The majority of the collection here comes from two Manchester businessmen of the 19th century, Jesse Haworth and Martyn Kennard.

In the large Nature Discovery and Living Worlds areas, the stuffed animals come with all-action poses and a skeleton of sperm whale floating at first floor level. The chamber here is lovely, a large iron hall, with at the far end graceful bridges one above the over as the staircase doubles back to take you up each floor. The Vivarium on the top floor near to this hall has snakes, lizards and frogs. The Nature's Library section has an astonishing collection of insects and butterflies pinned in cases.

Of course there's a T-Rex skeleton, or rather a cast of one, in the fossils section. Popularly named Stan, he has a skull five feet long, hips 12 feet from the ground and teeth 12 inches in length. He's the size of a bus. The original Stan was excavated by the Black Hills Institute, USA, in 1992.

The Manchester Gallery is odd, random rather than logical, based on mind-mapping rather than clear description. There are some special items such as a Roman altar found in 2008 close to the Roman fort site in the city (p136). This was erected by German-born Aelius Victor in the first century AD.

There are special events and exhibitions throughout the year and a café.

Manchester Museum

Clockwise from top: the Garratt train, Power Hall, sundial in 1830 station, Textiles Gallery, Air and Space Gallery, Revolution Manchester, city made Rolls Royce

Museum of Science and Industry

Lower Byrom Street, Castlefield, City centre, 0161 832 2244, M3 4FP. Free with suggested donation. Walk three p133. Every day 10am-5pm.

Now part of the Science Museums Group the Museum of Science and Industry in Manchester (MOSI) is the largest of its kind in the country. People of all ages, especially families, will enjoy visiting MOSI and despite the name, you don't have to be a budding scientist to understand it.

The range of exhibitions is huge, covering steam engines, space, cotton, gas, water, electricity, computers, photography, aviation, Manchester's history, the city's part in pioneering achievement and also a planetarium. The buildings, unusually for a museum, play their part too, spread out across seven acres, wandering from railways to aviation becomes an event in itself. They also comprise some of the most important structures in the city - especially the 1830 station building, which is the oldest in the world and the first of its kind.

The heart of the museum is the Power Hall with its impressive and frequently operating steam engines. A highlight is Beyer-Garratt articulated steam locomotive, the largest exhibit. Made at Beyer Peacock's Manchester factory in 1930, this Garratt ran on the South African Railways until 1972. There's also a replica of Novelty from 1929, one of the trains tested for the Liverpool and Manchester Railway. Don't miss the Haydock Colliery beam engine or the superb 1907 McNaught engine from Firgrove Mill.

The Textiles Gallery is another working machines extravaganza. This underlines Manchester's significance in the world trade of textiles and follows the production process through the finishing stages of design, dyeing, printing and making-up to recycling. It's a vigorous and good looking gallery.

Closer to the main entrance is the Revolution Manchester Gallery which takes a look at Manchester's extraordinary legacy with regard to pioneering innovation in science and industry – a few of these are described on p75-76. Exhibitions feature such greats as John Dalton, Ernest Rutherford and Joseph Whitworth.

Across the road from the main entrance is the Air and Space Gallery, housed in a former market hall, featuring a Shackleton bomber, a Japanese suicide plane, and something like a flying toast rack which turns out to be a replica Triplane 1 from 1909 developed by Manchester's AV Roe and the first British aircraft with a British engine to fly. In this building Manchester's automotive achievement is also examined and there's an early Rolls Royce, manufactured in the first company factory in Hulme, Manchester.

At the far end of the site are the most important historical buildings, Liverpool Road Station and its neighbouring warehouse. Both date from 1830 and were the terminus for the first passenger rail system, the Liverpool to Manchester Railway (p218). On weekends there are steam train rides at the site.

At the same end of the site is the now faded and old-fashioned but still interesting Making of Manchester exhibition about the city's history, with underneath a reconstructed sewer in Underground Manchester which explores how advances in sanitation were of immense importance in urban life.

The Experiment section is hugely popular with families, as is the 4D cinema with moving seats, water spray and air jets. Artworks feature throughout the museum and there is a rolling programme of temporary exhibitions as well as cafes for refreshment. For those who want to take their interest in science and industry further there is a comprehensive archive and study centre.

National Football Museum

Urbis Building, Cathedral Gardens, City centre, M4 3BG, 0161 605 8200. Free with suggested donation. Walk one p103. Mon-Sat 10am-5pm; Sun 11am-5pm.

Of course it helps but you don't have to like football to appreciate this museum. The energetic and engaging displays and the manner in which they have been put together makes for a lively visit. The art surrounding football is particularly strong here and includes a ceramic footballer from Picasso plus Spitting Image puppets such as those of Gary Lineker and Paul Gascoigne.

The museum provides a home for the largest collection of football memorabilia assembled - more than 140,000 objects. It's arranged over three floors with the atrium space dedicated to the museum's Hall of Fame.

National Football Museum

Highlights include a 'Pepper's Ghost' video illusion exhibit featuring famous footballing personalities such as England World Cup winning legend Sir Geoff Hurst. Exhibit highlights include a shirt from the world's first international match played in 1872, the 1966 World Cup Final ball and the shirt worn by Maradona during the 1986 'Hand of God' quarter final match between England and Argentina.

Great fun can be had in the Football Plus section with twelve challenges to test visitor's footballing skills. There's the inevitable penalty taking opportunity but there's all sorts of accuracy, dribbling and passing tests too. There is a charge to attempt the Football Plus challenges. You can log-on to the museum's website after your visit and check your scores.

There are frequent temporary exhibitions, a cafe and a shop and the visit is especially recommended for families. The building is interesting. It was designed by Ian Simpson Architects and is called Urbis. It opened in 2002 and has a funicular style lift up the side of the building following the slope of the roof. The National Football Museum is the third gallery or museum to occupy the building in its short life.

Bridgewater Hall

Lower Mosley Street, City centre, M2 3WS, 0161 907 9000. Free. Walk one page 85. From 10am every day, except Sunday. Access to the auditorium is by appointment or on organized tours.

If you were strong enough you could pick up the Bridgewater Hall. Look under the prow-like entrance and there's a rubber seal. This is the contact between terra firma and auditorium of the Bridgewater Hall which is otherwise – all 22,500 tons of it - balanced on huge springs. These prevent traffic noise and vibrations from trams penetrating into the concert hall. It's worth ringing ahead to see if you can get into the spooky undercroft of the Bridgewater to view the springs. The silence is total and overwhelming.

The Bridgewater Hall opened in 1996 and was the first free-standing concert hall built in the UK since 1951. It's the home of Manchester's Hallé Orchestra, one of the oldest permanent professional orchestras in the world from 1858, presently under the direction of Sir Mark Elder the internationally acclaimed conductor.

The building was designed by Nicholas Thompson working for RHWL. A mixture of moods is dictated by the different materials and it all builds to the drama of the great glass prow pointing at the Town Hall, tying the building into city life.

There's another story as well. Apparently the architect was aware the building would stand on a ley line. New Age folk and others claim that these are invisible lines of energy which cross the world and which our ancestors, with their intimate awareness of Mother Earth, recognized and used as pathways. Some people say aliens travel on them too. The alleged ley line here goes from York Minister to Chester Cathedral, right through the building. So the architect thought it might be a good idea to harness that energy for the orchestra.

Inside, the holy of holies is the auditorium, a temple to music, hence the heavy, bronze, temple-like doorways. The design of the room is a cross between the traditional shoe-box style of the older concert halls and the vineyard technique where the seats fall in receding terraces. Up on high are the tremendous steel knuckles and mesh pattern of the ceiling supports. At the far end is the elegant organ from the Marcusson company in Denmark.

Perhaps the best of the artworks is by Derryk Healey. On the inclined plane of the auditorium wall, rising behind the main entrance, he's applied a flowing artwork intended to resemble the warp threads on a giant loom. The square in front of the hall is named after Sir John Barbirolli, the acclaimed Hallé conductor of the mid-twentieth century. It contains two sculptures: the marble Touchstone (1996) by Kam Yasuda, and the bust of Barbirolli (2000) by Byron Howard. The conductor's nickname in Manchester was Bob O'Reilly.

Bridgewater Hall

People's History Museum

Tom Paine's Desk

Two tables which changed the world

Manchester has two desks or tables, a kilometre apart, which can rightly claim to have changed the world. In the People's History Museum is the desk where Tom Paine wrote *The Rights of Man*. This 1791 book stated that popular political revolution is permissible when a government does not safeguard the natural rights of its people. It was enormously influential in the politics of the day and the following century. The desk has been brought to Manchester, Paine didn't write the book in the city. Meanwhile in Chetham's Library (p33) there's the desk where Karl Marx and Friedrich Engels studied and where it's popularly thought part of the *Communist Manifesto* was written.

Two Museums of Struggle

The People's History Museum and the Working Class Movement Library are a twenty minute walk from each other. They both occupy impressive buildings with one industrial in nature and the other charmingly domestic. They both, in different ways, explore the path to democracy in the UK, from a left of centre perspective politically.

The bigger of the two by far is the **People's History Museum** *(Left Bank, Bridge Street, City centre, 0161 839 6061. Free with suggested donation. Walk one p94. Daily 10am-5pm).*

The pair of buildings that make up the museum are interesting. The new block from 2007 is by Austin-Smith: Lord in COR-ten steel, weathering to orange. The tough material matching the theme of the museum and the tough struggle for votes and representation. The older building is the hydraulic power station or pump house by Henry Price from 1909.

Hydraulic power - water pushed round the city under extreme pressure - once provided the city centre's energy, driving the machines in textile warehouses, curtains in theatres and even the Town Hall clock.

The main gallery floors are divided into historical periods 'Up to 1945' and 'From 1945'. The former is themed in a progression of topics such as Revolution, Reformers, Workers, Voters following the path to democracy. There are displays on a number of social and political topics such as the Votes for Women campaign, the Peterloo massacre, the rise of the unions. 'From 1945' has themes on Citizens and Time Off.

The museum is notable for the magnificent union banners it holds, on the 'From 1945' floor you can watch staff working on banners in the conservation centre. In the basement is a well-used archive centre.

There is a mixture of exhibits in glass cases, film and audio footage and hands-on activities, giving a good balance of information and entertainment.

There is a programme of changing exhibitions, collaborations with artists and a good cafe.

Over the river and left up Chapel Street is the **Working Class Movement Library** *(Jubilee House, 51 The Crescent, Salford, M5 4WX, 0161 736 3601)*. This occupies a delightful late-Victorian building opposite Salford Art Gallery and Salford University on The Crescent. There are books to get lost inside and elegant rooms in which to ruminate or debate.

Maxine Peake, actress and campaigner, is never out of the place, so you might be in good company. As Lynette Cawthra, the Library Manager, says: "There's no shushing here, only friendly people, comfy chairs and the offer of a cup of tea while you settle down with a good book. The Working Class Movement Library exists to tell the story of people's fight for a fairer world. This is not dreary politics but a place of ideas, of questions and of demands. The collection covers everything from working life to political life, to union life, to sporting life. There are lots of free events."

There are three floors of this library, gallery and museum. The Library came out of the work of two remarkable people, Eddie Frow and Ruth Haines, who spent their spare time and money travelling round Britain, gathering new items for the collection. By 1960, the collection was being consulted by historians and academics.

Notable items include a first edition of Sam Bamford's *Passages in the Life of a Radical,* issued as a part-work. The first issue stopped in the middle of a sentence so you had to buy the next one just to find out how the sentence ended. There's a diary from Ralph Cantor, a man from Cheetham Hill, Manchester, who died in 1937 fighting as an International Brigade volunteer in the Spanish Civil War and a badge in the shape of a portcullis with the Suffragette colours of purple, green and white. These were given to women when they came out of prison having served a sentence for undertaking illegal activities in support of women's suffrage. Then there are the books of course.

Working Class Movement Library

Whitworth Art Gallery

The University of Manchester, Oxford Road, Manchester, M15 6ER, 0161 275 7450. Free. Re-opening in February 2015 so check ahead for opening hours.

The Whitworth Art Gallery, administered by the University of Manchester, has one of the chief collections of British watercolours, historic textiles, engravings, prints, wallpapers and excellent work from modern and contemporary artists. Individuals represented include Durer, Rembrandt, Hogarth, Piranesi, Turner, Blake, Morris, Madox-Brown, Rossetti, Van Gogh, Picasso, Moore, Bacon, Lowry, Freud and Hockney. Sculptors of the calibre of Epstein and Paolozzi feature. There are 55,000 pieces in the collection and the textiles and wallpaper collections are displayed in such a way as to always maintain interest. The £15m redevelopment by MUMA architects doubles the exhibition space, engages fully with the park outside, boosts the study areas and greatly enhances the catering and shop areas.

It's one of several re-inventions for the gallery. The Whitworth was founded in 1885 through the will of Sir Joseph Whitworth, the archetypal Victorian entrepreneur. He is chiefly remembered as the father of precision engineering pio-

Ancient of Days by William Blake, c 1827

neering among other things a universal screw gauge. He came from humble birth in Stockport and rose to international fame and a knighthood, never forgetting that it was the duty of those fortunate in life to spread their wealth.

The main terracotta facade of the Whitworth dates from the first years of the 20th century by JW Beaumont architects and while strong is never beautiful. The interior of the Whitworth marks a complete change of mood. Designed by Roger Bickerdike, it is one of the great public areas from the 1960s to remain in the North West. It is everything Beaumont's design isn't: light, open, welcoming and perfectly tuned to the display of art. The floating mezzanine and the big windows are inspired. MUMA aim to continue Bickerdike's work.

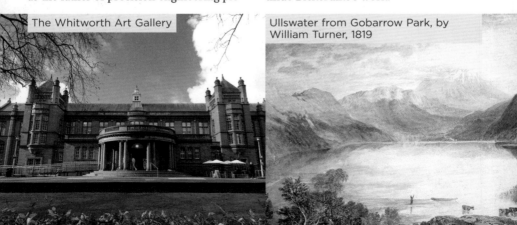

The Whitworth Art Gallery

Ullswater from Gobarrow Park, by William Turner, 1819

Gallery of Costume Platt Hall

Platt Hall, Platt Fields Park, Rusholme, Manchester, M14 5LL, 0161 245 7245. Free. Mon-Fri 1-5pm; Sat- Sun 10am-5pm

The gallery is organised as a timeline of fashion beginning with the 18th century. Shoes, handbags and clothes are all given their own sections. Pieces by well-known designers are everywhere. For example, a pair of '80s Manolo Blahnik shoes, a Balenciaga hat from 1954, a 2005 Philip Treacy hat worn by the Countess of Wessex to Ascot and dainty, ladylike handbags dating back to 1910. Elsewhere you'll find mini-skirts of the '60s, maxi dresses of the '70s, power dressing of the '80s, the beginning of the cult of celebrity in the '90s and the DIY retro 2000s - each era is marked by mannequins modelling an array of examples. The building, Platt Hall, is a delight in itself; the gallery is sewn into an elegant Georgian house from 1754 on the edge of Platt Fields Park. Timothy Lightoler was the architect and produced a model of Palladian symmetry, a geometric game of balance and precision. The staircase starts in one flight, splits and curves back in two, to the first floor. This is a staircase to glide up or down. The plasterwork is delightful in the dining room, complimented by *Widow*, a dress constructed from 100,000 silver pins. There is a programme of temporary exhibitions.

HOME

First Street, City centre, M15 4FN. Free. Walk three p130. Open daily.

Manchester's new 'new production centre for international contemporary art, theatre and film' opens in the first half of 2015 with the merged Cornerhouse arts centre and Library Theatre company. It will have a 500-seat theatre, a 150-seat flexible studio space, a 500m2, 4m high gallery space, five cinema screens, digital production and broadcast facilities, a café bar and restaurants. Its aim is to 'redefine the contemporary arts centre, creating a space where ideas, hopes and moments of wonder ricochet off walls and lodge themselves in the headspace of audiences old and new'. £25m HOME is part of the First Street development area and is designed by Dutch practice Mecannoo.

Gallery of Costume dining room

International Anthony Burgess Foundation

Chorlton Mill, 3 Cambridge Street, City centre, M1 5BY, 0161 235 0776. Free. Walk three p129. Mon-Fri 10am to 4pm. Access to the collections is by appointment.

Housed in a former 19th century textile mill this space is dedicated to the engaging Manchester writer, Anthony Burgess (1917-1993). Burgess was most famous as a writer, especially of *A Clockwork Orange*, but he was a polymath in reality. One brief biog reads 'English author, poet, playwright, composer, linguist, translator and critic'. All money left in the Burgess estate was left to the Foundation by Burgess's second wife Liliana. As Andrew Biswell, the director says, "The place is for everybody with an interest in eating, drinking, literature and life. We're a library, a reading room, a performance space, and a cafe. There's also a small museum devoted to Anthony Burgess, his private library, his dictionaries, furniture of his and an archive."

Jewish Museum

190 Cheetham Hill Rd, Manchester, M8 8LW, 0161 834 9879. £4.50 adults, £3.50 concessions. Sun-Thu 10am - 4pm; Fri 10am-1pm.

This is housed in the former Spanish and Portuguese Synagogue from 1874 and designed in the Moorish style by Edward Salomons, a Manchester Jewish architect. Inside there are 'objects, documents, photographs and oral histories charting the many stories and experiences of Manchester Jewish life'. There are regular tours of the area, the old centre of Manchester Jewry. Important Jewish figures associated with the city include Chaim Weizmann, first President of Israel, and writers Maisie Mosco, Jack Rosenthal and Howard Jacobson. Just down the road, the first true Marks and Spencer store opened in the 1890s.

Anthony Burgess fans

Elizabeth Gaskell's House

84 Plymouth Grove, M13 9LW, 0161 273 2215. £4.95 adults, £3.95, concessions, children under 16 free. Weds, Thu, Sun 11am-5pm.

Gaskell House on Plymouth Grove has reopened after a £2.5m restoration. The scale of the place is enjoyable. This is a liveable home, not a 'stately home'. It is chiefly associated with Elizabeth Gaskell, the novelist, who lived for many years and hosted a roll call of mid-19th century luminaries including Charles Dickens, Harriet Beecher Stowe, John Ruskin,

Gaskell House

Charles Halle and Elizabeth's good friend, Charlotte Brontë. The house has been restored to how it might have looked in the 1850s. You can see the dining room where Elizabeth wrote, the study of Elizabeth's husband William, the lovely drawing room where Charles *Hallé*, the man who created Manchester's *Hallé Orchestra* taught piano to Marianne Gaskell. The original architect was probably Richard Lane and the building would have been finished by 1838. There's a café and shop downstairs.

Greater Manchester Police Museum

57a Newton Street, City centre, M1 1ET, 0161 856 4500. Free. Tue (other weekdays by appointment for groups) 10.30am-3.30pm

A former police station built in 1879, and now brimming with artefacts from Manchester's law enforcement past: old uniforms, weapons, and equipment are abundant. The bleak prison cells transport

Police Museum

you into the clogs of a locked-up criminal whilst tales of the criminal underworld and the heroics of the city's police enliven the exhibits. Friendly staff will answer any questions you have about Manchester's finest thugs. You can also find out if any of your Manchester ancestors had a dark past.

Heaton Hall and Park

North Manchester, M25 2SW, 0161 773 1085. Free. Daily until dusk.

Heaton Park, one of the largest municipal parks in the country, has undergone a transformation in recent years with money spent across the 600 acres. Despite this the main reason for visiting the park, Heaton Hall, is rarely open. Manchester City Council blame government cuts. The house is considered one of the best neo-Classical homes in the country. It was built in 1772 for the Earl of Wilton by James Wyatt and is a building of lovely symmetry: end pavilions and colonnades linking to a domed central block guarded by life-size bronze lions. The interior is superb, a harmony in pastel. The Etruscan Room above the Salon is simply gorgeous, displaying a complex of delicate patterns and deities by Biagio Rebecca. 100 metres to the north east, is the Temple. This offers a wonderful belvedere, south across the city and east and north to the Pennine Hills. Another fine estate building is the Dower House.

Heaton Hall interior

Heaton Hall Dower House

Down by the lake you can see part of the façade of the old Town Hall of Manchester, re-erected on this site early in the 20th century. If you feel in the need of some recreation, there is fishing, bowling, golf, Segway riding and an excellent pitch and putt course. There's a good Animal Centre and an excellent playground. On certain days you can take a trip on the old trams that run through the lower end of the park. Tucked away in the wooded area to the west of the house is the excellent walled garden maintained by volunteers.

Heaton Hall

Heaton Park has a place in sporting history. Horse races were held in the park in the 19th century until the crowd became too riotous and drunken. The organisers then moved the races to Aintree, near Liverpool. The Grand National, in part, owes its origins to this large public estate. In music history it will be remembered for two reasons. In summer 2012 the Stone Roses played three come-back gigs to an audience of 225,000; in 1909, William Grimshaw brought a super-sized gramophone to the park and played opera to crowds of up to 40,000. Pope John Paul II visited in 1982.

Holy Name of Jesus and other churches

Built in 1871, the **Roman Catholic Holy Name** *(339 Oxford Rd, Manchester , M13 9PG, 0161 273 1456)*, is the dominant religious presence on Oxford Road. It is the most important work by Joseph Aloysius Hansom, a versatile man who also invented the two wheeled Hansom Cab. The building is impressive in scale especially when viewed from the rear where flying buttresses proliferate. The original design was to have had a 73m (240ft) spire but Hansom died so the tower was finished off by Adrian Gilbert Scott with huge Gothic arches. This is said to have inspired his brother Giles Gilbert Scott's design for Liverpool Anglican Cathedral tower.

The interior of Holy Name is breathtaking. Designed for a Jesuit community it is light, spacious and seems to almost glow. The church is rib-vaulted with terracotta and also faced with terracotta. Much of the decoration and detail was the work of Hansom's son, Joseph, with his masterpiece here, the High Altar, a feast of architectural detail. In the '50s Bing Crosby joined the choir while playing Manchester. In 1985 Morrissey of Manchester band The Smiths, name-checked the church in the song *Vicar in a Tutu*.

There are many other churches to visit within five or six miles of the city centre, but always ring ahead to see if they are open. The stately and grand **St Augustine**, *Pendlebury, by GF Bodley (0161 727 8175)* has been called 'one of the English churches of all time'. To the east of the city, the parish church of **St Michael**, *Ashton-under-Lyne (0161 343 4305)* has a set of late medieval stained glass depicting the life of St Helena. **St Leonard**, *Middleton (0161 643 2693)* comes with Norman elements and one of the oldest war memorials (1524). **St Margaret**, *Prestwich (0161 773 2698)* provides one of the best collections of woodwork in the region. Here craftsman Arthur Simpson provided between 1899 and 1920 an essay in the joys of the Arts and Crafts movement. On Chapel Street, Salford, close to the city centre, lies the **Catholic Cathedral** *(0161 817 2210)* of 1885 by Weightman and Hadfield. This has a beautifully sharp spire and an impressive east window.

Holy Name church

Ordsall Hall

322 Ordsall Lane, Salford, M5 3AN, 0161 872 0251. Free. Mon-Thu 10am-4pm, Sun 1pm-4pm.

Ordsall Hall ghost webcam

Lost in a sea of social housing between the city centre and the Quays lies a dream of 'Olde Englande'. Ordsall Hall is part of an estate more than a millennium old, in the 1300s it became part of the Radcliffe family estate and their home from the 1350s. After several changes of ownership, in 1875, it became a working mens' club for employees of Haworth's Mill in a suburb that was now solidly industrial. There was a billiard and a skittle alley in the Great Hall. In 1896, Earl Egerton restored the building adding a church, St Cyprian's, and turned the hall into a training college for the Church of England. After WW1 there were various community uses, Salford Corporation bought it in 1959, demolishing the church.

The north western front, hidden from the main road, is both impressive and pretty. The bay windows that allow light to flood the building are especially lovely as is the four leaf, quatrefoil, decoration. The Tudor Radcliffes liked the simple grace of the *quatrefoil*, so the box hedges outside the hall have been laid out to reflect this. The house would have been originally surrounded by a moat.

Inside, the Great Hall has splendid oak spere trusses on stone bases supporting the roof. There's a dais at one end and a minstrels gallery above. Behind the hall is the Star Chamber with its star patterns in the ceiling, one of which could be removed so people could spy on those below. There's the Great Chamber too with its rare 1360 wall paintings of pomegranates, a symbol of fertility and unity, an excellent choice for the marital bedroom. There's a good exhibition area too, a cafe and a short section on Pre-Raphaelite artist, Frederick Shields, who lived in part of the hall between 1872-1875. You can see his work on p27 in St Ann's Church. The hall is allegedly very haunted. There's a ghost webcam as the picture on this picture shows. Ordsall has a packed roster of events.

Ordsall Hall

Lark Hill Place, Salford Art Gallery

Museum of Transport

Boyle Street, Cheetham Hill, 0161 205 2122. Wed, Sat, Sun & Bank Hols, every day in August, 10am-4.30pm. £4 adults £4, £2 concessions, free to children under 16.

The Museum of Transport is packed with an array of mainly public service vehicles from the horse bus to the Metrolink, including double-deckers, fire engines and lorries, all lovingly restored in the on-site workshops. It's a volunteer-run museum. with a good gift shop for enthusiasts of die-cast vehicles and an interesting events programme - on special occasions, expect to see Museum of Transport buses about the streets.

Pankhurst Centre

60-62 Nelson Street, Chorlton on Medlock, Manchester, M13 9WP, 0161 273 5673. Free. Open on Thu only 10am-4pm

This house was the home of Emmeline Pankhurst and was where the Women's Social and Political Union was formed in 1903, in 1905 after a protest at the Free Trade Hall (p89), the WSPU became militant and was christened the Suffragettes. The Pankhurst parlour has been reconstructed as it may have looked in 1903, there's period furniture and displays about the family. The rest of the building is a Women's Centre with workshop and training rooms and is not open to the tourist public.

Salford Museum and Art Gallery

Peel Park Crescent, Salford, M5 WU, 0161 778 0800. Free. Tue-Fri 10am-4.45pm, Sat-Sun 10am-4pm.

The complex here opened to the public in 1850 as the Royal Museum and Public Library. It's been described as the first 'unconditionally free' public library in the UK. The 'Picture Gallery' is attractive with a good collection of Victorian and Edwardian artworks. A highlight at the head of the stairs is Perigal's very large Fancy Dress Ball from 1828. This is crammed with mini-portraits of the city's great and good in their costumes. Perigal was hoping that people would pay to be featured or those featured would want copies. The other main attraction is a recreation of a Victorian Street called Lark Hill Place. This was created in 1957 when central Salford was being re-developed. Many of the shop fronts were saved and restored. Inside the buildings are authentic objects. The recreation is set at teatime on a winter's afternoon and is very entertaining. You can dress up in traditional Victorian costume to liven things up further.

The Universities

The University of Manchester, Manchester Metropolitan University (MMU) and associated colleges are strung along Oxford Road south of the centre for a mile. The University of Manchester was created in 1851 under the will of local manufacturer John Owens, see Walk one p90. For the University areas in the city centre see Walk two p116/117. Formally recognised as the Victoria University in 1870 the University moved to its present location shortly after. The departments of the university associated with science and technology, claim the 1824 Mechanics Institute as their ancestor. The University (38,430) and MMU (33,490) together make up easily the largest concentration of students in the UK.

Areas of interest include the main Gothic block by Town Hall architect Alfred Waterhouse succeeded by his son Paul. Public access to Christies Bistro in a former library is available all through the week. Connected to Christies is the showpiece Whitworth Hall. Manchester Museum is part of the same complex.

A little north of the old university block is the Royal Northern College of Music with a cafe open to the public from where the superb processional way to the main auditorium begins. By Bikerdike, Allen,

Whitworth Hall

Rich & Partners from 1973 this beautifully balanced pedestrian way makes up for the austere exterior.

Further north again, the Manchester School of Art, MMU, is a collection of buildings. The original School of Art from 1881 by GT Redmayne contains the Holden Gallery frequently open to the public. Next door is the former Chorlton-on-Medlock Town Hall where in 1945, the Fifth Pan-African Conference took place with figures such as Jomo Kenyatta in attendance. Decisions taken would lead to the African nations pushing for early independence. The extension to the rear from 1897 has fine terracotta work. The new School of Art building on Boundary Street West from 2014 by Fielden Clegg and Bradley is magnificent, a fretwork of stairs, bridges and balconies with views into student work areas.

School of Art, MMU

Victoria Baths

Hathersage Rd, Chorlton-on-Medlock, Manchester, M13 0FE, 0161 224 2020. Weds Tours take place from April to October at 2pm. First Sun of each month, noon-5pm. Open Days take place on the first Sunday of each month from April to November.

Detail, Victoria Baths

Victoria Baths, no longer functioning as such, were opened in 1906 by Lord Mayor J Herbert Thewlis who described it as a 'water palace of which every citizen of Manchester is proud'. It cost £59,000, apparently 'no expense was spared', giving it three pools, segregated by class and gender, and a marvellous interior of glazed tiles and stained glass windows. The complex was designed under the direction of city architect Henry Price, at a time of city-wide investment in local amenities.

Closed in 1993, it was the first successful bidder for Restoration, the BBC show that aimed to rescue crumbling buildings. It has had £5 million of work done in recent years, thanks to the indefatigable work of the Victoria Baths Trust and Friends.

The main attraction on any visit is the fantastical interior weave of terracotta, mosaics, ironwork, woodwork and stained glass, all typical of the period and all delivered to a very high standard. The rigid class system of the age is displayed through the cricketer in stained glass over the first class entrance and the boxer over the second class entrance. The Turkish Baths is particularly enticing as is the clever emphasis of the watery theme throughout the building with, for example, fishy mosaics close to the entrances. Occasionally a pool is refilled with water for special events. Theatre companies, musicians and artists regularly exploit the building's virtues. Not that this is new. The famous swing orchestra of Phil Moss used to perform in the 1950s on a temporary floor over the first class pool.

Detail, Victoria Baths

Swimming occasionally returns to Victoria Baths

Industrial Suburb – Ancoats, mills, canals and houses

Ancoats, in the north of the city centre, can claim to be the first industrial suburb. Fields until the late 1780s it was soon a network of housing, mills, workshops and canals. It was to Ancoats that poor southern Italians came in the late 19th century and set up a distinct community.

Begin a short walk at the junction of George Leigh Street and Great Ancoats Street, with on the north side the smooth beauty of the **Daily Express Building**, a former newspaper office and printers, by Sir Owen Williams from 1939. The translucent glass and black glass building is delivered in *streamline moderne*, or futuristic art deco. The building looks the most contemporary in the city despite the subsequent seven decades or so.

On the other corner here is the **Methodist Women's Night Shelter** from 1899 and now offices. It looks almost domestic and included a coffee house and a home for women who needed 'further care and discipline'.

Follow George Leigh Street to Cornell Street, turn left, and then right into **Anita Street**. The housing here is municipal from the 1890s. The street was originally called Sanitary Street but the residents preferred something less utilitarian. Dominating the houses is **Victoria Square**, a slum replacement tenement of 1897, of, originally, 283 flats around a central court-

Ancoats Cutting Room Square

Ancoats Peeps

Ancoats Daily Express Building

Ancoats 1913 view of mills on Redhill Street

Mc CONNEL & CO. LTD.
ANCOATS MILLS
MANCHESTER
1913

yard. Now accommodation for the elderly it failed in its purpose in 1897 as the rents were too high for the slum dwellers.

Turn right in front of Victoria Square on Sherratt Street and head for the church. This was **St Peter's** from 1859 by Isaac Holden in the round arched Romanesque style. It has a beautiful lofty interior which has been reborn as the Hallé Orchestra's rehearsal space.

Right on Blossom Street is **Cutting Room Square** with cotton bale benches and images of abandoned mill interiors. The artwork in the square comes from artist Dan Dubowitz who also created Peeps, a series of iron and brass metal spy holes scattered through Ancoats.

Leave the square to the right of the church, Hood Street, turning first right into Murray Street passing between the canyons of factories to the Rochdale canal (p130) on Redhill Street. Turn and look back at the mills, renovated into offices, studios or apartments. You've just passed the oldest, **Murray's Mill** of 1798, with the most recent, on the left, towards the city centre, **Royal Mill** from 1911-13.

French writer Alexis de Toqueville commented in the 1830s about the largest here, owned by **McConnel and Kennedy**: '1,500 workers labouring 69 hours a week...three quarters of the workers in (the) factory are women and children.' This was Manchester

as 'shock city of the age'. To visitors the scale of the new industrial processes was beyond their range of experience. 'Here are buildings seven to eight storeys, as high and as big as the Royal Palace in Berlin,' said the German architect Schinkel in 1825.

Walk down Redhill Street to Great Ancoats Street. To the right, close to the junction with Jersey Street is Maurice Shapero's remarkable 2012 building for charity **42nd Street**. White steel gates at the front, and brushed aluminium round the back on Pickford Street.

Cross Great Ancoats Street, at Redhill Street, to view **Brownsfield Mill** from 1825. The building was leased by Humphrey Roe who set up with his brother, Alliot Vernon Roe, in 1910, the UK's first aircraft factory, creating the company AVRO. Brownsfield was also where Manchester artist LS Lowry worked (p143) from 1912 until 1952 at rent collecting company Pall Mall Properties. Return down Great Ancoats Street to the start point.

Ancoats 42nd Street building

Manchester City Centre

0   100 metres   200 metres   ¼ mile   400 metres

approx. 5 minutes

Each grid square represents ¼ mile, and approx. 5 minutes walk
(based on an average walking speed of 3mph)

- Buildings of interest
- Green/open spaces
- Rail stations
- Metrolink tramline & stops
- Car park
- On-street parking for disabled drivers
- ❶❷❸ Metroshuttle bus stops (Routes 1, 2 & 3) - FREE
- T Taxi ranks
- Traffic restricted areas
- Restaurants & Bars
- WC Toilets (all with disabled access)
- Accredited accommodation (August 2013)
- Post Offices
- Visitor Information Centre
- Help Points (Press button for help and advice)
- Principal shopping areas

Noma

Northern Quarter

Piccadilly

Gay Village

Cinatown

Petersfield/Convention Area

Castlefield

Spinningfields

Central Retail District

Oxford Road University

N

© Marketing Manchester 2013
Information correct at time of print
Contains Ordnance Survey data
© Crown copyright and database right 2010

PRACTICAL INFORMATION

Manchester's Visitor Information Centre

45-50 Piccadilly Plaza, Portland Street, City centre, M1 4AJ, 0871 222 8223, www. visitmanchester.com Mon - Sat 9.30am-5.00pm, Sun 10.30am-4.30pm

Manchester's visitor information centre is run by a team of experienced staff armed with leaflets, brochures and maps. They will have directions from A to B, ideas to keep the kids busy, souvenirs for friends and family and are available seven days a week. The centre sells discounted tickets to attractions throughout Greater Manchester including official match tickets and experiences for both Manchester United and Manchester City. It also sells tickets and serves as one of the starting points for the many and varied walking tours of Manchester.

City hosts

Keep a look out for city hosts. These are part of a Business Improvement District (BID) initiative, and provide practical and tourist information in the main shopping areas of Market Street, Exchange Square, New Cathedral Street, St Ann's Square and King Street. They work 363 days a year during business and retail hours.

The tour was more difficult than he first thought

Guided Tours

The best way to learn about the city is through a guided tour, these usually cost between £7-£12. The themes are endless. The Discover Manchester tours are regular tours across the city centre covering the city's past, present and future. Otherwise there are tours focussing on specific areas of Manchester's history, architecture, pubs, personalities and ghosts. There are several ways to book tours: direct through the Visitor Information Centre, through the guides themselves or through agencies such as Manchester Guided Tours (07505 685942). Ghost tours underground in the Haunted Underworld are run separately by Jonathan Schofield (07876 235638) and Flecky Bennett of Manchester Ghost Walks (07787 757642). Another tour agency is New Manchester Walks (07769 298068). The above tours are principally walking tours, tour buses run in the summer months through Manchester Bus Tours (07831 461565).

Emergencies

Phone 999 for police, fire and ambulance. For non-urgent police matters call 101. For health related matters visit the Accident and Emergency Department of **Manchester Royal Infirmary** at Oxford Rd, Manchester M13 9WL, 0161 276 1234. As for security in general, it's a big city be careful, but an undue degree of cautiousness is not required. After 10pm on weekend nights levels of drunkenness can be high and that's just among guidebook editors.

Post offices and bureau de change

The main post office is at 26 Spring Gardens, M2 1BB. This acts as a bureau de change should you wish to change money, as does the post office in the Town Hall Extension, M2 5DB. Both 0345 722 3344 Many central banks offer bureau de change facilities the same facility as does Marks and Spencer on 7 Market Street, M1 1WT, 0161 831 7341.

Getting around

There should be a smart ticketing system across all modes of public transport by 2017. Otherwise aside from buying tickets for individual journeys or return journeys across the city day tickets are the most convenient way to travel. They let you hop on and off services as often as you please. The cost is fixed. These start from £4.20 for adults and £2 for children. Group and family tickets are available from £6. All the day tickets (except Wayfarer) can be bought from the bus driver, station booking office, train conductor or Metrolink ticket machine. Wayfarer, the most comprehensive of the tickets, can be bought from Transport for Greater Manchester Travelshops and staffed rail stations, adults from £11, children from £6, family from £21. www.tfgm.com

Metroshuttle buses

There are three free buses around the city centre all in bright colours and clearly distinguished by the numbers 1, 2 and 3. The routes are shown on the map on pages 60-61 and they connect all major sights, stations, bus stations and so forth.

Taxis

All taxi fares are metered. Taxi fares from hackney (black) cabs can be cheaper than comparable services in many European cities and are highly regulated. Hackney cabs can be hailed in the street when their yellow light is illuminated. Expect to pay £8-£9 to MediaCityUK from Albert Square in the city centre, £7-£8 to Old Trafford stadia or to the Etihad Stadium. MANTAX (0161 230 3333) are a good contact for hackneys. Mini-cabs, or private hire, have to be pre-booked, but might be a little cheaper again. All are clearly marked with yellow cab signs and are either silver or white. Never get into an unmarked car with the driver claiming to be a mini-cab driver, these are uninsured and potentially dangerous. Streetcars (0161 228 7878) are the leading city centre provider. All the cab companies have their own app which can be downloaded if desired.

Kids Manchester

All the museums and galleries listed in the Places to Visit section have regular children's activities, family workshops, interactive displays and so on, such as Experiment in the Museum of Science and Industry or the Vivarium at Manchester Museum. The same goes for venues in the Sports section such as Chill Factore, Manchester Climbing Wall and the BMX centre. An attraction aimed solely at children is **Legoland Discovery Centre** (Barton Square, The Trafford Centre, M17 8AS, 0871 222 2662) with its rides, its city dioramas, 4D cinema. Prices for one adult and a child over 3-years-of age start around £16 but half that if booked online. Also in the Trafford Centre is **Sealife Manchester** (Barton Square, The Trafford Centre, M17 8AS, 0871 221 2483) featuring more than 5,000 creatures including sharks, seahorses, octopus, jellyfish and rays. Prices from £14.95 but again much much cheaper if booked online. There are walks through the main aquarium dressed in diving gear available too. The best thing is to book a combination ticket online for £19 for both attractions for an adult and a child. The city centre has events throughout the year aimed at children and there are small playgrounds in front of the Cathedral and in Piccadilly Gardens.

South west panorama. Neil Dimelow, 2011, Home series. Drawn from City Tower, Piccadilly. Images available from neildimelow.com

North west panorama. Neil Dimelow, 2011, Home series. Drawn from City Tower, Piccadilly. Images available from neildimelow.com

North east panorama. Neil Dimelow, 2011, Home series. Drawn from City Tower, Piccadilly. Images available from neildimelow.com

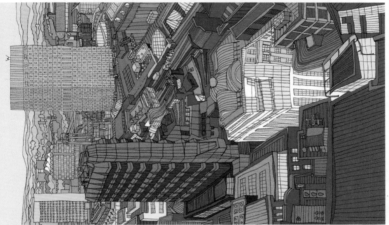

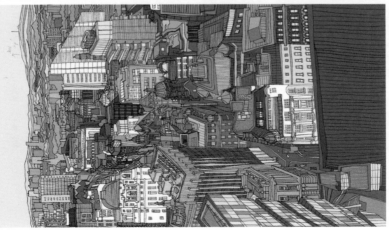

South east panorama. Neil Dimelow, 2011, Home series. Drawn from City Tower, Piccadilly. Images available from neildimelow.com

MANCHESTER IN QUOTES

Manchester is quotable. Over the centuries people have loved or hated it. It's not a place that attracts neutral opinion.

Manchester's size makes the social processes more visible. You can see how things are developing. Where they might end is another matter. Perhaps it'll be the first place to show us whether our new cities work. Manchester, as the Mancs love to tell you, is ahead of the game.

Jim McClellan, Esquire Magazine, 1998

Manchester became the centre of the universe. The best drugs. The best clothes. The best women. The best bands. The best club. Suddenly everyone wanted to be from Manchester; and if you were a Manc everyone wanted a part of you. For a big city, Manchester is just small enough.

Anthony H Wilson, broadcaster, music impresario, commentator.

'If proximity to great sporting events, an excellent reference library, a fine art gallery, the best curry houses in the Western world and some of the unlikeliest looking transvestites on the planet are considered pertinent, then Manchester deserves its ranking.'

Howard Jacobson, writer, winner of Man Booker prize, in 2011 as Manchester makes Conde Nast's best cities list.

This was the city which gave voice to 'the Manchester School' - the free-market liberals who did so much to define Victorian politics. Its heroes were Richard Cobden and John Bright, men who believed in the unalloyed power of commerce to deliver progress. Their acolytes transformed Manchester into 'the last and greatest of the Hanseatic towns - a civilisation created by traders without assistance from monarchs or territorial aristocracy'.

Tristram Hunt, The Observer, 2006

Look again at those buildings. As examples of frozen energy they fill you with amazement. Some Mancunians must have been giants. What dreams did these people have? And do they still have them?

Charles Jennings, Up North, 1996

I would like to live in Manchester. The transition between Manchester and death would be unnoticeable.

Mark Twain, American writer, 1846

I lived so far north of the city centre the postman was Norwegian. You can tell people in Didsbury are posh, they have grapes on the table when no-one's ill. There is an energy about Manchester that seems lacking in other cities, and if you see what the pigeons can do to a statue in Albert Square, the birds have it too. People think it always rains in Manchester. Not true, though I admit it's the only town in the country with lifeboat drill on the bus routes.

Les Dawson, comedian

We like annoying people. It's a Manchester thing. It's a trait. We like pissing people off.

Noel Gallagher, former Oasis song-writer

Yes I have had a tan. I went to Los Angeles and got one there, but it didn't make it back. You're not allowed to come through customs with a tan.

Morrissey on his Manchester complexion, 2009

Manchester is a remarkable instance of the good effect freedom has on trade. As this town is neither city nor corporation, but probably no more than a village, every man is at liberty to follow what occupations he pleases, without being subject to the restraint of particular laws.

Anon, The Travels of Tom Thumb over England and Wales, 1754

Manchester and Liverpool have a strange relationship. You can tell a joke in Liverpool and they won't understand it in Manchester. That's because they can't hear it.

Ken Dodd, comedian

In the evenings, the street life in Manchester is about the same as in London, only more crude. Yesterday in the Theatre Royal there were fifty people in the stalls and a dozen in the boxes. The bar, the foyer and the lounge of the theatre were dominated by prostitutes who offered themselves in a most shameless manner. When I went home I encountered two drunken middle-aged women workers, who, like the men, tried to haul each other into pubs in order to carry on drinking.

Jakob Venedey, 1845

Will tourists from New Holland or Michigan be someday amusing themselves with digging up antique steam engines at Manchester?

Richard Cobden, letter from Rome, 1827

If I should be so blessed as to revisit again my own country, but more especially Manchester, all that I could hope or desire would be presented before me in one view

Robert Clive, letter from India, 1744

Everything in the exterior appearance of the city attests the individual powers of man; nothing the directing power of society. From this foul drain the greatest stream of human industry flows out to fertilise the whole world. From this filthy sewer pure gold flows. Here humanity attains its most complete development and its most brutish; here civilisation works its miracles, and civilised man is turned back almost into a savage.

Alexis de Tocqueville, Journeys to England & Ireland, 1835

Because Manchester has never blown its own trumpet, it has never featured prominently on the tourist map of Europe. If Manchester were in France or Germany, we would visit it in droves. In fact, in many ways, it is the perfect city-break destination: accessible, reasonably compact, but blessed with a bewildering variety of attractions... Architecturally, Manchester is a mess, but a glorious mess.

Max Davidson, 'Manchester: another angel of the north', The Telegraph, 2010

I will not praise Manchester. I will agree with you that it rains there every day, that it is the ugliest city in Britain, that it is cocksure and conceited. I will, I say, agree to all this. You may say anything disagreeable you like about Manchester, and I will not care. Nevertheless...I have stayed in Athens, and Athens is a marvellous city; I know my Paris, and Paris is not without fascination; I have been to Cairo, and bazaars of Cairo seemed to me so wonderful that I held my breath as I passed through them. But these places are not Manchester. They are not so glorious as Manchester, not so vital, not so romantic, not so adventurous... But already I have broken my word: I have begun to praise Manchester in my second paragraph. Let me begin a third.

Gerald Cumberland (pseudonym for Charles Frederick Kenyon), Set Down in Malice, a Book of Reminiscences, 1919

What Art was to the ancient world, Science is to the modern: the distinctive faculty. A Lancashire village has expanded into a mighty region of factories and warehouses. Yet, rightly understood, Manchester is as great a human exploit as Athens. From early morn to the late twilight, our Coningsby for several days devoted himself to the comprehension of Manchester. It was to him a new world, pregnant with new ideas, and suggestive of new trains of thought and feeling.

Benjamin Disraeli, Coningsby, 1844

A wondrous town is Cottonborough! Vast – populous – ugly – sombre. Full of toiling slaves, pallid from close confinement and heated air. Full of squalor, vice, misery: yet also full of wealth and all its concomitants – luxury, splendour, enjoyment. A city of coal and iron – a city of the factory and the forge – a city where greater fortunes are amassed, and more quickly than in any other in the wide world. But how – and at what expense?

William Harrison Ainsworth, Mervyn Clitheroe, 1858

No provincial city in the United Kingdom, perhaps, is the subject of so general an interest, as the city of Manchester. Its fame has penetrated wherever the elevating influences of civilization have found their way, and the products of its industry, and the impress of its power, may be seen in every corner of the inhabited globe. A main source of England's greatness, there is no wonder that every Englishman should be anxious to gaze on its multiplied operations and vast appliances.

George Bradshaw, Bradshaw's Illustrated Guide to Manchester, 1857

We are here tonight standing in the centre of a district more wonderful in some respects than can be traced out on the map of any other Kingdom of the world. The population is extraordinary. It is extraordinary for its interests and industries, for the amount of its wealth, for the amount of its wages, and for the power which it exercises in its public opinion on and over the public opinion of the nation. But still, for all that, although the present and the past have been so brilliant. We must bear in mind that great cities have fallen. Therefore let us not for a moment imagine that we stand on a foundation absolutely sure and absolutely immovable.

John Bright, speaking at the banquet to celebrate the opening of the new Town Hall, 1877

All roads led to Manchester in the 1840s. Since it was the shock city of the age it was just as difficult to be neutral about it as it was to be neutral about Chicago in the 1890s. If Engels had lived not in Manchester, but in Birmingham, his conception of 'class' and his theories of the role of class in history might have been different. In this case Marx might not have been a communist but a currency reformer. The fact Manchester was taken to be the symbol of the age in the 1840s and not Birmingham... was of central political importance in modern world history.

Asa Briggs, Victorian Cities, 1963

John Dalton was a man of regular habits. For fifty-seven years he walked out of Manchester every day; he measured the rainfall, the temperature—a singularly monotonous enterprise in this climate.

Jacob Bronowski, The Ascent of Man, 1976

I came to the conclusion that the inhabitants here are of a different spirit which makes them want to enjoy life a little more.

Johann George Büsch, 1777

As for the Town Hall in Albert Square, once you have seen its silver plate and paintings and busts, its marble columns and mosaic floors, its stone staircase climbing past a blaze of stained glass, all other town halls fade into insignificance. What a world it represented – cotton and shipping and commerce, the like of which we shall never see again. It's a wonder they didn't use gold bars instead of bricks and stone.

Beryl Bainbridge, English Journey, or, The Road to Milton Keynes, 1984

In those days, for a Mancunian to visit the capital was an exercise in condescension. London was a day behind Manchester in the arts, in commercial cunning, in economic philosophy. True, it had the monarch and the government and was gratuitously big. It had more history than Manchester, but history was no more than a tourist frippery. When foreigners came to Manchester, they came to learn, not to feed ravens and snap beefeaters. Manchester was generous and London was not. London had something of the air of Chorlton-cum-Hardy.

Anthony Burgess, Little Wilson and Big God, 1986

I feel close to the rebelliousness and vigour of the youth here. Perhaps time will separate us, but nobody can deny that here, behind the windows of Manchester, there is an insane love of football, of celebration and of music.

Eric Cantona

Far, far away in the distance, on that flat plain, you might see the motionless cloud of smoke hanging over a great town, and that was Manchester – ugly, smoky Manchester; dear, busy, earnest, noble-working Manchester...

Elizabeth Gaskell, Libbie Marsh's Three Eras, 1847

You've got the fastest growing economy in the UK. Manchester is the number one choice for young people going into further education. And it's obvious why. There's the most amazing sense of optimism here. You know what's coming. The word - but. If Manchester has the fastest growing economy in Britain, it also faces some of the greatest social challenges.

David Cameron, launching the Breakthrough Manchester Report, 2007

By no stretch of the imagination is Manchester a picturesque city. It is however emphatically if unconventionally beautiful. In common with all things beautiful is it fundamentally flawed. It has a compulsion to preen and show off, it is narcissistic, contrary and wayward, and yet you cannot help but love it. It is admirable and maddening.

Chris Lethbridge, Change and Contradiction, Diverse City, 1998

For Manchester is the place where people do things. It is good to talk about doing things, but better still to do them. 'Don't talk about what you are going to do - do it.' That is the Manchester habit. And in the past through the manifestation of this quality the word Manchester became a synonym for energy and freedom and the right to do and to think without shackles.

Sir Edward Abbott Parry, What the Judge Saw: Being Twenty-Five Years in Manchester By One Who Has Done It, 1912

'Do not judge these industrial towns by their faces: they are the most alive places in England; they are more interesting than the little dead country towns which we so like to look at: think of Manchester and Birmingham with their concerts, theatres, parks, art galleries, cathedrals. Manchester in one of its crimson smoky sunsets is a sight never to be forgotten for beauty. To someone who likes people as well as buildings, the industrial towns are the hope and life of England.'

John Betjeman, future knight and Poet Laureate, 1943.

Just what Orwell never said

The currently most overused quote about Manchester is false. Across the city you'll see 'Manchester, the belly and guts of the nation' attributed to George Orwell in *The Road to Wigan Pier*. In 2007 the satirical character of Sleuth on Manchester website Manchester Confidential admitted he'd provided this quote in error to now-defunct museum Urbis in 2002. As Sleuth wrote: 'Sleuth is now sort of proud of it. Orwell might not have said it but he should have done. And now everybody thinks he did'.

I still..... have yet to gaze upon (Manchester's) cathedral...containing some of the richest medieval wood carving in England - or, for that matter, upon Marx and Engel's old rendezvous in Chetham's, Europe's first free public lending library. But I have sailed in a narrow boat, heard one of the world's great orchestras playing Stravinsky and drunk the cheapest ale in Britain, although not quite at the same time. Can a man ask for more?

Jim Gilchrist, The Scotsman, 1998

Manchester is legion but also corduroy and a dog

There are more than fifty Manchesters around the world.

Most of these are in the USA but there are several spread around all parts of the old British Empire. In Massachusetts there is a holiday resort called Manchester-by-the-Sea.

Strangest of all is a Manchester in a country that was never part of the British Empire. In the Amazon rainforest in northern Bolivia on the Rio Manuripi, a hundred miles and more from the nearest road, is one of the world's most humble Manchesters.

Indeed there are probably more Manchester namesakes around the world than for any other UK town or city. These derive from emigrants settling in recently colonised areas or because Manchester, as the embodiment of industrial progress, seemed a good title for energetic towns wanting to gain reflected glory.

But that's not the end of it.

The city's industrial fame in the nineteenth century led just about every country in the world to nick-name their first industrial area, especially if characterised by textiles, as Manchester.

Thus Osaka was the 'Manchester of Japan', Ahmedabad was the 'Manchester of India', Gabrovo, the 'Bulgarian Manchester' and Norrkoping was the 'Manchester of Sweden' and so on.

Manchester 'Things'

And then there's the commodities, beasts, trousers.

The **Manchester Terrier** is a fierce 'ratter', originally a killer of vermin, but now more likely to be pampered and preened and shown off in a dog show.

In Australia go into a Department Store and ask for '**Manchester**' and they'll know exactly what you mean: the bed linen department. Manchester was all about the cotton industry so linen was referred to by the city name, just as 'China' refers to the crockery section.

The **Manchester Seven** were seven engineers who were hired from local company Platt Brothers by Godai Tomatsu. In 1867, in Kagoshima they helped set up a textile factory, the first modern industrial concern in Japan, a country which had for centuries been closed to the outside world.

Manchester Hosen is another word for corduroy and was common in Northern Germany and parts of Scandinavia. It still has widespread use.

Manchester Tart, a shortcrust pastry based, jam, coconut and custard dessert. It's origin is unknown. And the Manchester Egg, a short-lived take on the Scotch Egg with black pudding and a pickled egg in the ingredients.

Madchester, the period in the late 1980s and early 1990s when Manchester's musical influence was at its height as evidenced by the success and style of The Stones Roses and Happy Mondays, the band who coined the phrase Madchester.

Manchester School is a 19th century liberal economic philosophy arguing free trade would lead to a more equitable society. See the History section for a full description.

Osaka, the Japanese Manchester

SIGNIFICANT CITY

'FIRSTS' were inevitably going to take place in Manchester. In the nineteenth century Greater Manchester became for better or worse, 'the world's first modern industrial city': the potent symbol of how urban society had changed. As such it helped push the world into the modern age. This pioneering spirit still continues, underlining the region's creativity and initiative. Manchester, through the University of Manchester, has 25 Nobel prize-winners more than all but six nations.

The list below is only a selection of Greater Manchester Firsts - there are many more.

'Manchester is the place where people do things. Don't talk about what you are going to do, do it. That is the Manchester habit. And through the manifestation of this quality, the word Manchester has become a synonym for energy and freedom and the right to think and to do without shackles.' Judge Parry, 1912.

'There is an energy about Manchester that seems lacking in other cities, and if you see what the pigeons can do to a statue in Albert Square, the birds have it too.' Les Dawson, Manchester comedian.

Politics, Religion and Society

The Free Trade Movement/ Manchester School – This grew out of the Anti-Corn Law League and resulted in Manchester being the only British city to get a philosophy named after it: The Manchester School. The leaders of the Manchester School believed trade should be allowed to flourish without government interference - which too frequently was both nationalistic and aggressive. Twisted by Margaret Thatcher and Ronald Reagan into neo-liberalism in the 1980s, it underpins the globalised nature of trade in 2010.

The Anti-Corn Law League – This was the first modern political movement and began life in the 1830s. It employed full-time administrators, teams of public speakers, mail shots, lobbying and the latest technology: the new telegraph. Its methods were the model for later lobbying groups.

Vegetarianism – The movement began in 1809 in Salford Bible Christian Church, inspired by the sermons of the local preacher named, of all things, the Rev. William Cowherd. A vegetarian cookbook

Manchester from Kersal Moor, 1852, by William Wyld: the industrial cataclysm is coming

Emmeline Pankhurst

was published here by Martha Brotherton from 1812 and her husband, Joseph, was the first fully vegetarian MP.

Votes for women – Emmeline Pankhurst founded the Women's Social and Political Union in 1903. This body went militant and was nick-named the Suffragettes. Earlier in 1867, the National Society for Women Suffrage was founded in Manchester by Lydia Becker.

TUC – The first general meeting of the Trades Union Congress was held in 1868 in the Mechanic's Institute, Princess Street.

Shakers – Ann Lee, founder of the Shaker religion, was born in Manchester in 1736. She emigrated to America in 1786, taking her visions with her. The strict religious sect is now chiefly known for their austere furniture design.

Right to Roam/The Mass Trespass – A breakthrough for public access to open private land occurred in 1932 when Benny Rothman from South Manchester led the Kinder Trespass in 1932. Salford songwriter, Ewan MacColl, wrote 'The Manchester Rambler' to mark the event.

Science and Industry

Atomic theory, meteorology, colour blindness – John Dalton is a scientific colossus of Manchester. His atomic theory (1803), with its pioneering work on the constitution of elements, was the precursor of all modern chemistry, whilst his lectures on meteorology turned the study of weather into a science. He was the first to describe colour blindness.

First Law of Thermodynamics – Law of physics concerning the mechanical equivalence of heat discovered by James Prescott Joule (1819-89): the unit of energy is titled the 'joule'.

Precision engineering – Sir Joseph Whitworth (1803-87) was the father of precision engineering. His work finding true planes allowed him to gain accuracies in tool making up to 0.000001 inch. He was the first to develop a standard screw thread and first to design a mechanical street cleaner.

Cast iron beam – The introduction of cast iron beams strong enough to span large distances was the work of Eaton Hodgkinson and Sir William Fairbairn for bridge building, in particular the Britannia Tubular Bridge across the Menai Straits. They also began the large-scale use of plated wrought iron. Fairbairn (1789-1874), an engineering giant, was responsible for advances in boiler making and invention of the riveting machine.

Bessemer Process – It was at William Galloway's foundry at Knott Mill, Manchester, in 1855 where Henry Bessemer perfected the mass-production of steel through the removal of impurities from iron by oxidation.

Steam hammer – Invented in 1840 by James Nasmyth at his Patricroft factory.

Industrial estate – The first purpose-built industrial estate was Trafford Park in 1896.

Earth density – John Henry Poynting established the mean density of the earth in 1891. The Poynting Robertson Effect helps explain the effect of radiation from the sun.

Splitting the atom, the atomic nucleus – Ernest Rutherford, working at Manchester University, discovered the nucleus of atoms and later how to split them in 1919. His assistant was Hans Geiger of the Geiger Counter fame.

Computers – The first computer with a stored programme and memory, nicknamed 'The Baby', was developed at Manchester University in 1948 by Professors Tom Kilburn and Fred Williams.

Obstetrics – Doctor Charles White pioneered new practices in obstetrics, including the use of fresh water and fresh air for women after giving birth.

Test tube baby/IVF – The first child of in vitro fertilisation (IVF) was Louise Brown born in Oldham General Hospital in 1977 through the work of Patrick Steptoe and Robert Edwards.

Medical ethics – Dr Thomas Percival, in the late 18th century, founded the science of medical ethics.

Graphene - The Nobel Prize in Physics for 2010 was awarded to Andre Geim and Konstantin Novoselov at the University of Manchester 'for groundbreaking experiments regarding the two-dimensional material graphene', the so-called 'world's thinnest material.

Activated Sludge System – Fame comes in all forms and this method of bacterial sewage disposal from 1913 is standard across the globe particularly where land is at a premium.

Hypnotism - James Braid introduced the word 'hypnotism' to the world. This led from his studies of what had been called 'mesmerism'. He was also an innovator in the treatment of club foot.

Hans Geiger and Ernest Rutherford in Manchester

Transport

Modern canal – In Britain, this was the Bridgewater Canal in 1761: a totally artificial waterway independent of natural rivers.

Railway – The world's first passenger railway system began operating from a purpose-built station on Liverpool Road in 1830. It was the success of the Liverpool and Manchester Railway that launched the railway revolution.

Submarine – The first mechanically powered submarine was launched in 1880 to the designs of Hulme curate, the Rev. George Garrett. He also invented an armour-plated mortarboard for academics under attack.

Swing aqueduct – The first and only swing aqueduct in the world is at Barton, west of the city. Built in 1893, it carries the Bridgewater Canal over the Ship Canal together with 800 tons of water.

British plane and aviator – Local man, AV Roe, designed and flew the first totally British aeroplane in 1908. Roe pioneered the enclosed cockpit and single joystick. In 1928, one of his Avro Avians, made in Manchester, became the first plane to complete a solo flight to Australia.

Trans-Alantic flight – Former Manchester Central High School students, JW Alcock and AW Brown, were the first to fly the Atlantic Ocean non-stop in 1919.

First municipal airport – Manchester established the first municipal airport in the UK in 1929.

Trams – Trams were reintroduced on to UK streets in 1992 with the Metrolink service.

Arts

Professional, permanent orchestra – This was the Halle Orchestra, set up in 1858 by German Charles Halle who was later knighted for his work. There is debate whether Liverpool's Philharmonic Orchestra is actually the earliest.

Repertory theatre – Ann Horniman began British repertory theatre in 1908 at the Gaiety, Peter Street.

Art Treasures Exhibition – Following the success of London's Great Exhibition with science and industry, Manchester, in 1857, began a trend for international art exhibitions - with 16,000 works this remains the largest temporary art exhibition in history.

Top of the Pops – The now defunct TV show was first broadcast from Rusholme in 1964, headlined by The Rolling Stones and The Hollies.

Roget's Thesaurus – Whilst first secretary of Manchester's Portico Library, Peter Mark Roget began his helpmate for wordsmiths: the Thesaurus of English Words and Phrases.

Manchester International Festival – Manchester's main arts festival takes place every two years (it began in 2007) and was the first to only programme new and original works.

Sport

The Football League – The world's first professional football league was set up in 1888 in the Royal Hotel, Piccadilly.

European Cup, treble – Manchester United was the first English football team to win the European Cup in 1968. In 1999 they became the first team to win the **Holy Trinity** – European Cup, FA Cup and League Championship – in one season.

Crowds – The only time the crowd at an English club match has exceed 84,000 was at Maine Road in 1934, when Manchester City played Stoke City in the FA Cup 6th round. The actual attendance was 84,569 and City won.

Civic Achievement

Gas supply – Manchester Corporation Gas, the first in the country, was set up in 1818 at a cost of £40,000.

Municipal parks – Phillips Parks, Queens Park and Peel Park opened in 1846 to become the first municipal parks.

Water – Manchester led the way in providing the citizens of the new big cities with a supply of pure, fresh water when it opened its Longdendale Reservoirs in 1851.

Municipal libraries – Salford Borough Library opened in 1850, followed in 1852 by Manchester's which operated the first Children's Library from 1862.

Free public library – Perhaps the nation's first free, public library opened as Chetham's Library, off Long Millgate, in 1653.

Miscellaneous

First casualty of English Civil War – This was Richard Perceval, linen weaver, shot on Market Street, 1642.

Bullfighter – Frank Evans from Salford was Britain's first matador and has fought many times in Spain.

Marks & Spencer – Despite a market stall in Leeds, the first Marks & Spencer store opened in Manchester in 1894.

Rolls-Royce – In 1904, Frederick Royce met Charles Rolls at the Midland Hotel where they set up the famous company.

UFO landing pad – In Hulme Park, there is a UFO airport located on ley lines. Honest. Manchester likes to think ahead.

Rolls Royce memorial in Hulme Park

Watch Your Step – I'm Drenched

In Manchester there are a thousand puddles.

Bus-queue puddles poised on slanting paving stones,

Railway puddles slouching outside stations,

Cinema puddles in ambush at the exits,

Zebra-crossing puddles in dips of the dark stripes --

They lurk in the murk

Of the north-western evening

For the sake of their notorious joke,

Their only joke -- to soak

The tights or trousers of the citizens.

Each splash and consequent curse is echoed by

One thousand dark Mancunian puddle chuckles.

In Manchester there lives the King of Puddles,

Master of Miniature Muck Lakes,

The Shah of Slosh, Splendifero of Splash,

Prince, Pasha and Pope of Puddledom.

Where? Somewhere. The rain-headed ruler

Lies doggo, incognito,

Disguised as an average, accidental mini-pool.

He is as scared as any other emperor,

For one night, all his soiled and soggy victims

Might storm his streets, assassination in their minds,

A thousand rolls of blotting paper in their hands,

And drink his shadowed, one-joke life away.

Adrian Mitchell

Puddle on Deansgate

Weather and Geography

Sun setting and the storm clouds gathering. View south west from the Pennine hills into Manchester

It rains every day in Manchester, it never stops, there's just relentless precipitation.

That is of course totally false. It's not even the rainiest city in the UK, it just has that reputation. Of course you just never know in Manchester, it might be glorious sunshine in the morning, heavy rain at noon but by evening there'll be a beautiful sunset. In fact the light effects through the day, with the sky on constant manoeuvre, is worth noting. As a 1936 guide to Lancashire's industry put it: 'the climate is equable and mild but the weather of the whole district is subject to constant daily variations of temperature and humidity'.

The simple fact of the matter is that Manchester's in the west of the country, backed up against the Pennine hills, and in the path of the prevailing south westerly Atlantic weather systems. This means the west is wetter than the east of the country but it also means it rarely snows.

Manchester has an average rainfall of around 860mm a year (rain on 149 days), Cardiff has 1,150mm (149 days), Glasgow 1,120mm (170 days), Plymouth 1,000mm (142 days). They are all cities on the west of the UK. The UK city with least rainy days is Ipswich, close to the east coast with 107. Expect average temperatures in Manchester in spring of 5C to 12C, summer 11.4C to 22C, autumn 7C to 14C, winter 1.5C to 7C. Remember these are averages so in summer it can be much hotter and in winter much colder.

By the way Manchester's latitude is 53 degrees, 46 minutes north which puts it opposite the southern end of Hudson Bay in Canada. Compared to the extremes there, the climate is positively benign – thanks to the Gulf Stream.

Geography

Manchester lies 56km (35 miles) from the west coast, on a plain within an armpit of the Pennine hills. At Manchester Town Hall the city is 40m (130ft) above sea level. On the Pennines 25km (15 miles away) the land rises to 600m (2,000ft). The principal river is the River Irwell which flows for 63km (39 miles) from the hills in the north to confluence with the River Mersey 13km (8 miles) south west of the city. The bedrock under the city centre is formed of Triassic sandstones. This was the original building material of the city and was a bruised red colour. It was replaced by harder yellow sandstones for many of Manchester's stone buildings as the red sandstone was easily worn away by acid rain in the industrial period. It was Robert Angus Smith in 1852 in Manchester who was the first to tie acid rain and atmospheric pollution together. Across the region there are deep clays deposited after previous ice ages and these provided the material to make the abundant red brick. There are rich coal seams as well, many still remaining despite human exploitation for hundreds of years.

View north east across the northern part of the city centre

City Walks

Getting beneath the skin of Manchester with tours looking at the city's past and present

WALKING THE CITY

Most of the walking tours in this large section of the book are in the city centre. The city centre is flat and no more than four square kilometres in area, brimful with things to see and stories to tell.

The key is to look above ground floor level where you'll find a degree of flashiness especially with the Victorian and Edwardian buildings. These acted as bricks and mortar advertisements for their proprietors.

Thus, there is an anthology of styles, not only are neighbouring buildings different from each other, but often the same building completes startling architectural acrobatics with wild patterns, a crazy riot of window decoration and grinning gargoyles and sculptures. There's good work from the last few years too.

You won't find much in the way of space. As the world's first industrial city, Manchester grew where capital demanded in a country where the individual's rights to do as he wished with his property took precedence over planning consent for many decades – in some respects not much has changed. As such there was no desire in the commercial centre for grand parks or boulevards. Only now is open space being considered seriously, although not seriously enough for many people.

TIP

The walks are designed to be used without a map but should you require a map there is one on pages 60-61. Otherwise there are instructions throughout the text as to whether to turn left and right and so on. Where elsewhere in the book there is a larger description of a building the page number appears in brackets, e.g. (p48).

Prince Albert struts in shadow across the Festival Pavilion at Manchester International Festival

Walk One

Civic Centre, Convention Quarter, St John's, Spinningfields, Deansgate, St Ann's, Cathedral, Cooperative area, Exchange Square

Start at the door of the Town Hall (p14) in Albert Square, designed by Alfred Waterhouse and completed in 1877. The Square takes its name from the **Albert Memorial** which predates the Town Hall by ten years.

Jubilee Fountain gargoyle

The memorial was designed by Thomas Worthington. Under the canopy is a statue of Prince Albert by Matthew Noble. Manchester had always liked the German consort of Queen Victoria. Albert appreciated the need for industrial progress and education – his interest fitted the city's self-interest. The memorial, which predates Gilbert Scott's in London, is swathed in heraldry and sculptural details including Art holding a pen and scroll, Commerce resting upon a ship's prow and other idealised representations of the Prince's interests. The remarkable structure was threatened in the 1970s after years of neglect when one councillor suggested it'd be best to break it up and use it to fix roads rather than spend money to repair it. Fortunately he was ignored.

A little to the north of the memorial, again by Thomas Worthington, is the **Jubilee Fountain** from 1897, commemorating Queen Victoria's 60th year on the throne. This was adapted from an earlier, simpler structure, placed here to mark the opening of a new fresh water supply from Thirlmere in the Lake District in 1894. The Manchester coat of arms and the gargoyles are beautifully realised.

The Thirlmere aqueduct is 96 miles (155km) in length, and is the longest gravity-fed aque-

duct in the country. There are no pumps along its route, the water flows at a speed of 4mph and takes just over a day to reach the city.

Close to the fountain is the only statue in the Square that turns its back on the Town Hall. This is the statue of **Bishop Fraser**. A Church of England cleric he was known as 'the bishop of all denominations' through his good works for people of all faiths. His back is turned because he's looking down Cross Street towards the Cathedral.

In the south west corner of the square is the beautiful former Methodist meeting house the Memorial Hall (architectural picture, left) from Thomas Worthington from 1866, now **Albert Square Chop House**. It's a model in Venetian Gothic of how to enrich a streetscape without dominating it.

The other statues in Albert Square are those of politician and demagogue **John Bright**, **Oliver Heywood**, a banker and businessman notable for his philanthropy and leadership and **William Gladstone**. Gladstone, a Liverpudlian by birth, was four times British prime minister for the Liberal party and, in a mostly Liberal city such as Manchester, very popular.

Mario Raggi, the sculptor, has given Gladstone back in death the fore-finger on his left hand. Gladstone had shot that off as a young man. The statue is popu-larly known as 'the man hailing a taxi' for obvious reasons.

Leave Albert Square by Mount Street. **The Town Hall Extension** (p20) is on the left. On the right the extravagant lion and unicorn, symbols of Crown authority, around the door of **Velvet Restaurant and Bar** indi-cate how it was Manchester's first purpose built Inland Revenue Building from 1876 by Pennington and Brigden.

Next on the right is the **Friend's Meeting House** from 1829 by Richard Lane. The architect of the Town Hall, Alfred Waterhouse, was apprenticed to Lane but rejected the neo-Greek classicism shown here for the new fashion of the Gothic revival. Quakers played a huge part in Manchester life, leading the city in its anti-slavery policies. One of the most notable being the scientist John Dalton a pioneer of atomic theory and the man who discovered colour blindness. He died in 1844. Lovers of the macabre can still view see his eyeballs pre-served in a glass jar (above) in the Museum of Science and Industry (p53).

The Lion and the Unicorn guard the gates

The white Portland stone walls of the circular **Central Library** (p31) are on the left, one of Manchester's team of superb libraries. Across Peter Street is the brown and red terracotta mass of the **Midland Hotel**. This was built in 1903 by Charles Trubshaw for the Midland Railway Company. The building mixes stylistic motifs with wild abandon but is one of the city's most eye-catching structures. On 4 May 1904 Charles Rolls met local manufacturer Frederick Royce in the hotel. Together they created the Rolls-Royce Motor Company. Inside Simon Rogan's celebrated French Restaurant diners have included Winston Churchill and General Patton. The Beatles were refused entry because they were dressed inappropriately. Or maybe because they were from Liverpool.

Previously the Midland was the site of the Gentlemen's Concert Hall where Liszt, Paganini and Chopin all played. Very polite. Next door was the People's Concert Hall, where the audience occasionally became so rowdy a wire net had to be hung over the stage to protect the performers. Less polite.

Follow Lower Mosley Street to the left of

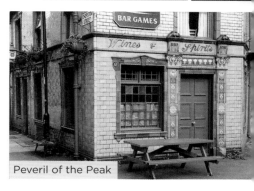

Peveril of the Peak

the hotel alongside the tramlines. Cross over and make for the **Bridgewater Hall** (p44). If you continue down Lower Mosley Street, you arrive at one of Manchester's finest period pubs, **the Britons Protection** which is over 200 years old and features local beers and over 300 whiskies. A few metres further east on Great Bridgewater Street is another classic pub, the **Peveril of the Peak**, which features the oldest continuously used table football machine in the country from the 1950s. Cross back over the tramlines after visiting the Bridgewater Hall and pass by the front of **Manchester Central**, the conference and convention centre of the city.

The Midland Hotel and Rolls Royce

Terracotta St George

Central Station has been re- invented as the convention, conference and exhibition complex **Manchester Central**. The original designer was Sir John Fowler with Sacre, Johnson and Johnstone, and it opened in 1880. It was built principally for the Midland Railway Company, and retains the widest unsupported iron arch in Britain after St Pancras in London. The brick arcades that elevated the station to track level are said to have used 34 million bricks, but also destroyed 225 houses and displaced over 1,000 people to provide space for the station. In 1969, it was decided Manchester had too many railway termini. Central Station was one of two to draw the short straw, and was closed. It re-

opened in the mid-1980s working for the now-defunct Greater Manchester Council, as Greater Manchester Exhibition Centre.

The most exciting part of the building is the interior. When it is empty, the visitor stands isolated in 10,000 square metres of uninterrupted space. It makes the individual feel reduced, so if you have friends with ego problems lock them in there. Next door and part of Manchester Central is the **Convention Centre** from 2000, a tasteful and elegant design from Stephenson Bell. From the elevated area in front of the complex, take note of the rear of the Midland Hotel. If you are lucky enough to arrive at sunset, the tiled building, in the dying light, seems to catch fire.

Walk down the left hand side of the Midland Hotel, turning left into Peter Street. The tiled and buff-coloured building is the former YMCA, now an office, **St George's House**. It was built in 1911, again in terracotta, with Art Nouveau panels and a fine copy of Donatello's St George. It was the first building with a reinforced concrete frame in the city and used to have a swimming pool on its top floor.

Manchester Central

Interior of Albert Hall

The next building is the former **Theatre Royal** (below right), now acquired by the Radisson Edwardian Hotel for conversion to bedrooms and function spaces. Built in 1845 by Irwin and Chester, this also featured water up on high, with a 20,000-gallon tank placed in the roof space as a fire precaution – the previous theatre had burnt down. The grand classical portico shelters one of the very few, if one of the very worst, external statues of Shakespeare in the country.

Some of the greatest Victorian and Edwardian actors appeared in the theatre, including Henry Irving, William Macready, Edmund Keen and Jenny Lind. The first production of *La Boheme* in English was performed here in 1897 with composer Puccini in the audience. Jean Eugene Robert-Houdin, a French magician sold out over many nights here in the 1840s. The renowned Houdini admired the pioneer trickster so much he stole part of his surname and made it his own. The place even hosted Take That's first TV performance on *Hitman & Her*.

On the other side of the road, you might be able to make out a blue plaque. This marks the site of the **Gaiety Theatre**. In the early years of the 20th century, Annie Horniman ran Britain's first repertory theatre from here. Horniman was a striking lady who dressed in elaborate brocade dresses, wore a monocle and

smoked a cigar. Her chief director, Lewis Casson, married celebrated actress Sybil Thorndike.

Next door is the **Free Trade Hall** (p88), now part of the **Radisson Blu Edwardian Hotel**. This is one of the most totemic of Manchester buildings, in some respects the heart of 'Manchesterness'.

The plaque on the wall here is dedicated to the Peterloo Massacre when fifteen people died for democracy.

Across the road a little further down the street is **Albert Hall** (left), built in 1910 as a Methodist meeting hall. The upstairs main room which can hold almost 2,000 people has been re-invented as a live entertainment venue after years of dereliction. When it was built, this building was strictly temperance, now the gigs are livened by alcohol. This change of use probably accounts for the angry ghost that supposedly haunts the building. Actress Maxine Peake triumphed in 2013 here reciting Percy Bysshe Shelley's *The Masque of Anarchy* commemorating the Peterloo Massacre which happened just a few metres away.

The tour continues on p90.

The tour continues on p90.

Theatre Royal

The Free Trade Hall – a symbol and a building

Now the Radisson Blu Edwardian Hotel and redeveloped by Stephen Barker, this is probably the only building in the UK named after an economic principle. Free Trade was the Manchester mantra of the mid to late 19th century, also called the Manchester School.

The Free Trade Hall stands on the site of the Peterloo Massacre and the two remaining 19th century walls were part of the third hall, completed in 1856, replacing temporary structures. The rest of the older building was destroyed by WWII bombing.

The wonderfully balanced design was by Edward Walters and is based on the Renaissance style of northern Italy. The main façade is decorated over the arcade with the coats of arms of the Lancashire towns that fought to rid Britain of the restrictive Corn Laws.

Above the windows of the first floor are carved figures by John Thomas representing the Arts, Commerce, Agriculture and the Continents. In the central panel Free Trade herself, spreading her arms to give and receive, bestows her favours upon the nation and Empire.

For 150 years the hall hosted political speeches but also readings, theatre, dancing. It was best known as the home of the Hallé Orchestra from 1858 to 1996. Notable guests have included several monarchs, Charles Dickens, David Livingstone, Benjamin Disraeli, David Lloyd George, Winston Churchill, Bob Dylan, Led Zeppelin, Queen, and the Sex Pistols. Bob Dylan, during his 1966 concert, was jeered and called 'Judas!' for moving away from folk music towards rock.

The move of the Hallé Orchestra to the

ST. PETER'S FIELDS
THE PETERLOO MASSACRE

On 16th August 1819 a peaceful rally of 60,000 pro-democracy reformers, men, women and children, was attacked by armed cavalry resulting in 15 deaths and over 600 injuries.

The Free Trade Hall

Bridgewater Hall led to the creation of the hotel. This was controversial given the history and symbolism of the place but justified because little survived of the original building, the acoustics of the Free Trade Hall were poor and Manchester had several music venues of the same size.

The history of the place is full of incident. For example in October 1905 the hall was hired by the government of the day, the Liberal Party. Winston Churchill and Sir Edward Grey were the main speakers – the latter the man who said in 1914, "The lamps are going out all over Europe. We shall not see them lit again in our lifetime."

Members of the Women's Social and Political Union (WPSU), later nick-named the Suffragettes, were present.

In their leader Emmeline Pankhurst's words: 'We made a banner with the words 'Will the Liberal Party Give Votes for Women'. We were to let this down over the gallery rail (but) it was impossible to get the seats we wanted. We cut out and made a small banner with the three-word inscription, 'Votes for Women'. Thus accidentally, came into existence the slogan of the suffrage movement.'

Two women were arrested at the event, Emmeline Pankhurst's daughter, Christabel, and Annie Kenney. They ended up in prison which was exactly what they wanted. The WSPU were suddenly big news.

Some years earlier, on 31 January, 1849, MP John Bright at a celebration at the Free Trade Hall had said: "As a people we have found out that we have some power. We have discovered that we were not born with saddles on our backs, and that country gentlemen were not born with spurs". He was speaking at a banquet of 3,000 guests celebrating the repeal of the Corn Laws, a symbolic victory of the middle classes, led by Manchester, over aristocratic land-owners.

Woodrow Wilson and 'The Great League'

In 1919 American President Woodrow Wilson visited the city. He was in Europe taking part in the negotiations following the armistice in WW1. He was a prime advocate of The League of Nations (the forerunner of The United Nations). He made a key speech to this effect in The Free Trade Hall.

'Manchester has been a centre of the great forward-looking sentiments of men who had the instinct of large planning, not merely for the city itself, but for the Kingdom and the Empire, and the world; and with that outlook we can be sure that we can go shoulder to shoulder together. I wish we could, not only for Great Britain and the United States, but for France and Italy and the world, enter into a great league and covenant, declaring ourselves first of all friends of mankind and uniting ourselves together for the maintenance and the triumph of right.'

St John Street

...tour continued from page 87.

On the left at this end of Peter Street behind the shabby glass building is a square in front of the impressive bulk of the **Great Northern Railway Company's Goods Warehouse**, built in 1898. This was formerly a three-in-one transport interchange. In a tunnel underneath goods could be shipped in by canal, on other floors there was road access, and through the great southern gates the main rail lines entered. Now it hosts a casino, a cinema, a bowling alley and several restaurants.

When Peter Street meets Deansgate, cross Deansgate and turn left. On the other side of the road is the luscious Deansgate façade of the Great Northern, all dressed up in the so-called 'streaky bacon' style, advertising the places and companies with which the railway company traded.

Take the first right into **St John's Street**, a handsome street of late eighteenth century buildings with some later insertions. St John's Street meets Byrom Street. On the left here in Byrom Street the houses have sweet Gothick doorways – a short lived fashion of the period.

Walk into **St John's Gardens** which was formerly the site of St John's church, finished 1769, demolished 1931. The cross in the gardens states there are the remains of 22,000 people here, new research places the figure at 24,113.

The dead include characters such as 67-year-old Thomas Raspo of Withington, 'a Frenchman, buried on 23 January 1824 who was clever enough to keep a wife and a concubine in the same house'. More significant is the grave of John Owens who died in 1846 and left £96,654 for the founding of a non-denominational university. This opened in 1851 and was the ancestor of the 25 Nobel prize-winning University of Manchester.

Only Owens' gravestone (and that of his father) remain. Even William Marsden who campaigned for the half-day holiday on a Saturday and gave working people respite from endless drudgery has lost his monument, although he's mentioned on the memorial cross.

St John's Gardens

Cannon as bollards

Leave the gardens the same way you entered and turn left on Byrom Street. At the entrance to the alleyway leading down the side of St John's Gardens, two cannon barrels stick out of the pavement acting as bollards. They are real cannon and mark the spot where in 1745 Charles Edward Stuart practised with his artillery in his abortive attempt to wrest the throne from the Hanoverians and return it to the Stuart kings.

After the cannon Byrom Street descends a short distance to Quay Street. The building at the junction here on the left is a Georgian building once home to prominent politician Richard Cobden and later the first building of Owen's College, the predecessor of the University of Manchester.

Over the road to the right is the **Opera House**, 1912, designed by Mills and Murgatroyd. Harold Leek came to the Opera House with the European premier of *Oklahoma*, the programme writer got his name wrong, and Harold Leek went away as Howard Keel. Later, in the 1950s, Sean Connery appeared in a production of *South Pacific*. Matt Busby came down from Old Trafford to see if the actor would sign for Manchester United. He refused, so United missed out on having James Bond play for them. The Opera House is still one of the key live venues especially for touring West End musicals.

Further up Quay Street again is the huge bulk of **Sunlight House**, a white Portland stone splash of Art Deco built by the flamboyant Joe Sunlight in 1931. Sunlight was a rags to riches entrepreneur, who fled with

his family as a 12-year-old refugee from Russia. The family name was anglicised. From small property speculations, Joe rose to be one of the country's greatest property developers. One of his passions was Hollywood and he went to extraordinary lengths to court the stars of the day, becoming friendly with Douglas Fairbanks – hence the name of the swimming pool on the site. His other passion was owning horses and gambling. On one occasion he is said to have lost £30,000 in one day, only to win it back on the next.

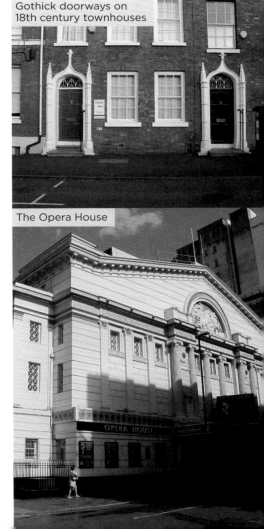

Gothick doorways on 18th century townhouses

The Opera House

The gap between the Opera House and Sunlight House, now occupied by a car park was set to be Manchester's first skyscraper. At 350ft high it would have been the tallest office in Europe for decades. But Joe Sunlight's extraordinary 35 storey

The skyscraper that never was

Hardman Square, Spinningfields

structure, proposed in 1948, fell foul of the planning authorities and was never built. Joe Sunlight, a self-made property magnate and architect never forgave 'the faint-hearted planners' in Manchester.

Cross Quay Street here and continue down Byrom Street by the side of the Opera House. At the taxi rank turn left into Hardman Square and the heart of the £1billion Allied London redevelopment area of **Spinningfields** with its lawns and bars.

Continue down Hardman Boulevard to the **River Irwell** walking under the flats of the Left Bank development. The Irwell is the border between the cities of Manchester and Salford on the far bank. Manchester has always been the dominant town and Salford largely a suburb but for crazy historical reasons the two administrations have remained separate.

Walk to the centre of the footbridge, below you may see rowers training and swans paddling. Only in the last forty years has 'the hardest worked river in the world' cleaned itself enough, after two centuries of heavy industrialisation, to sustain a varied wildlife. You might see herons standing on the river banks and brown trout swim in the depths.

Cross to the Salford side and turn right. The pub down by the riverside here is named after **Mark Addy**. Mark Addy was born in a rickety riverside house. Whilst helping out at his father's boat-hiring business, Addy rescued more than 50 people from the toxic soup that masqueraded as a river. After his last rescue of a child in 1889, he said, "to see the joy of his brother and sister when I brought them out, to feel their grip round my legs, and hear them thank me a hundred times, was more to me than all besides". Earlier he had been awarded the Albert Medal by Queen Victoria and had been given 200 guineas by the people of Salford. His death is said to have been hastened by swallowing so much filthy water.

River Irwell bridges

New Bailey Street is soon reached, turn right over the 1844 single arched bridge, but before you do look over the road to the bronze statue of **Joseph Brotherton**. This was erected in 1858 and came from the prolific sculptor Matthew Noble, who would later sculpt Albert for his eponymous memorial (p83) at the start of this tour.

Brotherton was one of the nineteenth century good guys. A cotton manufacturer and Salford's first MP from 1832, Brotherton campaigned against child labour and for improved working conditions in factories. He promoted with great energy the creation of public parks, museums and libraries. He was pro-Parliamentary reform, anti-war, a champion of anti-slavery in first the British Empire and then in the USA, and he considered the death penalty barbaric, campaigning vigorously for its abolition. He also argued eloquently the case for free non-denominational education which he thought would make people more tolerant of each other and less partisan. He was by conscience a vegetarian, a member of Salford's small but significant Bible Christian Church. His wife Martha wrote the first widely used vegetarian cookbook from 1812. By the fourth edition it contained over 1,200 recipes.

Brotherton wore a fresh flower in his lapel every day to remind himself of the potential for beauty in every circumstance. He died suddenly in 1857, on a bus into the city centre.

Cross over Albert Bridge back into Manchester and onto Bridge Street. **Albert Bridge**, was designed by Jesse Hartley one of the great Victorian engineers who was finishing off Liverpool's Albert Dock at the same time. From the centre of the span you can see the white Trinity Bridge, from 1996, by the Spanish engineer Santiago Calatrava. No modern European city dare be without a Calatrava bridge. Between the bridges on the Manchester side is Albert Bridge House, the tax office, from 1959 by EH Banks, and one of the more elegant International Modern style city buildings.

Civil Justice from the inside

Dramatic profile

The impressive buildings immediately on the right form the **People's History Museum** aka The Pumphouse (p46). Behind this is a magnificent structure with overhanging end elements and a huge glass wall. Of all the recent Manchester buildings this delivers the killer visual punch. It's the **Civil Justice Centre** by Australian architects Denton Corker Marshall. They've brought the city a building bold in form and striking in silhouette. It's also a monster; 81m (266ft) tall on 15 levels over 34,000sqm with 47 courtrooms (Technical, Family, County, Civil and High), 4 tribunal courts, 75 consultation rooms plus office and support space.

It's the biggest court complex to be built in the UK since 1882 and the Royal Courts of Justice in London. The most eye-catching parts externally are the protruding glass rooms floating one over the other, but even more the huge glass wall on the west. This is a stage for the performance of the heavens - reflecting the city back on itself. Catch it at sunset and sigh.

It's also a public building so you can enter free of charge, although your bags will be searched – security in a government building and all that. But the reward is one of the most jaw-dropping interiors you'll come across. Take the lift for superb views across the west of the conurbation.

The Civil Justice Centre with the People's History Museum in the foreground

Continue along Bridge Street and turn right before the Waitrose store and past the unassuming 1970s' Crown Court extension on the right and the Disney-esque but fun Oast House pub on the left. The 1960's Crown Court ceremonial entrance with its alarming Third Reich-like golden eagles follows next. Turn left up The Avenue at this point and continue to Deansgate.

In the little square here is the racy underground entrance to Australasia restaurant and on the other side of that is the equally racy – in a Victorian Gothic way – **John Rylands Library** (p35), one of the key Manchester attractions.

To the right here on Deansgate at the junction with Lloyd Street, is **Elliot House** from 1878 by Royle and Bennet originally for the School Board, then the Registrar's Office, offices, a replacement library and now a restaurant. It's in the Queen Anne style, the cherub lunette window surrounds are delightful as are the wizard heads – sage teachers and perfect kids for a School Board building.

The whole area of shiny Spinningfields was in the nineteenth century one of the roughest in the city. It was District 13 or the 13th District and on one occasion the police found 46 pubs being used as brothels. On the other side of John Rylands is Wood Street which still contains **Wood Street Mission**. This was founded in 1869 by Alfred Alsop to help alleviate the condition of destitute and down and out children and their families. It still continues its work today.

In front of John Rylands Library is a pedestrian crossing. Cross here and turn right and then

Angel of Education

left up pedestrianised Brazennose Street. There's a very odd 2011 sculpture of **Frederick Chopin**, the celebrated Polish composer and pianist at this junction, complete with his mistress waving a skinny arm. The artist is Robert Sobocinski and the work marks the 200-year-old relationship between Manchester and Poland. Chopin played once in the city in 1848. The sculpture amuses Manchester people, not only because it's so bad but because it makes them wonder whether the city should erect statues for everybody who visited once.

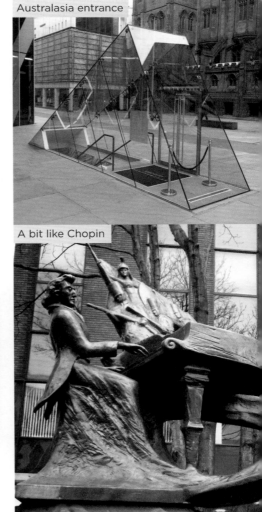

Australasia entrance

A bit like Chopin

Continue up Brazennose Street to Lincoln Square. The square houses one of the older pubs in the city, the Rising Sun, and one of the best restaurants, Wings.

The statue of **Abraham Lincoln** by George Grey Barnard, a gift from the USA, commemorates the letters of support Manchester sent Lincoln during the American Civil War, and the letters Lincoln sent back. Manchester workers saw the war as the righteous route to the abolition of slavery. Memories were fresh of the hideous conditions that had prevailed in the Lancashire factories earlier in the century. For many, the conditions had reduced them to a level comparable with the slaves in the USA. The letter was sent despite the Union blockade cutting off cotton supplies from the southern states and thus causing severe distress, including starvation, in the Manchester region.

Take the first left after Lincoln, under the Indian Bean trees with their huge summer

Abraham Lincoln

leaves. Immediately you'll see central Manchester's only Roman Catholic church, **St Mary's** (p28).

There's a covered alleyway to the right of the church take this and follow it under a second covered way to John Dalton Street and turn left to Deansgate. At the traffic lights turn right along Deansgate.

Deansgate largely follows the path of the original, 1,900-year-old Roman road through Manchester, which means, of course, it's straight. There are many possible reasons for the curious name of the street. The best story is that it was named after the Danes – the Vikings in other words – who burnt the little Saxon town in the ninth century. Thus Dean is a corruption of Dane and gate is a corruption of the Scandinavian word 'gata' meaning street.

Before turning right at pedestrianized King Street look over at the large white building on the other side of the road. This is **House of Fraser**, formerly Kendal, Milne and Faulkner. This was the city's first department store and has occupied more or less the same site since 1836 when it was called simply the Bazaar. The present building dates from 1939 and is a fine Modernist building of the period. If spotting footballers is your thing, take King Street West over the street here, and dip into either San Carlo or Cicchetti. Then wait five or ten minutes until one turns up.

Deansgate mapped, 1772

Cicchetti Restaurant

At the rear of House of Fraser is Southgate Street. The department store entrance on this street stands on the site of the Ermin and Engels Office where Frederick Engels, the German communist and writer, worked as a textile agent. Engels lived for 22 years on and off in Manchester and considered the office environment his personal prison, but he was committed to providing his friend Karl Marx with enough subsidy to allow him to continue his studies in the British Library. In 1869, after almost 22 years in Manchester, Engels celebrated his last day at work with a champagne dinner.

Walk up pedestrianised King Street. The enjoyable variety of façades reflects the independent nature of the businesses in former times. Jack Wills shop on the left is a classic brick Georgian town house, **35 King Street**, from 1736. In 1771 the house became a bank which in turn became the Manchester and Salford District Bank. The

whole area consisted of elegant houses in the eighteenth century, one of them became the house of Samuel Greg who created Styal Mill, now a visitor attraction close to Manchester Airport. In 1789 he married Hannah Lightbody, who despite her maiden name bore him six daughters and seven sons.

Double back and turn right through St Ann's Passage. The passage opens into the peaceful paved area around St Ann's Church (p27).

The square in front of **St Ann's Church** used to be called Acresfield. From 1227 it was the site of the town's annual fair. This took place over three days every September, largely for the sale of live-stock. In those unsophisticated times, the inhabitants would gather on the opening day at the entrance to the field. When the first animal entered, they would pelt it with acorns and beat it with whips. In the evening they'd get drunk. Simple pleasures.

View of St Ann's Square from St Ann's Church, looking north, with the domes of the Royal Exchange to the right.

Heywood's Bank (now RBS), stone harmony

Cotton Bud, best covered up

St Ann's Square was equally riotous in the eighteenth century and early nineteenth century when electoral hustings were erected. It was after one such occasion when the Liberals routed the Tories that Manchester MP John Bright said if he could find a real Conservative working man in Manchester he'd put him under a glass case. Given the overwhelming Labour sentiment in the city of Manchester presently, that sentence could be easily revisited.

With your back to the church, on the opposite corner right, is the beautiful Renaissance style **Heywood's Bank** (now the Royal Bank of Scotland) from 1848 by John Gregan, with next to it, down St Ann's Street, the brick and stone of the former manager's house. Oliver Heywood who created the bank was a philanthropist and the prime instigator of the Mechanics Institute. If you want harmony in architecture then this is it. The quality of the stonework is remarkable.

The tall white Portland stone building in the same block but fronting the square was the offices of shippers, **Manchester Liners**. It carries a fabulous relief of the Argo with the Golden Fleece (from the Jason and the Argonauts myth). In the square there is a statue of the free trader, Richard Cobden, whose house we've already seen on this tour, and a Boer War Memorial.

There's also a weak **Cotton Bud** fountain by Peter Randall Page, 1996. Tony Blair, soon to be Prime Minister, was the special guest at the launch that year and when the fountain began, he said, "Is that it?"

Turn left from the War Memorial and walk to the **Barton Arcade**, built in 1871 by Corbett, Raby and Sawyer. Inside the arcade, light floods in from the airy domes whilst the delicate balconies seem to float over the shops.

Make your way back into St Ann's Square to visit the **Royal Exchange** (p21). Return to St Ann's Square and walk across St Mary's Gate to New Cathedral Street, which runs alongside Marks & Spencer and Selfridges. The building they share was designed by Building Design Partnership (BDP).

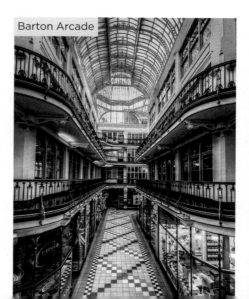

Barton Arcade

On the left of New Cathedral Street is the Shambles West development with more shops, including Harvey Nichols - also by BDP. On the extreme west is the huge glass shape of **No 1 Deansgate** apartments by Ian Simpson Architects perched on a lattice of steel girders.

The site occupied by **Shambles West** was for many centuries the **Market Place** – the heart of secular Manchester. Increasingly by-passed in the 19th century, it was effectively finished off by the Luftwaffe in December 1940.

Here the conduit ran with claret on the occasion of Charles II's return from exile in 1660, here Bonnie Prince Charlie, Charles Edward Stuart, halted on his abortive grab for the British throne and several months later the heads of two of his officers were displayed on the old Exchange. It was in the Market Place that Captain Mouncey was killed in a duel with Cornet Hamilton over a dog. More importantly here, away from great events, generations of countless Mancunians traded stories and goods and measured out their lives.

A most remarkable woman moved to 12 Market Place in August 1766. Elizabeth Raffald had arrived in the city three years earlier with her husband John. During her time in Manchester, Elizabeth ran a shop, a domestic servants' employment agency, an inside and outside catering business and two pubs. She also wrote the first Manchester Street Directory, the first best-selling English cookbook, *The Experienced English Housekeeper*, and in her last years assisted Dr White with his book on midwifery. And for the final twist: in the 18 years Elizabeth Raffald lived in Manchester, it is said she had 16 children. It's also said she died of exhaustion.

One of the long disappeared streets nearby was **Smithy Door**. The name was given when a visitor reneged on a debt to a blacksmith on the street. When the courts demanded proof of the debt the blacksmith removed his door and brought it to the court: the agreement had been scrawled in charcoal on the door.

The Old Market Place of Manchester before the bombs fell in 1940

Follow Cathedral Street north to **Exchange Square**. The design of the square by New Yorker Martha Schwartz includes curving paths between heavy walls. On higher ground to Corporation Street lie benches like the wheels of railway trains – a lame reference to Manchester's role as the city of the first successful passenger rail system, the Liverpool and Manchester Railway.

More interesting are the large but odd windmills slowly spinning on steel columns canted at different angles. The artist, John Hyatt, thought the reflection of the Corn Exchange in the windows of Selfridges, resembled a huge sandcastle, so he created these out-sized beach windmills.

The water feature at the lower part of the square follows the course of **Hanging Ditch**, a long disappeared natural water course that emptied over a waterfall or rapids into the River Irwell a short way to the west. This watercourse, together

Exchange Square

with the Rivers Irwell and Irk, formed a defensible position protected on three sides, inside which Saxon and Medieval Manchester developed.

Proceed down to the pubs of Sinclair's Oyster Bar and the Old Wellington Inn. Both were moved down the hill from their original site because they were in the path of New Cathedral Street. This wasn't the first time they'd been moved – they were jacked up to fit with a new square in the 1960s.

Sinclair's dates from the 18th century and has a charmingly complicated interior

Sinclairs Oyster Bar, Old Wellington Pub and the Mitre Hotel

floor plan full of nooks and crannies. For many years it was John Shaw's pub. His punch was so strong, you could only drink one pint if you were alone or a quart if in company. The city has a tradition that this is the derivation of the expression 'mind your Ps and Qs'. In the 19th century it was frequented by Lady Spittlewick, whose pleasure it was to consume at least 40 oysters each day. This habit continued until, in her advanced years, Lady Spittlewick was rushed to the Infirmary where she died. She'd choked on a pearl.

The Old Wellington is one of the city's oldest buildings, dating from the 1530s. The original elements of the timber frame are in the darker wood. A trip to the third floor ceiling space is especially rewarding. John Byrom, poet, wit and inventor of a phonetic system of shorthand, was born in the building.

He wrote a ditty about the confusion over who was the rightful King in the early 18th century, the Young Pretender, Charles Edward Stuart, or George II of the Hanoverian dynasty.

'God bless the King! (I mean our faith's defender).
God bless! (No harm in blessing) the Pretender.
But who Pretender is, and who is King,
God bless us all! That's quite another thing!'

Turn left in front of The Old Wellington and the Mitre Hotel and walk past the Cathedral Visitor's Centre with its medieval bridge beneath, to Victoria Street, passing the delightful **Mynshull's House** with its inscription describing the charity it supported.

Cross to **Victoria Bridge**, where Manchester and Salford kiss. The River Irwell swirls below. Note how high and proud the Cathedral sits above the waters – a good place to defend. It was around this point where the 'ford' of Salford lay. The first bridge was probably wooden-built a thousand years ago. The older one here was finished in 1839 and dedicated to Queen Victoria – note the royal orbs at the centre of each side. It was officially opened 12 years later by the Queen herself. A typesetter at The Times was dismissed when he couldn't resist amending the line 'Her Majesty passed over the bridge and duly declared it open' to one in which the 'a' in 'passed' was replaced with an 'i'. The bridge was also an important meeting and market place.

Victoria Bridge on a Saturday Night
Traditional Manchester ballad

Chorus

Hurrooh what a bother, this, that, and the other,
All jumbled together, - a comical sight!
My oath, I declare on'tis just like a fair on,
Victoria Bridge on a Saturday Night!

If troubled with pthisic, there are doctors with physic,
With lozenges, boluses, poppy's and pills,
With ointment for drawing, with baccy for chawing,
Would blister your chops, till you're red in the gills,
There's snuff for your noses, and salve for your toses,
With poultry and pigs, pickled pork, and police,
With pokers, and fendyrs, and Newspaper venders,
And Stretford black puddings a penny a piece.

Chorus

Hurrooh what a bother, this, that, and the other,
All jumbled together, - a comical sight!
My oath, I declare on'tis just like a fair on,
Victoria Bridge on a Saturday Night!

There's cab drivers calling, and fish women bawling,
Their cod – fish, and haddock, fresh flounder and fluke
With dory, and dab fish, and cockles, and crak – fish,
And beautiful salmon, just caught – with a hook,
There's lots of disparity, folks craving for charity,
Howling away, you would drop with surprise,
And some you will find are so desperate blind,
Sure they can't see at all till they open their eyes.

There's a newer footbridge that takes people over the river to the recent Greengate Square in Salford, but retrace your steps to the little gardens to the left of the wine shop. Here you can see the arches of the medieval bridge from around the 1400s that crossed Hanging Ditch and led to the Cathedral. It's now crowned by an excellent teashop, Propertea, co-owned by TV personality Yvette Fielding.

For a full description of the **Cathedral** turn to p24.

Walk between the Propertea and the Cathedral to the **Corn Exchange** – a complex building with a domed interior built largely between 1897 and 1903. Turn left down the cobbled street to Cathedral Gardens and a fine view of the **National Football Museum** (p44). The free of charge museum is housed in a striking structure, the Urbis building from 2002 by Manchester architects Ian Simpson Architects.

Continue walking north by the side of the 19th century brick building, the former **Manchester Grammar School** until it moved out of the city centre in the 1930s to a new site in the suburb of Fallowfield. The Grammar School was founded in 1515.

This building presently forms part of **Chetham's School of Music and Library** (p33). The 1420s' gatehouse to what was known generally as the College lies at the end of the Grammar School range.

Ahead is **Victoria Station**. The long façade of 1904 is impressive enough, but the

The National Football Museum

delight is in the detail. The outside canopy of delicate glass and iron advertising destinations from Bolton to Belgium is a joy. So is the interior white tile map of the former rail routes over a vigorous war memorial by George Wragge. The memorial features St George and the dragon, the latter representing German militarism.

Other details include the paneled booking offices and the blue and gold mosaics advertising the former shops and services. The domed restaurant, decorated with a riot of fruit and other goodies, is also a treat. Attached to the station is the monolithic **Manchester Arena** (1995). The best part, the impressive inner amphitheatre, has seating for 20,000 and plays host to major visiting acts.

Opposite Victoria Station lies the fine new building of **Chetham's School of Music** by Roger Stephenson from 2012. The new building provides rehearsal, recital and classroom space for just under 300 pupils - there are 74 practice rooms. It is clad in the Chetham's brick, a brick specially designed to give texture and variety and reflect the texture of stone found in the older buildings nearby.

By a twist of fate the original 1844 railway station part of which survives at a right angle to the present Victoria Station was designed by Robert Stephenson – a distant ancestor of Roger Stephenson.

Facing the station turn right and walk up to Corporation Street along Todd Street. Todd was formerly Toad Street and it was here where Ann Lee was born. She became 'Ann the Word' for the Christian sect called the Shakers. They believed her to be the female incarnation of Christ – largely because she'd told them she was. Following a revelation Ann and her followers emigrated to upstate New York in 1774 where they set up a community. Men and women lived separately and sex wasn't allowed. The sect became famous for its simple and severe furniture shunning sensuous curves.

James Sadler in a balloon

A simple Shaker chair

Cross over **Corporation Street** and turn left. Most of the buildings here form part of the co-operative movement. The first successful co-operative was created in Rochdale in 1844, with the headquarters moving here later in the century. At the junction with Balloon Street there's a statue of **Robert Owen**. Owen was a radical thinker and pioneer of co-operation. He was also an astute businessman. At 20 years of age, he was a manager in one of the city's cotton factories. Later he moved north and developed the famous New Lanark Mills, near Glasgow.

Balloon Street is so-called because it was from a garden close to this spot where pastry chef turned aviator James Sadler made a balloon ascent in Manchester in

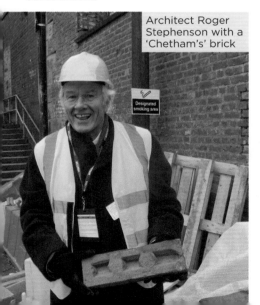

Architect Roger Stephenson with a 'Chetham's' brick

May 1785. It wasn't the first Manchester balloon ascent but it was the most notorious. He made another Manchester ascent later that May. This time things went wrong and he rose 13,000ft and travelled 50 miles before landing near Pontefract in Yorkshire. He was badly injured after being dragged 2 miles by the balloon before it threw him out of the basket and took off again. The incident also resulted in the death of a cow for which Sadler had to provide compensation.

If you appreciate the architecture of the International Modern Movement, you should follow Corporation Street to Miller Street and then turn right. Here is, first, New Century House and then, to the right off Miller Street, the cloud tickling Cooperative Insurance Society (CIS) tower, both dating from 1962 by Hay and Burnet, Tait and Partners.

In terms of quality, the 25-storey, 122m (400ft), **CIS tower** is superb. From viewpoints all around, it hunches over the north end of the city centre like an eagle over its eyrie – the body of the bird is the aluminum and glass curtain walled office block, the breast and the head are the protruding service tower covered by solar panels. The brief from the Cooperative Insurance Society was for an office block that could compete with the best in London or New York whilst providing the city with a building that pointed to the future. They took a design from Chicago of the Inland Steel Building by Skidmore, Owings and Merrill and filled the aforementioned brief perfectly.

There are occasional open days for visitors and inside there are some surviving interiors on the highest two executive floors, the 23rd and 24th. These are paneled with lovely pale wood inspired by the best Scandinavian interiors of the time. Trips onto the roof allow visitors a view 400ft straight down the attached girders – a tough decorative element to reveal the internal structure.

CIS Tower

View down the girders from the top

Interior

1 Angel Square

Over the road is the headquarters for the Cooperative Group, **1 Angel Square**, another tour-de-force. It opened in 2012 and is sat within a redevelopment area. It was designed by 3D Reid and is 70 metres high (230ft) with 320,000 sq ft of office space accommodating 3,500 staff. It is one of the most environmentally friendly buildings in Europe. Air is pulled in through the three huge - and sculptural - tubes outside and by a kind of modern witchcraft is converted into a ventilation system for the entire structure. In buildings with this much electronic kit the problem is keeping the structure cool rather than heating it up. The central Atrium which can be viewed from the main foyer is as awe-inspiring as that in the Civil Justice Centre, you could fit Manchester Cathedral inside.

Retrace your steps back down Corporation Street and continue past the Printworks leisure complex, once the largest newspaper production factory in Europe, through Exchange Square to the red postbox under the splendid twisted bridge by Stephen Hodder.

The postbox has been moved slightly since 1996, when it was smack next to the IRA van full of 3,500lb of explosives that devastated the city centre. As the blast crumpled walls and windows for hundreds of metres around, the 100-year-old postbox seems to have occupied some magical eye of the storm. Aside from paint scratches, it stood firm. A few days later a postman picked his way through the rubble, removed the letters and parcels and sent them on their way. If you really want to ensure your post arrives then this is the box for you – if you ever use anything as old fashioned as letters. Overseas visitors can use the box to post this book to relatives to show them how astonishing Manchester is.

The atrium at 1 Angel Square

The 'survivor' postbox

Walk Two

Grand Commerce, Enigmatic Gardens,
University, Village, Chinatown

Start the walk from the junction of Chapel Street and Cross Street.

The modern office block on the right of Chapel Street contains within itself, on the ground floor, the Unitarian **Cross Street Chapel**. This site has exercised an enormous influence on the city. At its heyday in the 19th century there were probably no more than 2,000 members of the congregation, yet the chapel provided the city with its first five mayors and the region with 12 MPs.

Part of the attraction was the liberal nature of Unitarians, a virtually dogma-free branch of Christianity. One of the ministers was the Rev. William Gaskell, the husband of the novelist Elizabeth Gaskell. Another member of the Congregation was Thomas Potter, who was a principal sponsor of the *Manchester Guardian* when it was established on 5 May 1821, price 7d. The first four words of the *Manchester Guardian*, now simply *The Guardian* newspaper, were 'A Black Newfoundland Bitch'. Napoleon had died the same day but that news wouldn't reach Manchester for weeks, so the 'paper immortalised a lost labrador on a front page made up entirely of advertisements. News did not replace ads on page one until 1952.

Behind the Pret-a-Manger sandwich shop here is **Back Pool Fold** an atmospheric, pungent, alleyway. The name refers to the moat of Radcliffe Hall, which was formerly in this area. The moat was the location of Manchester's ducking stool. This was an open-bottomed chair attached to a pole, which could be levered over blocks into the moat, ducking the miscreant in the water. It was used to punish 'lewde women and scoldes': prostitutes and women who tampered with weights and measures in the market place, although 'scoldes' could refer to nagging wives as well. Many of these

Elizabeth Gaskell

entertaining little passages between the major streets are medieval in origin, following old paths along field boundaries.

With your back to Cross Street Chapel turn left along Cross Street. The charming little pub on your right and across the road is **Mr Thomas's Chop House**, rebuilt in the present style in 1901. This little terracotta gem has an original green tiled interior – lovely to look at easy to clean. Turn first left. This is King Street, full of a variety of grand commercial premises.

The first building on the left is the former Lloyds Bank, **53 King Street**, now cleaned and showing off its beautiful white Portland stone. The bank occupies the site of the original Manchester Town Hall from 1825 until 1877. Part of the façade of the old Town Hall was rebuilt in Heaton Park. **53 King Street** is by prolific Manchester designer Charles Heathcote and dates from 1915.

Mr Thomas's Chophouse detail

It's in his typically muscular Baroque. Decorating the building is symbolic statuary, a patriotic Britannia, and a female personification of Commerce.

Previously the site contained the town house of Doctor Charles White (1728-1813). White was instrumental in establishing the first hospital in Manchester, the Infirmary. He was also a noted physician and obstetrician – his advocacy of fresh water and air greatly reduced mortality rates amongst women after they'd given birth.

For a while the house held the mummified body of Hannah Beswick. She'd been afraid of being buried alive. So in exchange for ensuring she was properly gone, she promised to leave a substantial bequest to the distinguished Doctor Charles White to help with his Manchester Infirmary. So when she died she was pickled, or more correctly embalmed, and placed inside a grandfather clock case in his house. Servants would check each morning to make sure she was still dead.

53 King Street

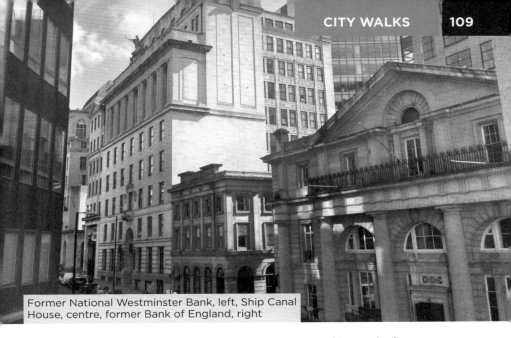

Former National Westminster Bank, left, Ship Canal House, centre, former Bank of England, right

The next building on the same side, is a striking black structure in tooled Swedish granite. It dates from 1969 and was formerly the **National Westminster Bank** by Casson and Conder. The architects wanted the bank to merge in with all the other smoke-darkened buildings around but their worthy ambition was made nonsense when the other buildings were cleaned. Before the bank part of the site had been the lawyer home of the Ainsworth family. One family member, William Harrison Ainsworth, became a novelist and it was his books that cemented the stories of Dick Turpin, Bonnie Prince Charlie and the Lancashire Witches into British consciousness.

Until fairly recent times King Street was purely the domain of finance and commerce: the splendid introduction into what was known as the 'Half Square Mile' in mimicry of London's 'Square Mile'. Technology, bank mergers and the changing needs of modern finance have left these buildings seeking new uses. Across the road is CR Cockerell's handsome classical building from 1846, formerly the **Bank of England**. This was the first permanent provincial branch of the bank. It is now shops and offices. Attached to it is the 82 King Street tower from Holford Associates in 1995.

Also on the right side of the street is the massive **Ship Canal House** by Harry Fairhurst, another epic early 20th century designer we'll encounter again. The building dates from 1929 in Portland stone. The bronze doors are particularly impressive. The problem of Manchester's street pattern denying good views of the city is graphically illustrated here: you have to lean at a spine endangering angle to get any view of the statue of Neptune at its roofline.

Attached to Ship Canal House is a bank, formerly **Atlas Insurance** building. Again the doors are magnificent, capped with a pained-looking Atlas in bronze hoisting the world.

Turn right here down Brown Street and Atlas's rear neighbour is the sweet former **Brook's Bank**, now Burger and Lobster restaurant, from 1868 with a gorgeous entrance alive with carved flowers under a three storey oriel topped by a metal corona.

Return to King Street which is rounds off with three very different buildings. On one side there is the pure white slice of towering efficiency that is Edwin Luytens' **Midland Bank** opened 1935, now Jamie's Italian, crowned by Gotham Hotel – the operators think the building looks like something from Batman's town, maybe the offices of the *Daily Planet*. Either way it's a clever structure reducing telescopically as it climbs to the pavilions on the roof. Go into the restaurant and have a look at the columns all capped with little bells on the capitals – a Lutyens' trademark, called Delhi Bells, after columns used for his work at New Delhi in India. Find an excuse to go to the toilets and seek out the former vault with its double key deposit boxes in pared down Art Décor-style steel. Here were once stored everything from gems and gold to the master tapes of Manchester bands Joy Division and New Order.

When the bank was decommissioned prior to the restaurant refit a problem became apparent. Some of the boxes hadn't been emptied. They still contained valuables but the owners or their descendants couldn't be traced so the Bank of England drilled the boxes open and found £1.1m in jewellery, deeds and assorted goodies. They also found a handgun.

Former Reform Club

Opposite the Lutyens' bank is the **Reform Club** building in a style called Venetian Gothic from 1871. This mad piece of High Victoriana has wild turrets on the two front corners, sculptured panels, granite pillars and carvings writhing all over its surface. Its architect was Edward Salomons. It was built as the city headquarters for the Liberal Party. On the first floor is a balcony from which such figures as William Gladstone, Winston Churchill and Lloyd George spoke. Behind the balcony is the magnificent dining room of the club with its huge oak ceiling, now a restaurant called simply Room. Curiously the lingerie shop Agent Provocateur has a fitting room occupying the most elegant, marble, washrooms for gentlemen in the city – of course no gents ever get in there now.

Former Midland Bank now Jamie's Italian

King Street terminates with the former **Lancashire and Yorkshire Bank** now Rosso Restaurant which has another splendid interior complete with dome and at the door lovely stained glass of red and white roses representing the two counties.

We take the street to the right but to the left here is Brown's Restaurant, formerly **Parr's Bank** by Charles Heathcote from 1902. If you have a thing for green marble the interior will make you swoon.

Follow **Spring Gardens**, down to **Fountain Street**. Both these locations take their name from the fresh water supply that bubbled up out of the fields here and was channelled in a culvert to the old Market Place.

Cross Fountain Street to Mosley Street. Over the road here is the classical **Portico Library**, with a pub below and the original use above. It dates from 1806 and is described on page 36.

Continue down the right side of the Portico Library down Charlotte Street and turn left onto George Street. A plaque on the wall marks where the **Manchester Literary and Philosophical Society** building stood before being destroyed in WWII. It still exists at the Metropolitan University and self-describes on its website thus: 'The Society was established in 1781, with the object of promoting the advancement of education and public interest in any form of literature, science, arts or public affairs. It is the first and oldest Literary and Philosophical Society in the World, and the second oldest Learned Society in the United Kingdom. Its past members include John Dalton and his gifted pupil James Prescott Joule, Peter Mark Roget, the originator of the Thesaurus; William Fairbairn the engineer; Henry Roscoe the chemist; Ernest Rutherford the nuclear physicist; Joseph Whitworth the precision engineer as well as Professor Tom Kilburn and Alan Turing, computing pioneers.'

The restored 1967 building at the junction of George Street and New York Street, now called **The Exchange**, was built by the

The gates of Armageddon - Guardian Exchange as it was

Ministry of Public Building and Works. It lies above the Guardian Royal Exchange. This was part of a network of four tunnel complexes to be built in London, Birmingham, Manchester and Glasgow to maintain links with the rest of Nato should the UK be attacked by Soviet atomic weapons. The generators entitled Marilyn (Monroe) and Jane (Russell) after the stars of the day still sit almost 60m (200ft) beneath the city. There is no public access to these sinister reminders of Armageddon as BT currently runs cabling down them.

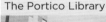

The Portico Library

Turn right on New York Street to Portland Street. Cross the road to the **Britannia Hotel**. This vast and faded building was formerly the S&J Watts warehouse which, occupying the whole city block, was always the biggest of the city's sole occupancy textile warehouses. It cost £100,000 in 1857/8 and the architects were Travis and Mangnall. Each floor has a different architectural treatment with Egyptian at the base rising through Italian Renaissance, Elizabethan and French Renaissance to four great roof projections lit by rose windows.

It's worth going inside to see the magnificent iron cantilever staircase rising from ground to top floor and the memorials to employees killed in the World Wars – including one of the most moving and beautifully crafted, Charles Jagger's indomitable bronze of the *Manchester Sentry* from 1921.

In its heyday, the warehouse would process the 1,000 large to small orders received each morning by close of business. In 1867, a journalist from Freelance magazine expressed his astonishment on encountering the building: 'I am not naturally of a sceptical or suspicious cast of mind. I have eaten sausages and kidney pudding without asking questions but when I was told that this was only a warehouse, I felt that it was necessary to draw the line of credulity somewhere.'

In the December 1940 blitz the whole area was hit by incendiary bombs. With the cotton bales blazing at thousands of degrees, many buildings were consumed, whilst others were demolished to prevent the fire spreading. One of those that had to be sacrificed was the S&J Watts warehouse.

The decision was passed to Chief Fireman Wilf Beckett of the company's own brigade. He refused to budge. Incredulous, the authorities cut off the supply of water to Beckett. The little volunteer force then fought the fires with blankets and sheets until the temperatures outside cooled. In 1941 the building received direct hits once more, and again Beckett and his band saved the day. Later that year he was honoured, on behalf of his men, at Buckingham Palace.

Charles Jagger's Manchester Sentry

Symphony in iron: Britannia Hotel stairs

Piccadilly from the 'Gardens' in the 1970s

Cross back over Portland Street and turn right, past Manchester Visitor Information Centre, cross the bus lanes and tram lines at Parker Street and turn left keeping the concrete wall on your right, until you reach a hole punched in it.

Look back at the vast bulk of what was **Piccadilly Plaza**. The broad concrete podium, the tall tower in the centre and the hotel on the left, is from the original 1965 complex by Covell, Matthews and Partners. The grey right-hand building is from 2001 and is beyond bad. City Tower, splendidly restored by Bruntwood developers, is a 1960s' beauty, looking as fresh as a daisy at 107m (351ft) complete with a racy and original decoration in moulded concrete of computer circuit boards. The hotel is bizarre with the reception several floors above the ground at car park level. Manchester had a plan at the time to divide pedestrians and traffic between ground access and high level roadways. Inside, climbing through several levels in the stairwell is a 1960s' resin artwork by George Mitchell that matches the crazed optimism of the age, and its brutal disregard for anything that had gone before.

Turn right through the hole punched in the concrete wall and you emerge into Piccadilly Gardens, or rather a collection of lawns. The Gardens were completely redesigned by the internationally renowned team of Japanese designer Tadao Andao at the beginning of the Millennium. Nothing much works and the whole city laughs at the mess the designers made and weeps at the cost of trying again. The wall is nicknamed the Berlin Wall.

There is one decent feature, the **Tree of Remembrance**, by Wolfgang and Heron from 2005; public art that seems to capture the reflective, sorrowful mood of its theme. It marks the many hundreds of civilians who died in the Nazi bombing of Manchester in World War II, particularly on 22/23 December 1940 – 'the Christmas Blitz'. Over the two nights around 500 German bombers dropped 467 tons of high explosive and 2000 incendiary bombs on the city and surrounding areas, almost 1,000 people died.

Piccadilly Plaza from the 'Gardens'

There's an entrance to Primark over the tramlines and Mosley Street here. The white Portland stone building to the right of Primark is the **Abbey National Bank**. The bank occupies part of Royal Buildings built on the site of the Royal Hotel where the world's first professional football league was ratified in April 1888.

On the other side of Piccadilly Gardens from Piccadilly Plaza are a row of Victorian and Edwardian statues. Walk to the first closest to the Abbey National Bank. In sequence here we have **Robert Peel** (erected 1853), reforming Prime Minister and local man; **James Watt** (1857), the important steam engineer; **Queen Victoria** (1901); the **Duke of Wellington** (1856), national hero of Waterloo.

The remarkable neo-Baroque canopy of white limestone containing the terrifying statue of Queen Victoria in full regalia – the stern matriarch of nation and Empire - is notable for the insults it's always attracted. Designed by Edward Onslow, one contemporary called it, 'At once the most pretentious, the most incoherent and the most inept of any sculptural monument one has ever seen in England.'

Leave Piccadilly Gardens down the street called Piccadilly leading to Piccadilly Station. In the 18th century, before Manchester became independent minded, deferential locals gave borrowed London names for various streets, hence Piccadilly.

Queen Vic's worst statue

Number 77-83 on Piccadilly by Clegg and Knowles from 1877 is a crazy mix of styles with two lazy workmen sculpted close to the turret on the roof.

Further down the street, the 18th century New Brunswick pub is passed, once a grand townhouse on the fringe of Manchester. Then comes a superb textile warehouse from 1898. The first is now the **Abode Hotel, 107 Piccadilly**, with a lovely tiled stairwell, and an entertaining stripy, bold Baroque on the outside. The architect was Charles Heathcote and the client was Horrocks Crewdson and Company, textile manufacturing giants in Preston whose main selling operation was here in Manchester. There's an extension at the back. The company were the pioneers of ready-to-wear dresses.

Lazy workmen on Piccadilly taken from the car park opposite

Over the road and a little further down is the **Malmaison Hotel**, 1-3 Piccadilly and formerly the warehouse of Joshua Hoyle Ltd. It's by Charles Heathcote, from 1904 creating an odd building of various styles – known for obvious reasons as Eclecticism. Joshua Hoyle was one of the first companies to provide insurance against injury to their employees.

Turn right here on Auburn Street and cross the tramlines at Aytoun Street to Minshull Street. The mighty **Crown Courts** complex over the Rochdale Canal was designed by Thomas Worthington and opened in 1871 as the City Police Courts. It's all fancy Italian Gothic in its older parts with an attractive clock tower, a little like the one Worthington designed for his rejected entry for Manchester Town Hall. There's some lively carving if you walk round the building.

Minshull and Aytoun Streets are named for Barbara Minshull and Roger Aytoun. Aytoun came to Manchester from Scotland in 1769, was 6ft 4", handsome and in full military uniform even though he wasn't in the army. At Kersal Races in Salford he wooed Barbara Minshull, one of the wealthiest people in the North West, owning much of the land in Manchester south east of Portland Street. Three weeks later they married. It was a scandal. Aytoun was in his twenties, Minshull was 65.

She survived another 14 years. During this time and subsequently Aytoun squandered Minshull's fortune on wine, women and recruitment. Finally his military aspirations were met when he raised a Manchester volunteer regiment which fought at Gibraltar in the wars with Napoleon. One of Aytoun's recruitment methods was brawling in pubs. If the fight was won the loser had to join up. Aytoun gained a nickname from this, 'Spanking Roger'.

Crown Courts from City Tower

London Road Fire and Police Station from the south east

The road by the canal here is Canal Street and the Gay and Lesbian Village but turn left for now on Minshull Street and follow the street to the junction with Whitworth Street and turn left. The vast empty building on the right is **London Road Fire and Police Station** from 1906 by Woodhouse and Willoughby. It is another festival of brick and terracotta but this time alive with stylised sculptures and even eagles on the tower looking out across the city for any tell-tale signs of smoke. At one time there was accommodation for forty police and firemen and families, stables, a bank, library, gym and playground in the building.

Now it's the mother of all planning battles between the city and the owners who for almost thirty years have refused to do anything but let the building decline.

Double-back to the main junction and lights here and cross to the narrow tree-lined Coburg Street on the far side of Fairfield Street. Follow the street to Granby Row and the gardens area. The mighty building on the right is now part of the University of Manchester but was built as the **Manchester Technical College** in 1902, in response to growing competition from Germany and America challenging Britain's industrial ascendancy. It's crowned – although this can only be seen from the Whitworth Street side of the building – by the **Godlee Observatory**, home of the Manchester Astronomical Society. This wonderful space can be visited every Thursday, if you book with the Society online.

The pedestrianised and garden area of Granby Row has some entertaining sculptures. The twisted steel cable, *Technology Arch* is by Axel Wolkenhauer from 1989. Behind in the railway arch and even more spritely is Thomas Dagnall's *Archimedes*, with a euphoric expression, caught at the very moment of springing from his bath and shouting 'Eureka!'

Archimedes under the arches

Celebrating Modernism

Continue past *Archimedes* and down the flying stairs and you're in the heart of concrete Modernism in Manchester. Most of the buildings here are by Cruikshank and Seward and were designed for the University of Manchester, Institute of Science and Technology in the sixties. The latter merged with the University in 2004. The area provides a lesson in the architectural fashion of the period, its joy in diverse, almost naive, geometric shapes, its delight in spatial planning, its glee in changes of level. You can almost hear the architects chortling as they drew. Take a look at the stairs and bridge you've just descended, very elegant and great fun.

Retrace your steps to Wolkenhauer's *Technology Arch* and turn left, immedi-

ately you arrive at Kerry Morrison's **Vimto bottle**. This giant sculpture marks the spot where John Noel Nichols invented the popular Manchester soft drink in 1908. Still going strong today, it was intended as a temperance replacement for alcohol. The name came from 'vip and vim tonic', unfortunately an anagram of vomit.

The pedestrianised street adjacent to the Vimto sculpture is Granby Row, where the Plug Riots took place in 1842. These were called by the Chartist movement after the House of Lords rejected a petition demanding an extension of the vote to working men. The name of the riots came from striking workers stopping production by removing the boiler plugs from the steam engines in their factories.

Follow Granby Row down to Sackville Street and cross over. On the west side of Granby Row there are two classic Manchester packing warehouses, converted to residential use. In these gargantuan structures finished cloth went for quality control and was labelled and baled for shipment and storage before it was ready for export. The buildings hosted several tenants. **61-63 Granby Row** is first up on the left by GH Goldsmith from 1908, red brick, Portland stone dressings, and Art Nouveau special effects, a big bold confident building.

Vimto for energy

61-63's neighbour, **Orient House**, has a façade that could be from a Hollywood blockbuster of the 1930s based in Ancient Rome. Also by Goldsmith from 1914, this is all bluster, white faience and a giant Ionic colonnade. It's amusing when you remember it was a textile warehouse. Round the back of the building it's all different, the Bauhaus movement would have been proud of the original utterly functional grid of glass, steel and concrete.

Orient House

Cross over Princess Street and continue between more epic packing warehouses along the cobbled road, note the vast iron gates through which the cloth would arrive and leave. The streets have iron kerbs too as stone kerbs would shatter under the iron wheels of the delivery carts.

The road curves right over a darkly impressive view and a steep drop into the River Medlock. On the left is the 1840s' railway viaduct, on the right there is a cliff face of huge late Victorian and Edwardian packing warehouses.

Look into the river and on the right you'll see an arch. This was once an entrance to

an 18th century tunnel transporting goods by canal boat towards Piccadilly and long since silted up by factory waste dumped into the river. This raised the level of the river bed by up to 2m (more than 6ft).

View over the Medlock and the backs of buildings from Edwardian Manchester

Twisted Art Nouveau gate, Lancaster House

Follow the cobbles to Whitworth Street under the wonderful twisted Art Nouveau iron gate - when closed this describes a perfect circle. The warehouses on each side here, **India House** on the left, **Lancaster House** on the right, are by Harry Fairhurst between 1905 and 1906. Across the street and down to the left is the white **Bridgewater House** from 1912 by the same architect. This whole section of street is magnificently scaled and full of crazy terracotta reliefs, sculptures, towers, rippling bays.

As these buildings were being raised the UK cotton industry centred on Manchester's Royal Exchange was producing more than six billion linear yards of finished cotton, the nearest rival was Japan producing 56 million linear yards.

Cross Whitworth Street and turn right, glimpsing down Beaver Street, one of the few remaining tall city centre chimneys belonging to a former Pumphouse (p46). Cross Princess Street at the lights and walk to Sackville Street, turn left. On a bench in Sackville Gardens, to the right, is a sculpture of **Alan Turing** (1912-1954) sat on a bench. He worked at the University of Manchester and is widely regarded as the father of theoretical computer science and the study of artificial intelligence. He committed suicide by eating a cyanide injected apple, his favourite pantomime as a child had been *Snow White*. The reason for his depression is unclear, although his prosecution for homosexuality in 1952 and his treatment with oestrogen injections as an alternative to prison were probably factors, especially as the conviction meant he was denied access to secret government work. Some people have denied he committed suicide and believe his death was an accident.

Alan Turing gets birthday love, June 23

Continue up Sackville Gardens, over the canal and turn left at Canal Street and walk down to Princess Street. This is the **Gay Village**. The Village, as an idea, has been around for several decades – at least since the Sixties. Some people recall a competition in which a name for the area, 'Gaysville', was suggested. There was a flea market 30 years ago on August Bank Holiday, including a tripe-eating contest to raise money.

The original impetus for the Village seems to have arisen because this canal-side location was a warehouse district of the city centre, little frequented by shoppers and office workers during the day or by revellers during the evening. Close to main transport links, it also developed as a red light area. In an age of gay suppression and repression, this twilight zone became an obvious place of rendezvous for 'queers' within pubs such as the New Union.

Major TV dramas which have featured the Village include the legendary *Queer as Folk* and *Bob and Rose* (both by Russell T Davies) and *Cold Feet*. Novelists to have written about the area include Nicholas Blincoe with *Manchester Slingback* and

Definitely the Village

Coronation Street creator Tony Warren in the brilliant *Behind Closed Doors*.

Manto bar here was an important moment in Village life when it opened in 1992. For the first time a Village bar had plate glass windows, nothing was hidden.

At Princess Street turn right. This part of Princess Street is 'palazzo land', a style of warehouse based on Italian Renaissance palaces adopted after Charles Barry's 'palazzo' design for Manchester's Athenaeum Club completed in 1837. The 'palazzo' delivered a simple but stately design allowed plenty of light whilst not wasting too much space on decoration. The

Pride weekend on Canal Street

main salesrooms with cotton samples were on the upper floors, the first floor provided the counting house and the administration whilst the lower basement contained the machinery, the steam engines and the boilers. A large iron gateway led from the rear or the side of the building through which the textiles were distributed.

One of the buildings on the right, three up from the canal is the **Mechanics Institute**, a lovely example of a 'palazzo' but not a warehouse, instead a place for self-improvement and education of 'the artisan classes'. It dates from 1854 and was designed by J Gregan. It was in here the Trades Union Congress was created in 1868. In an earlier building in 1851 Mrs Dexter had lectured on the thorny subject of 'bloomerism', in otherwords should women wear trousers.

Continue up Princess Street until the traffic lights and cross over Portland Street. Turn right on Portland Street and straightaway you'll encounter a delightful row of mainly 18th century buildings, which include the **Circus** and **Grey Horse** pubs. All the smaller older buildings here used to be pubs as well. At second floor level,

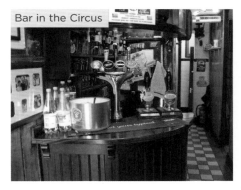
Bar in the Circus

long rows of windows allow increased light into what was a workshop – usually for the intricate task of handloom weaving. The Circus is, inside and out, a remarkable survival of a modest 19th century city pub and has probably the smallest bar in the country.

Mr Hardy operated a largely equestrian circus from close by in the 1790s. The success of the venture led the local landlords to rename their pubs in its honour. In 1797 Mr Hardy went on tour, first to Liverpool and then to Dublin. After a warm welcome in Liverpool, the troupe boarded a ship to Ireland but at the last minute Hardy was called back to Manchester on

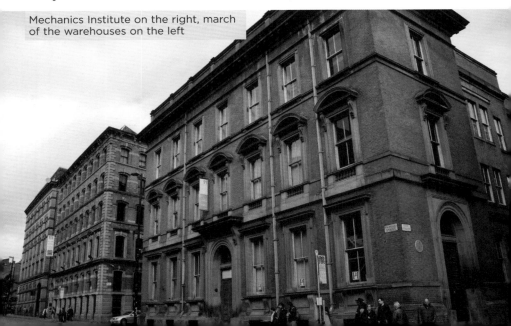
Mechanics Institute on the right, march of the warehouses on the left

business. In rough seas the ship foundered, and horses and performers were lost. Two centuries later the pubs still commemorate Mr Hardy's brief candle flicker of showbiz success.

Facing the Circus turn right on Portland Street and take the first left down Nicholas Street. Ahead on the right is the **Chinese Arch**. This magnificent structure from 1987 is decorated in red and gold dragons and phoenixes: colours and symbols of luck and prosperity. Erected as a token of friendship between the Chinese people and Manchester, it was the first true Imperial Chinese arch in Europe.

Manchester's **Chinatown** really got going in the 1970s. There was a combination of factors that led to this. Hong Kong's speedy urbanisation in the second half of the 20th century resulted in the destruction of farms and villages causing many people to try life abroad. In the UK, the port of Liverpool, 50km (30m) west of Manchester declined - Liverpool has the oldest Chinese community in the West, the ships that used the port having recruited Chinese sailors or laundry workers for over 150 years.

Velvet Crab in Hunan Restaurant

Meanwhile in Manchester the textile warehouses in the area gradually became redundant as the trade moved elsewhere giving Chinese entrepreneurs a central area to create restaurants next to the city's business district. This in turn led to a corresponding growth in the services developed to serve them and their customers. Over time a distinct quarter developed with the arrival of medicine shops, health centres, financial and legal services, supermarkets, old people's homes and Sunday schools.

Chinese Arch

There had been signs of decline recently as huge Chinese supermarkets developed on the city fringes, but in the last couple of years the solidly Cantonese nature of Chinatown - reflecting Britain's colonial links with Hong Kong - has fractured and new waves of immigrants from Mandarin speaking areas, together with a large Chinese student body, have breathed new life into the area. Thai, Japanese food and other Far Eastern restaurants have joined the party to make this one of the more exciting areas to dine out but also to stock up on once rare foods for home consumption.

Continue along Nicholas Street with the Chinese Arch on your right, and turn left on George Street to the junction with Princess Street. The building first on the right is the aforementioned former **Athenaeum Club** from 1837 by Charles Barry, now part of the extension of Manchester Art Gallery. It's a balanced and bold building, the first 'Manchester Palazzo', maybe based on Palazzo Pandolfini, Florence.

The Athenaeum promoted adult education and provided reading and newsroom facilities – the 1873 lecture hall survives on the top floor with some impressive plasterwork. It was self-consciously grand and in lovely Roman script declares beneath the cornice 'For the advancement and diffusion of knowledge'.

Speakers at the Athenaeum included Charles Dickens who in 1843 delivered a

Athenaeum Club detail

powerful speech in support of universal education. He said: "(Some have said) a little learning is a dangerous thing? Why, a little hanging was considered a very dangerous thing, according to the same authorities, with this difference, that, because a little hanging was dangerous, we had a great deal of it; and, because a little learning was dangerous, we were to have none at all." The still surviving Athenaeum Amateur Dramatics society, associated with the building, claims to be the oldest in the world.

Continue down Princess Street, passing the Atheneum's neighbour on the right, **Manchester Art Gallery**, also by Charles Barry, from 1824-35 (p37), the city's best neo-Greek building. From this point there is a fine view of the rear of Manchester Town Hall (page 14), revealing its scale.

Cross the tramlines and Mosley Street. St Peter's Square is to the left but continue to Cooper Street and turn right and first left to Kennedy Street where two late Georgian pubs survive. Note the weavers' window on the second floor of the **Vine Inn**, meanwhile the **City Arms** has a very well-preserved interior. The Wetherspoons pub here, the **Waterhouse**, was formerly the office of Slater Heelis solicitors who represented the police and yeomanry after the Peterloo Massacre.

Return to Princess Street and cross over to the Cenotaph, the war memorial and this tour's conclusion.

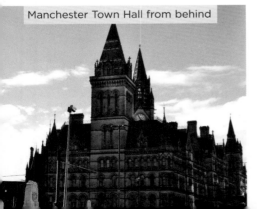
Manchester Town Hall from behind

Walk Three

Theatres, Tiles, Mills, Canals and Castlefield

START the walk at the **Cenotaph** at the rear of Manchester Town Hall (p14) in St Peter's Square.

The Cenotaph or War Memorial was erected in Manchester in 1924 on the western side of the square and moved here in 2014. It's an impressive and elegant commemoration by Sir Edwin Lutyens, the most prominent British architect of the day, who would build again in Manchester with his Midland Bank on King Street – see Walk Two, p110.

A guest of honour at the unveiling of the Cenotaph was Mrs Bingle from Ancoats, who'd lost her three sons in WW1. Capping the monument is a fallen soldier covered in a great coat, his Tommy's helmet at his feet.

Follow the arcade of the Town Hall Extension (p20), perhaps taking the opportunity to admire the Rates Hall, by entering the building at the far end.

Turn left at Central Library (p31) and cross to the very tall modern building, **One St Peter's Square**, which contains Fumo restaurant. This huge office building by Glen Howells architects has attracted criticism, some people complaining it overwhelms the library, but its clean lines and clarity have been praised by others.

St Peter's Church in the 19th century

In between the Library and One St Peter's Square, **St Peter's Church** used to stand, an elegant classical building, the portico of which was transferred to the Gaskell Reading Rooms (now Belle Epoque restaurant) in Knutsford, when the church was demolished in 1907.

The transfer was completed by eccentric Manchester glove manufacturer and would-be architect, Richard Harding Watt. He died as an old man after falling from the roof of a horse-drawn carriage. He was standing on the carriage so he could see the houses he'd designed on Legh Road, Knutsford, over high boundary hedges; suddenly the horse pulling the carriage lurched from a piece of paper blowing in the road and it was bye, bye, Mr Watt.

Cross Oxford Street at One St Peter's Square and turn left, away from Central Library. Very soon on the right you reach **Princes Buildings**, a buff terracotta façade with Art Nouveau details, best at roof level with chimneys linked by a jolly curved parapet. This was by IRE Birkett and erected in 1903 as shops, offices and warehousing.

Over Chepstow Street is a McDonalds with script high on the façade reading the **Picture House**. This was the first purpose

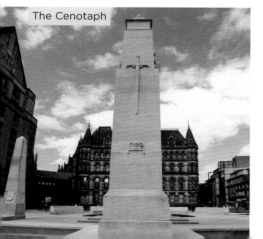
The Cenotaph

built cinema in Manchester. On the opposite side of Oxford Road is the giant arcade at first floor level of the **Louis Behrens & Sons** warehouse. Behrens was a German Jew and came to Britain to join his brother in the textile industry.

After The Picture House is a dreary multi-storey car park, the site of the **Manchester Hippodrome**. Performers who strutted its boards included Sarah Bernhardt, Ellen Terry, Lily Langtree, Anna Pavlova, Gracie Fields and George Formby. According to Terry Wyke in *Manchester Theatres*, ukulele legend Formby 'was so fond of the theatre that a reproduction of the proscenium arch was placed over his grave' during his funeral.

Two mighty packing warehouses face each other across the road here. On the left is **St James's Buildings** by Clegg, Fryer and Penman from 1913. The latter is a vast Baroque style edifice in gleaming Portland stone with broken pediments, heavy cornices, a crazy little temple-like tower and a sumptuous entrance hall and stair. It was in a club under St James's Buildings in the 1970s where Warsaw played their second gig in 1977. They returned as the influential group Joy Division the next year and were spotted and signed to Factory Records. After the death of lead singer Ian Curtis they changed their name again to

St James' Building entrance

Oxford Road with St James's Buildings, Churchgate House, Palace Theatre and Refuge Assurance

Behren's Warehouse

Churchgate House, on the right, formerly the Tootal Broadhurst Lee & Co building, by J Gibbon Sankey from 1898, is more restrained but still very grand with bands of brick and terracotta. The corner details of the building, the ceramic giants – Atlantes in architectural parlance - were probably designed by WJ Neatby, the renowned head of the architectural department of tiling specialists Doulton – subsequently Royal Doulton.

'Atlantes' hold up Churchgate House

Pass over Rochdale Canal and the **Palace Theatre** is on the left. Built in 1891, refaced in 1956 it contains a gorgeous auditorium from 1913. Charlie Chaplain has appeared on the stage, as have a whole roster of top-flight stars including Frank Sinatra and more recently key performers at Manchester International Festival such as Damon Albarn, Lou Reed and Marina Abramovic.

Oxford Road Station

The theatre district of Manchester has often majored in music and dance. It was John Tiller in Manchester in 1890 who created the eponymous Tiller Girls. He wanted to make the dancers more coordinated, so he had them link arms. With high kicks and perfect timing they became famous from New York to Paris.

Distinctive roof of Oxford Road Station

At the road junction here, take the ramp to your right to **Oxford Road Station**, a fine timber station from 1960 by Max Clendinning, described as 'one of the more remarkable and unusual stations'. The surviving furniture, ticket office, cafe and ceilings, full of sweeping movement, are perfect for a station – yet surprisingly gentle. The prow at the entrance is echoed by two similar motifs behind: Manchester fantasists insist the resulting profile influenced Jorn Utzon's design of Sydney Opera House.

With your back to the station take the steep stairs down to The Salisbury pub and then climb the cobbles back to Oxford Road.

The Tiller Girls in action

Dominating everything here is the Palace Hotel, formerly the Refuge Assurance building, an insurance company. One of the most colourful descriptions ever given to a Manchester building is CR Reilly's from 1924, who thought it resembled 'a tall young man in flannel trousers escorting two charming but delicate old ladies in lace'.

It's worth looking more closely at the **Palace Hotel**, so cross the road at the pedestrian crossing to the left. It was built in stages between 1891 and 1930. The first part, by Town Hall architect Alfred Waterhouse, rose at the corner of Oxford Road and Whitworth Street where the doorway is capped by a terracotta castle, a symbol of security for those trusting their money with the Refuge Assurance. There's dazzling tilework just inside the porch, often with an intertwined RA. There's more tilework inside the main lounge, while the huge 1910 entrance under the 66m (217ft) clocktower is equally impressive. The quarters on the clock feature a stylised Manchester bee (p207).

The roof of the building was chosen for the closing scene of classic British film noir, *Hell is a City*, with Stanley Baker, from 1959.

Cross back over Oxford Road and turn immediately right after the railway bridge, down New Wakefield Street, with its bars and graffiti-art on the railway arches.

At the junction with Great Marlborough Street is **Student Castle** from 2012. The building is by Manchester practice Hodder+Partners and is tall. At 106m (almost 350ft) it's the fourth tallest building in the city. It cost £28.5m, is 37-storeys and provides self-contained studios and apartments for 520 people. Across the road is the **Green Building** by Terry Farrell & Partners from 2005. The circular building has a turbine on the roof to provide for electricity generation.

Student Castle from the south

Dazzling tiles in the Refuge Assurance, now the Palace Hotel

Turn left on Great Marlborough Street. On one of the 19th century brick buildings on the right is a plaque marking notorious **Little Ireland**. Friedrich Engels, German communist and Manchester resident for almost 22 years, described the area in his 1845 book *The Condition of the Working Class in England*: 'The cottages are old, dirty, and of the smallest sort, the streets uneven, fallen into ruts and in part without drains

SITE OF
LITTLE IRELAND
LARGE NUMBERS OF IMMIGRANT
IRISH WORKERS LIVED HERE IN
APPALLING HOUSING CONDITIONS
BUILT   C. 1827
VACATED   C. 1847
DEMOLISHED   C. 1877

or pavements; masses of refuse, offal and sickening filth lie among standing pools in all directions; the atmosphere is poisoned by effluvia'.

The area seemed to sum up the worst of the unregulated industrial revolution, in the words of another commentator, Alexis de Toqueville, Manchester was where 'everything in the exterior appearance attests the individual powers of Man: nothing the directing powers of Society'.

Anthony Burgess's piano and writing desk

Little Ireland (plaque, top centre) was largely and inadvertently 'slum-cleared' by the railway. Oxford Road Station and the railway arches arrived in 1849 as part of the **Manchester South Junction and Altrincham** line destroying Engels' broken cottages, but not without incident: three railway arches collapsed killing workmen.

This area was once one of the major manufacturing districts of central Manchester. Chorlton Old Mill here was built for social pioneer Robert Owen in 1795 before he left Manchester to set up New Lanark Mills close to Glasgow, now a World Heritage Site.

Palace Hotel tower from Cambridge Street

Follow Great Bridgewater Street as it becomes Lower Ormond Street on the other side of Hulme Street, and on the right before the junction with Chester Street is the mucky but glumly-striking mountain of brick that is **Chatham Mill**. This dates from 1820 with an extension of 1823. Inside the former cotton-spinning mill is a 21st century hive of creative industries, designers and fashionistas.

Turn right on Chester Street and right again on Cambridge Street. Some of the recent student residences here are fake mills: a curious turn-around in reputation for the 'dark Satanic mills'.

Cross over Hulme Street and immediately on the right, within the Birley cotton mill, now apartments, is the **International Anthony Burgess Foundation** with its café, performance space, archive and library. The very entertaining Anthony Burgess, famed for his novel *A Clockwork Orange*, is profiled in the history and people section of this book.

The factories on both sides here were pioneers in waterproof cloth production. This happened when the local manufacturer, Birley's, combined with Charles Macintosh in the late 1820s – hence the generic name for the raincoat 'the Mac'.

Continue down Cambridge Street to Whitworth Street West, passing *Hotspur House*, a textile mill that became a printers publishing the *Hotspur* boys' action comic and other titles. It launched in 1933 and bizarrely contained an offer for an electric shock machine with the words: 'It's a great prize, absolutely harmless and will give hours of fun. Just watch your pal's face when you give him his first electric shock!' There's an old Township of Manchester marker on the building before the city expanded in the early 19th century.

Turn left on Whitworth Street West, looking briefly to the right at the **Ritz Ballroom** from 1928. This is the city's longest continuously running music venue. Its sprung dance floor featured in the 1961 film A Taste Of Honey, the 'kichen-sink' drama set in 1950s' Salford, originally a play by 18-year-old Shelagh Delaney. It also hosted the first gig of Manchester cult band, The Smiths, in 1982.

Follow the railway arches to the junction with Albion Street. On the right here is **Hacienda Apartments**. These stand on the site of a warehouse that bizarrely, so far from the sea, became a yacht showroom and then in 1982 became the famous Hacienda nightclub, financed by Factory Records, led by Anthony (Tony) H Wilson and money from the band New Order.

It appeared on the cover of magazine *Newsweek* as the most famous club in the world in the eighties and is seen as the

Township of Manchester boundary sign

The Hacienda Apartments

spiritual home of acid house music and rave culture, with DJs Mike Pickering and Graeme Park leading the scene. It closed in 1997 after problems with security and spiralling debt.

The Hacienda then transmuted into history and subsequently has had museum and gallery exhibitions devoted to it, leading to a backlash amongst Manchester commentators who claim the sentimentality regarding its legacy stifles new ideas.

Path down to Rochdale Canal at Deansgate Locks

Under the rail arches to the left is the route into the **First Street** development. Follow the path and turn left into Tony Wilson Place, named after the Factory Records boss, broadcaster, Hacienda associate and original dreamer and thinker. Nearby streets are named after other Manchester personalities.

HOME lies on at the far side of Tony Wilson Place, designed by Mecanoo architects, and the latest addition to the official arts scene of Manchester. There are two performance venues - a 500-seat theatre and 150-seat flexible studio space, five cinema screens, gallery space to display contemporary art, a cafe bar and restau-rant. Patrons include local boy Danny Boyle, director of *Slumdog Millionaire* and the London Olympic's opening ceremony.

Retrace your steps to Whitworth Street West and turn left over Albion Street and then cross Whitworth Street West and take the path down to the Rochdale Canal and follow the towpath, opposite the rows of bars occupying the old railway arches.

Rochdale Canal opened in 1804 and was the first canal link between east and west coasts across the Pennine hills. The canal is 32 miles long and has 92 locks. In 1845 it handled 979,443 tons of trade, now tourists navigate its length.

View across Castlefield at Middle Warehouse

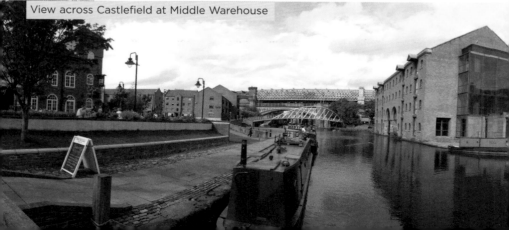

Follow the canal past lock 91 and under Deansgate and take the first path off the canal to the left, which brings you on to Castle Street.

You are now in Castlefield, an area with a peculiar sort of beauty, perhaps a peculiar sort of *Manchester* beauty, where water and brick combine powerfully and viaduct after viaduct leap over canal and wharfside. It is one of the strongest urban landscapes in the UK, a place where the Romans settled Manchester and where the oldest industrial age canal meets the oldest passenger rail station in the world.

Cross straight over the cobbles of Castle Street past a cogwheel sculpture onto a high platform over the Bridgewater Canal basin. You're standing on the remains of Grocers' Warehouse, designed by James Brindley who also designed much of the Bridgewater Canal with John Gilbert. This canal opened in 1765, the first true UK artificial navigation for industry.

Take the stairs, on the left, down to the canal basin. Grocers' Warehouse is ingenious. Under the building is a tunnel carrying the River Medlock. The overflow of the canal water into the tunnel caused a waterwheel in the warehouse to turn allowing coal and goods to be lifted from the canal to the road level.

The **Bridgewater Canal** brought coal from the Duke of Bridgewater's collieries at Worsley 11km (7m) away. It was one of those lurches in technology that enabled the fires of industry to burn brighter. The Duke was laughed at for his enterprise and the canal nearly broke him with its cost of £200,000, yet just a short time later it was returning £80,000 a year.

James Brindley, the engineer, used to say "water is like a giant, safest while lying on its back" which resulted in the Bridgewater Canal being the fastest in the country. There are no locks to slow the movement of traffic down as the canal follows the contours of the landscape.

Brindley also loved to consume huge quantities of food and drink. For particular binges it was said he had a waistcoat with a top button that when raised by pressure from the food gathering in the belly beneath would pop and warn Brindley with engineering precision to stop eating.

The former church, on the left, was the *Congregational Chapel* from 1856 by Edward Walters, completed in the same year as his Free Trade Hall (see Walk One, p88). In more recent times it was the recording studio of Pete Waterman and hosted artists of the calibre of Kylie Minogue and...er...Steps. According to legend this was where Rick Astley recorded 1987 hit, *Never Gonna Give You Up*. Waterman gave up the building in 2006.

From the foot of the stairs take the black bridge on the left, over the canal arm, and follow the towpath. Across the canal, the

red sandstone bedrock under Manchester can be spotted, above that is the splendid restoration of **Eastgate**, an 1870s' warehouse, with a water tower now topped by a light box.

The path passes **Middle Warehouse**, now called Castle Quay, occupied by apartments and a radio station. The warehouse

Summertime at Duke's 92

The Lock Keeper's cottage garden

Iron power

dates from 1831 and incorporates two large boat arches. Then comes the **Wharf** pub with its well-maintained outdoor area. On the other side of the canal is the oldest of the warehouses in the area, the elegant Merchant's Warehouse, 1825, with sweet modern glass extensions.

Take the white curve of **Merchants Bridge** from 1996 by Whitby Bird and Partners. From the middle you can see fourteen bridges, including the mighty cast iron railway viaducts of 1877 and 1893 and the smaller iron arched railway bridge of 1849. All of these are sprung from castellated columns or piers in a remarkable act of Victorian double-think. The Roman Fort of Manchester (p136) was close by, the remaining vestiges of which were largely destroyed by the railways, but the Victorians thought they'd remind viewers of the destruction with their little castles.

There's a good view of lock 92, the last lock, on the Rochdale Canal here as it joins with the Bridgewater Canal.

Walk past **Barca** bar, originally opened in the 1990s, and once partly owned by flame-haired Manchester crooner Mick Hucknall of Simply Red (he's got red hair, supports United and the Labour Party – hence Simply Red).

Better bars and businesses lie to the right, over Rochdale Canal, **Dukes 92** and Albert's Shed, the former previously stables for the canals. Also to the right, but on this side of the canal is the quaint, and in this cityscape unlikely looking, **Lock Keeper's Cottage** from the early 19th century.

After Barca Bar turn left and left again under the railway bridge, then the iron viaducts, and another brick viaduct and into the **Outdoor Arena**. This is the scene of sporadic events through the city calendar. In 1994 over 20,000 people gathered in and around the Arena to hear, via big screen, the president of the International Olympic Games announce that Sydney had won the right to host the games, not

Manchester or the other competing cities. There was a silent pause for a few seconds and then the whole crowd started singing the Monty Python song, *Always Look on the Bright Side of Life*.

Leave the Outdoor Arena up the stairs at the far end, close to the Castlefield Hotel over the canal arms to the left. On Liverpool Road, cross the road and turn left. You're walking by the side of the **Museum of Science and Industry, MOSI** (see p43), Britain's largest such museum located in several important buildings.

There's a plaque on the wall in the buildings close to the junction with Water Street. These announce these modest buildings as the **Liverpool Road Station** of 1830, part of the Liverpool to Manchester Railway (now part of MOSI). This launched on 15 September 1830, it launched the Railway Age. This was the first recognisably modern railway system and the first passenger one. The Prime Minister, The Duke of Wellington opened the line, and it was an immediate success.

Liverpool Road Station

The station building is modest for such epoch making changes, almost domestic, as though the designers had no idea of how a station should look. The handsome house at the bottom of the site was the Station Agent's residence. The pub over the road, the Commercial Hotel, opened at the same time and is therefore the oldest railway hotel anywhere, the modest ancestor of the Midland Hotel, see Walk One (p85).

Castlefield Outdoor Arena

Retrace your steps up Liverpool Road and turn right down Potato Wharf, a cobbled street, the name recalling how the vegetables from west Lancashire came into the city on the canals.

Under the railway arch, turn left towards the Youth Hostel car park to view **Giant's Basin**. This is another example of James Brindley's genius - slightly altered. It is the 1760s' overflow of the Bridgewater Canal into the River Medlock which flows in a tunnel underneath and exits the canal basin over the cobbles of Potato Wharf nearby.

Again retrace your steps, to Liverpool Road and then right, up to the junction with Lower Byrom Street. The curved brick building here is the Sunday School from 1827 of the demolished St Matthew's Church. Both were designed by Sir Charles Barry, who'd later design the Houses of

Detail of former markets now Air & Space Gallery

Giant's Basin

Parliament. To the right is the entrance to MOSI.

Continue up Liverpool Road, passing, the **Oxnoble** pub. This is probably the only pub in the UK named after a potato. The Oxnoble was a low grade spud: Manchester people said they gave it to the animals while in Liverpool they ate it. In Liverpool they said the reverse.

On the other side of the road is the Air and Space gallery of MOSI. This is part of a pair of former market buildings selling the vegetables that gave the Oxnoble its name. The buildings are by Travis and Mangnall from 1876 and 1878. There are cotton flowers at chest height on the columns and red roses for Lancashire at the capitals.

The blue post box close by dates from the years after WWII when air mail was sent via blue boxes not red.

To the right are reconstructed remains of Mamucium, the Roman Fort of Manchester, first built here in AD79 – see page 136.

The White Lion pub dates from the 1770s and is part of a range of buildings hosting weaver's cottages with their distinctive second floor workshop windows providing light for fiddly textile work completed in the home.

Continue up to the Deansgate junction. The building to the left, containing, the Cervantes Institute and Dimitris Restaurant was once the **Free Library** designed by Meek and Allison in 1882.

Dominating everything is **Beetham Tower** by Manchester's Ian Simpson Architects. This is 47 storeys tall, split between the Hilton Hotel and private apartments and was completed in 2006 at a cost of £150m. At level 23 is Cloud 23, the viewing

Beetham Tower, tall and thin

bar and top floor of the Hilton. The building looks top heavy, cantilevered out at level 22, to give more living space to the apartments above.

At 168m (551ft) Beetham Tower is easily the tallest building outside London. Opinion is divided over its merit as it delivers a starkly simple profile to the city although its slender profile from east and west is dramatic: with a ratio of 1:10 it is one of the thinnest skyscrapers anywhere.

The architect himself, Ian Simpson, lives on the top floor duplex that spans the whole building and includes an internal garden of lime, lemon and oak

trees. Manchester magazine *Manchester Confidential* conducted a poll in 2009 asking whether people liked Beetham Tower and after almost 9,000 replies it was 60-40 in favour, although one reader remarked that Ian Simpson reminded him of *Lord of the Rings* character Sauron staring down from his high fortress.

The top glass element puzzles many people but is there to balance the lower cantilever. The fact the glass element whistles and moans in high winds increases the controversy over Beetham Tower, leading to spoof suggestions the other skyscrapers of Manchester should be calibrated to whistle popular hits together on windy days.

ROMAN MANCHESTER

It must have been the cohorts of 20th Valeria Victrix legion, under General Agricola, who spotted Manchester's potential in 79 AD – a memorable year, especially for the citizens of Pompeii whose city was wiped out by the eruption of Mount Vesuvius.

The Romans recognised the strategic value

Roman Manchester
as it may have looked

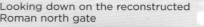

Looking down on the reconstructed
Roman north gate

of the rounded bluff over the confluence of the Rivers Irwell and Medlock. The Romans stayed for over three centuries. Their fort was garrisoned, at its peak, by an 800 strong mixed force of infantry and cavalry. This was an auxiliary regiment, not native Romans, but recruits or conscripts from the other provinces.

Primarily the place was military in character but as often happened outside Roman forts a civilian settlement grew which accommodated the unofficial wives of the soldiers and attracted artisans and craftsmen, who set up furnaces and workshops.

During excavations in the seventies a Christian 'magic square' dating from 175 AD was found. This coded inscription spells the word Paternoster, the opening words of the Lord's Prayer in Latin. It's the oldest evidence of Christianity in the country.

Seven roads met at the fort, more than at any other site in the North. Future movements of people and resources would, for convenience sake, move along these routes and come directly through Manchester. Roman authority officially abandoned Britain in 410 AD and eventually the Saxons moved in.

Manchester's name

The Victorians thought Manchester's Roman name was Mancenion and that's how it appears in Ford Madox Brown's Town Hall mural. Some Manchester men translated this fancifully as 'city of men'. Modern scholarship now believes the name to have been Mamucium or 'breast-shaped hill' – a very different notion. Meanwhile the Latin word 'castrum' meaning fort was twisted into the 'chester' element of the city's name. Bravissimo, a lingerie retailer, once used the real Roman name in a Manchester promotional campaign.

Walk Four

The Quays, the Imperial War Museum North,
The Lowry, MediaCityUK

The Quays, formerly Manchester Docks, makes for a fine circular walk of around twenty minutes without stops, but you'll want to stop and you'll want to visit buildings. The architecture, the engineering and the huge expanse of water creates a spectacular modern urban landscape. Not all the buildings are classics, but the combined effect is powerful. Sport even joins in with Manchester United closing off the view to the south.

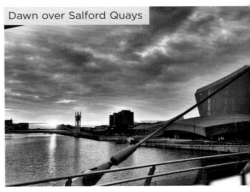
Dawn over Salford Quays

A bonus is the quality of the light as it bounces off the water and ricochets off the steel and aluminium buildings. Dawns and sunsets are often stunning, but beware the wind that can come howling down Manchester Ship Canal. The lighting scheme across the Quays makes an evening walk rewarding too. The easiest way to access the area is by tram from the city centre to the MediaCityUK stop.

There's a history of Manchester Ship Canal on page 225.

Start the walk at The Lowry arts centre and cross the footbridge nearby. This was finished in 2000 to the designs of Casado

of Madrid. It was engineered by Parkman's of Salford and constructed a short distance down the canal at the dry dock on the other side of the Imperial War Museum North. It was then floated into place. It is a lift bridge, the whole walking area lifting in its cat's cradle of wire and steel, around 20m (65ft) or so, to the great pulley wheels on the four pylons.

In the summer months Mersey Ferries from Liverpool travel up and down the canal and the bridge opens to let the

The Lowry

Mobile childcare solution

vessels through. Standing in the centre, the view encompasses the Imperial War Museum North, The Lowry, the city centre, Manchester United Football Club and in the distance the Pennine hills.

Turn left after the bridge to view the art-works, there's a small playground too. The best of the works is the furthest away, *Silent Cargoes* by SITE. This commemorates the canal and the adjacent area of Trafford Park which it served. The artwork takes the form of an arrange-

IWMN

IWMN with United looming behind

ment of industrial artefacts and products, machinery, tools, barrels, cotton bales seemingly abandoned on the wharf side. Scattered through the work are gloves and caps, as though the workers have just come off shift. This gives the work an air of melancholy. The industrial world might have been mucky but there was an honour in manufacturing which is less easy to discern in a nation increasingly employed in the service industries.

Retrace your steps, but at the bridge continue on this side of the canal to the **Imperial War Museum North – IWMN** *(Quay West, Trafford Wharf Rd, Manchester M17 1TZ, 0161 836 4000. Free. Open daily 10am-5pm).*

If the museum is open, walk round the building to get a feel for this unusual structure, before entering at the main entrance, on the other side of the building away from the canal. IWMN was designed by Daniel Libeskind and opened in 2001. Prior to working in Trafford he built the Jewish Museum in Berlin, subsequently he has worked on the masterplan for the World Trade Center site in New York following the terrorist attack on September 11, 2002.

Libeskind's buildings are all about statement and concept. For the Imperial War Museum North Libeskind placed a ceramic tea pot in a plastic bag and dropped it out of the window. Three of the broken shards he arranged as a world shattered by war in a pattern representing the three theatres of land, sea and air war. The resulting building is deliberately disorientating with few right angles or level floor plates. Thus it reflects the confusion of war. The main permanent exhibition lies in the Earth Shard. The exhibition areas here, the 'silos', provide a blank canvas for the light and sound shows that regularly transform the space.

The message of the museum is stated as War Shapes Lives. This is delivered without judgment, the facts and stories laid before visitors, and covers conflict since WW1. The exhibits come from the Imperial War Museum's own collections. The stories told are very moving, the exhibits can be terrifying. A nuclear bomb seems modest in size, perhaps a couple of metres long, the map on the wall nearby shows you the large area of Northern England it would have devastated were it to have been dropped.

Libeskind's connection to the World Trade Center site has an echo in the 7m (23ft) section of twisted steel from the toppled buildings. The pick of the artworks is

IWMN

Gerry Judah's *Crusader*, a beautiful large white sculpture contrasting with the darkness of the subject matter which depicts destroyed buildings on a cross.

No visit would be complete without ascending to the 29m (95ft) viewing platform in the Air Shard which gives great views over the Greater Manchester conurbation. Visitors walk over a metal grille looking straight back down to the floor beneath. The temporary exhibitions are always worth visiting and there are plenty of activities for kids and of course, a cafe and a shop.

IWMN and a perfomer in front of Twin Towers shard

The landscaping on the canal side of IWMN leads to the second footbridge on the route. This was finished in 2011 and was designed by Gifford Engineering and Wilkinson Eyre. It weighs 450 tonnes, and has two spans of 65m (213ft) and 18m (63ft). It swings through 71 degrees to give a 48m (158ft) navigation channel.

On the same side of the canal as IWMN is ITV Granada with hints - over the modest facade as you cross the bridge - of the set of the longest continuously running TV soap anywhere, *Coronation Street*. This began in December 1960, written by Tony Warren and based on working class life in the streets of nearby Ordsall.

The footbridge takes you into the heart of **MediaCityUK**, the nation's largest concentration of media, principally occupied by almost 2,500 BBC staff, who started to arrive in 2011. The first building on the right is **Quay House**, which broadcasts *BBC Breakfast, Match of the Day, BBC Radio 5 Live, North West Tonight* and *BBC Radio Manchester*. On the left is **Bridge House** where *Blue Peter, Mastermind, Dragons' Den, CBBC*, and *BBC Bitesize* are produced.

The route from the bridge opens out into the main square of MediaCityUK with its large screen. The dominant building is **The Studios** with is varied colour scheme. This contains seven high definition studios, the largest with an area of 1,160m^2 (12,500sqft). One of the studios is occupied by the BBC Philharmonic Orchestra and sat on hydraulic jacks to insulate it from noise coming from other studios.

The next building along, facing the excellent small park, is **Dock House** and contains the BBC's Research and Development, Religion and Ethics departments and BBC 6 Music. Several Radio 4 programmes are made here. **Orange House**, next door, contains the restaurant Damson, more ITV space and the University of Salford's media departments.

There are several apartment blocks behind the media buildings. The BBC moved so many of their departments to the banks of Manchester Ship Canal in an effort to lessen the London-centric metropolitan tone of their output. It's cheaper to be here than in the capital as well.

The architecture of MediaCityUK from Wilkinson Eyre, Chapman Taylor and Fairhursts has been criticised as a 'crazed accumulation of development, in which every aimlessly gesticulating building sports at least three different cladding treatments. The overriding sense is one of extreme anxiety on the part of the architects about the development's isolation'.

You can see what Ellis Woodman, the writer of this, meant and that might

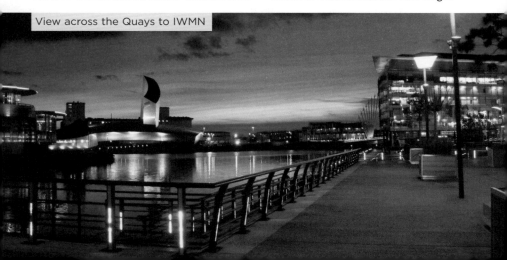

View across the Quays to IWMN

MediaCityUK

Swimming in Dock Nine

have seemed the case in 2011. Now MediaCityUK can be appreciated better. With a playground in the small park plus the Blue Peter garden, the area is becoming very popular with locals and visitors and especially families. The Dockyard pub selling Manchester beers and simple food has helped.

Walk through the park area to the main road and turn right. On the left is the long expanse of Dock Nine, bordered by apartments and at the far end several shoddy examples of 1980s' architecture. The swing bridge in the middle of the dock arm was moved here from the main canal in the '80s. Over half a mile in length Dock Nine was big enough to hold 10 large ships. The

problem is those ships kept getting longer making transit through the locks and up to the head waters infeasible. The last cargo vessel arrived at this end of the canal in 1982.

The change in character has enabled the atrociously polluted waters to be cleaned. The process is on-going: if you look carefully, twenty metres down Dock Nine, you might see bubbling whirlpools oxygenating the waters. These have worked so well there are open water swimming sessions on Saturdays in Dock Nine and an annual triathlon.

Straight ahead is the Lowry. Walk towards the building and then turn left to circumnavigate it. At the far end is the artwork

MediaCityUK

Where the Wild Things Were by Unusual Artists (that's their name). The idea is that the giant blades of elephant grass 'suggest places beyond the canal, where ships sailed to and from'. Continue round the far side of Lowry and underneath the footbridge and along the promenade here facing Manchester United on its ridge over the canal. The promenade leads to the Helly Hansen Watersports Centre where visitors can partake of dinghy sailing, windsurfing and power boating.

Retrace your steps with the bland Lowry Outlet Mall on the right, back to **The Lowry** arts centre *(Pier 8, Salford Quays, M50 3AZ, 0843 208 6000. Free but suggested donation. Gallery open Sun-Fri 11am-5pm, Sat 10am-5pm)*. This stainless steel building was designed by Michael Wilford and comprises theatres, an art gallery, a restaurant, a shop, conference areas and Salford Tourist Information Centre. It opened in 2000 and kickstarted the proper redevelopment of the Quays and attracts several hundred thousand people each year.

Inside the Quays building

The Lyric theatre has 1,750 seats, the Quays, 460. There's a smaller Studio for 150 too. The exterior of the main auditorium rises in steel panels above a mass of sharp geometric forms, cones, cubes and circles. These are swathed in glass allowing a view of people circulating around the interior. The view from the inside out is good while the views across the building are remarkable. The foyer is overlooked by balconies opening from the first floor, and the restaurant bar is crossed by a bridge whilst the outer shell of the Lyric is punctured by balconies and staircases.

The colours are overwhelming, oranges and deep purples in the entrance area, in stark contrast to the silver exterior. Wilford wanted this building to be very democratic, appealing to everyone and he thought the colour scheme aided this.

The galleries devoted to Manchester artist Laurence Stephen Lowry, and to temporary and visiting exhibitions, are on the north facing side of the building to prevent damage from the sunny south but there is plenty of light streaming in from the neighbouring promenade windows.

There's irony with the dedication of this building to Lowry. A space that is as colourful as an HG Wells' dream of the future commemorates an artist who inhabited a hermit's cave of imagination. A building that attracts thousands to its shows marks a man who shied from human relationships. Meanwhile the industrial scenes Lowry painted have disappeared outside his dedicated art centre under apartments, shopping centres and studios.

Inside The Lowry

The Lowry

Laurence Stephen Lowry (1887-1976)

Lowry was born in Old Trafford and lived in Greater Manchester in various homes all his life. He was eccentric but hardly in the typical mould of the Bohemian artist. He was massively introverted, never had an adult relationship, was a teetotal, non-smoker and funded his painting by rent-collecting. His early life was submerged by a strong mother who ridiculed his attempts at being an artist. Despite this he plugged away and his work gradually gained fame during his lifetime, its deceptively simple nature and frequently homely themes appealing to a broad audience. He is famous for his industrial scenes but should also be remembered for his eerie and desolate landscapes and seascapes. His Head of a Man (*Red Eyes*) is probably his masterpiece, a twisted self portrait from 1938.

Coming from the Mill (1930) was described by Lowry as 'his most characteristic mill scene' and is shown below. It carries all the main Lowry themes. He painted industrial scenes, because as he said, 'I lived on the spot'. The figures are simplified, part of a crowd, de-individualised. 'The ghostly figures are symbols of my mood,' he said. The people rarely have faces and they are frequently hunched. They always seem on the move as well as though in permanent transit or limbo. The painting has the characteristic dome Lowry always included, and shows a town that was 'part real and part imaginary'. The houses are ones he would have seen in his rent-collecting walks, their familiarity is what appealed to Lowry who said, 'I have put most of my tenants in my pictures'. A dog as usual is included. Lowry thought animals free unlike the automaton humans. 'You never see the sun in my paintings,' Lowry said, another reflection of his introversion. In fact he only ever used a palette of five colours, white, black, blue, yellow and red. The horse and cart in the picture is typical too. By the 1930s cars were commonplace, yet Lowry rarely painted them, never allowing technological advances to animate his vision of industrial Britain.

Coming from the Mill (1930)

The North West of England is one of the most diverse in Britain if not Europe. Human works vary from stone to brick, from slate-roofed terrace to thatched cottage, from towering mill to stately home. From the north to the southeast there is tough millstone grit moorland followed by limestone uplands. To the south lies a gentle rolling countryside of villages and meadows. All the areas offer fine walks and all have places to visit.

Brass Art's, Time Capsule, Tatton Park Art Biennial

Regional attractions

Clockwise from top: Dunham, Lyme, Tatton, Tatton, Dunham, Tatton, Lyme, Lyme.

Stately homes and gardens

The top three 'stately homes' close to Manchester lie just to the south of the city. All have a range of entrance charges depending on whether you're just visiting the house or garden or both and all have cafes, shops and playgrounds. There are special events throughout the year. Look out for promenade theatre in summer and Tatton's Biennial contemporary art fair with the next in 2016. Also at Tatton every year is the annual Royal Horticultural Society Flower Show.

Lyme Hall and Park *(Disley, Stockport, SK 12 2NR, 01663 762 023)* has a stirring location in a bowl below the higher hills but still far above Manchester and Cheshire plains. The family of Lyme were the Leghs. The building is made up of Elizabethan elements with later alterations, particularly by the celebrated architect Giacomo Leoni in the 1730s. The result is a handsome house built around a gorgeous Renaissance courtyard. Highlights include Grinling Gibbon's woodcarvings and Mortlake tapestries. High in the building is the bedroom that housed Mary Queen of Scots. When the weather was wet and cold the impressive space of the Long Gallery was used. The house is set in 1,377 acres of parkland containing red and fallow deer. There are also formal gardens with fine plant specimens and a Dutch walled garden. From the Elizabethan hunting tower to the north, there are wide views across the North West of England.

Tatton Park *(Knutsford, Cheshire, WA16 6QN, 01625 537 4400)* is set in the calm beauty of the gently undulating Cheshire countryside and within its own 1,000 acre deer park. The elegant Georgian mansion is by Samuel and Lewis Wyatt and was formerly the home of the important Egerton family. Amongst many qualities, the house has fine furniture and decorations and a large and interesting library. The principal glory of Tatton Park, though,

is its exceptional garden, said to be amongst the top ten in the country. There are 50 acres of formal garden crammed with variety and beauty at all times of the year. The Japanese Garden, 1910-12, was created by Japanese gardeners – it's the oldest genuinely Japanese garden in the West. The parkland is wonderful for a stroll at any time of the year. This has free access via various public paths but the best way to enter is from the top of King Street in Knutsford. The park has two large lakes or meres and there is swimming, sailing, fishing and riding. You can also visit the 15th century Old Hall and the Home Farm.

Dunham Massey *(Charcoal Lane, Altrincham, WA14 4SJ, 0161 941 1025)* is smaller than Lyme Park or Tatton Park but the closest to the city. The house is red brick with a stone-faced centre. There are elements dating from the 17th century, although most of the building is early 18th century. The house was opened to the public on the death of the Earl of Stamford in 1976. The most famous feature of the house is its collection of Huguenot silver. The garden is lovely and large and contains an exquisitely kept parterre, an aromatic orangery and a busy Edwardian water garden. Outside the garden is the informal parkland area, which stretches over a couple of hundred acres. To add grace to the landscape of grass and tree, there is a herd of fallow deer – every year there are up to 20 fawns produced. Close to the house is an attractive and working Elizabethan water mill. The modern visitors centre is a glorious design by Brownhill Hayward Brown.

Aside from these three but further afield, 64km (40 miles) east, is one of the greatest stately homes. **Chatsworth House** in the Peak District National Park has State Rooms that belong in a royal palace, while the grandeur of the gardens are underlined by the Great Cascade.

Historic houses

Bramall Hall *(Hall Rd, Bramhall, Stockport SK7 3NX, 0161 474 2020)* in Stockport is a timber-framed Elizabethan manor house set in a 60-acre park. It retains many original features including rare 16th century wall paintings regarded as some of the most important in the country depicting birds, animals, people, flowers and demons. They alone make the journey here worthwhile. **Hall I'th Wood** *(Green Way, off Crompton Way, Bolton 01204 332370)* is an attractive part-timbered, late medieval merchant's mansion where Samuel Crompton invented the Spinning Mule in 1779. **Smithhills Hall** *(Smithhills Dean Road, Bolton, 01204 332377)* is a fine half-timbered and stone mansion with many original features from medieval and Tudor periods. **Wythenshawe Hall** *(Altrincham Road, Wythenshawe, 0161 998 2331)* is often closed so ring ahead to see if it's open. Much of the house dates from the 16th century, the most notable rooms being the dining room and the drawing room. The Horticultural Centre in the surrounding park adds to a visit's interest.

Shadowy wall painting in Bramhall Hall

Public buildings

Without doubt the grandest public building outside the city centre in Greater Manchester is **Rochdale Town Hall** *(The Esplanade, Rochdale, OL16 1AB, 01706 924773)* a magnificent Gothic Victorian Town Hall, a sumptuous display of civic pride and wealth. The building is set off by the grand civic space it has been given, the gardens on three sides and the parish church high on the steep bank behind. It was built between 1866 and 1871 to the designs of William Crossland. The building is 100m long. The tower is 50m tall. The latter used to be taller and had a spire constructed of wood, but this burnt down and was replaced with this better stone version, in 1883, by Alfred Waterhouse, the architect of that other Gothic masterpiece, Manchester Town Hall. The interior has a giant staircase leading up to the Great Hall with a hammerbeam roof, a large mural of the Magna Carta and stained-glass windows depicting British monarchs. **Bolton Town Hall** *(Victoria Square, Bolton, BL1 1RU, 01204 333 333)* is Classical in inspiration and dates from 1873, designed by William Hill. The building dominates the town centre with its six-column Corinthian portico reached by a wide staircase and its tower given a French cap and cupola. Inside is the impressive Great Hall.

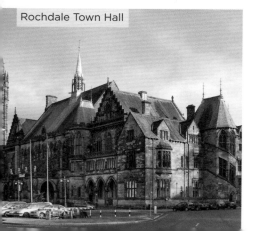
Rochdale Town Hall

Mills, Trains, Planes and The Stars

Quarry Bank Mill *(Styal, near Manchester Airport, 01625 527 468)* is a National Trust property and one of the best days out in the area. The museum is housed in a spinning mill built by Samuel Gregg in 1784. The museum is fully working with skilled demonstrators operating original machinery and giving a display of the different processes needed to take cotton from raw material stage to finished product. The model village of Styal nearby is worth a visit. Totally unspoilt, it has handsome brick houses, a school, a shop and a church. An essential on every visit is a walk through the very attractive 250 acres of Styal Country Park, with its river and woodland walks. **East Lancashire Railway** *(Bolton Street Station, Bury, BL9 0EY, 0161 764 7790)* is a volunteer-run attraction. For a modest price, you can take a journey in a steam train, or sometimes a veteran diesel, the eight miles or so up to Rawtenstall and back. The journey is a pleasant one with the Irwell Valley narrowing and the hills and moors pressing in. A bicycle can be taken on the train for free. Special events include Santa Specials, Thomas the Tank Engine Days, and drive-an-engine-yourself sessions.

The Runway Viewing Park *(Sunbank Lane, Altrincham, WA15 8XQ, 0161 489 3932)* sits close to Manchester Airport runway with viewing mounds to gaze at airplanes and extensive aviation collections in other parts including a DC10 and an RAF Nimrod. Pride of place goes to the sleek Concorde housed in its own special hangar and surely the most lovely plane ever built. You will have to book ahead (08715 22 11 00) for a tour of Concorde to gain access. **Jodrell Bank Discovery Centre** *(The University of Manchester Macclesfield, SK11 9DL, 01477 571 766)* is 33km or

20miles, from the city centre but this radio telescope is included here because it is operated by the University of Manchester. The main saucer, from 1957, rears over the Cheshire countryside like a huge abstract sculpture and was the first to track the Soviet satellite, Sputnik. There are planet, star and space pavilions. Outside a 35-acre arboretum allows the visitor to contemplate the gifts of Mother Earth.

Concorde in its hangar

Greater Manchester's Museums and Galleries

There are a huge range of local museums and galleries across Greater Manchester, most of them free. Ring ahead for opening times as these may vary at short notice.

Bolton Museum, Art Gallery and Aquarium *(Le Mans Crescent, Bolton, BL1 1SE, 01204 332211)* is a fine building with permanent and touring exhibitions of paintings, photography, sculpture and contemporary ceramics. In the museum there is an aquarium, a good natural history section and a notable Ancient Egyptian collection. Bolton-born Thomas Moran's celebrated

Stockport Air Raid Shelters

Regiment in 1881, known as the Manchesters. It has recreations of trench life in WW1 and five Victoria Crosses won by the regiment's soldiers.

Rochdale Pioneers Museum *(Toad Lane, Rochdale, OL12 ONU, 01706 524 920)* This museum is housed in the original building where Britain's first successful working class co-operative began in 1844. The museum provides an insight into the principles and ideals of co-operative philosophy. **Stockport Air Raid Shelters** *(Chestergate, Stockport, SK1 1NE, 0161 474 1940)* makes for an interesting museum housed in former tunnels carved out of the soft red sandstone. These were designed to protect thousands of people for prolonged periods of time from the threat of German air attack. The visit involves a descent into the 1940s' gloom to experience the sights and sounds of the Home Front. The **Stockport Hat Works Museum** *(Wellington Road North, Stockport, SK3 OEU)* is housed in a former mill in the town centre and traces the history of hat making from a cottage industry using beaver and otter fur to today's fashion designs. **Touchstones Rochdale** *(The Esplanade, Rochdale, OL16 1AQ, 01706 924492)* is a well-designed recent museum depicting the social history of this important town and the people who animated it. The town's art collection is also located here, together with the local studies department.

painting *Evening Camp, nearing the Upper Colorado River*, 1882, is a hymn to the undeveloped American West – ring ahead to check if it's on display. **Gallery Oldham** *(Greaves Street, off Union Street, Oldham, OL1 1AL, 0161 770 4653)* is a smart modern gallery by Pringle, Richards and Sharratt and houses a permanent collection of work, including paintings by Dante Gabriel Rossetti, Sickert and Hockney. There are temporary exhibitions too. Check out the extraordinary panorama taken in 1879 by Mr Knott. **Museum of the Manchesters** *(Ashton-under-Lyne Town Hall, OL7 0QA, 0161 343 2878)* illustrates the history of the 63rd and 96th Foot Regiments, which merged to become the Manchester

Evening Camp, nearing the Upper Colorado River

The Moors

'Moors are a stage for the performance of Heaven, any audience is incidental', wrote poet Laureate, Ted Hughes. The Pennine Hills surround Manchester on three sides, at their closest a mere 16km (10 miles) away. Most of these upland areas are characterised by the vast spaces of the moors, often forming a series of plateaux wide open to all that the elements can throw at them. Often the plateaux break and crash into deep ravines and dells, where scrub woodland fights with ferns and nettles.

The edges of the heights themselves are frayed into crags such as those at Cown Edge Rocks near Glossop or the accurately named Windgather Rocks at Kettleshulme. In fine weather, the Moors are beautiful and dramatic, mingling fresh air with long views and sheep. On some days a total silence seems to descend, broken only by skylarks or a gentle breeze whispering through the coarse grass. On several of the Moors to the east of the city, the heather burns purple in late summer.

But there is something ambiguous about the Moors too. If there is beauty here it is imperfect. This is no Alpine idyll or lowland English pleasantry. In bad weather, there is a dark primeval quality, that has fascinated writers for centuries. It's as if the Moors have their own person-ality: one traumatised by the human abuse of deforestation, quarrying and industry. Emily Brontë understood this well in *Wuthering Heights* – set on the Haworth Moors 25 miles northeast of the city. So did Ted Hughes who captured the raw, hard beauty of the hills in his celebration of Pennine moors, *Remains of Elmet*, and quoted above.

Of course, the name Moors is tarnished in Manchester with the word murderer. Saddleworth Moor was the chosen loca-tion for Ian Brady and Myra Hindley when they buried their child victims in the '60s. One body remains lost up there. As do others from other times. In the deep peat pleats around Kinder, Bleaklow and Black Hill are the scattered wreckage of a large number of planes, including Spitfires, Lancasters, several US Liberators and a Superfortress.

Sometimes it feels appropriate that a common bird call up here is the cry of the curlew: if all that is cold and sinister about the Moors could be caught in one sound it is that. Yet similarly all that is bright and fresh about the Moors is contained in the twitter of the skylark.

The Moors are about extremes. Everybody should take the opportunity to claim their own bit of the southern Pennines.

The Moors

Peel Tower

Ramsbottom and Holcombe – a Moorland Walk

This walk features steam trains, sculpture, a charming small town, a steep climb and great views. It's a walk in the Pennine Hills, 22km (14 miles) north of Manchester, of about 5km (3 miles) and rises up (330ft) 1,100ft. Good walks in the gentle country-side south of the city can be made through the grounds of Dunham Massey and Tatton Park, page 147.

Part of the joy is getting to Ramsbottom. Take the Metrolink tram out of Victoria Station, Manchester, to Bury and walk ten minutes, it's signposted, to Bolton Road Station. This is the main station for the volunteer-run East Lancs Railway which usually operates during the weekends. Buy a ticket for Ramsbottom Station which sometimes has a black pea seller outside. A tub of black peas, a traditional Lancashire dish, will set you up for the walk but make sure you put plenty of vinegar on them.

Take Bridge Street, to the right of the Railway pub. Bridge Street is full of charming independent businesses including delicatessens, an excellent antique shop plus a fish and chip shop which still uses dripping to fry the food.

Bridge Street, Ramsbottom

Tilted Vase sculpture

Bridge Street opens out into the Market Place. Edward Allington's two-ton *Tilted Vase* sculpture from 1998, part of the Irwell Sculpture Trail, dominates the space. It's an epic work reflecting the classical facades around but with its bolted sections recalling the industrial revolution.

Cross straight over the busy road and continue up Carr Street, resisting the temptations (or not) of the award-winning Chocolate Cafe and its hand-crafted chocolate. At the Rose and Crown pub, turn sharp left into Tanners Street with its traditional terraced houses. Turn right up the even steeper Rawson's Rake which takes you past the impressive Emmanuel Church from 1853 and into Holcombe Village. Here views start to open out and straight ahead you can see your destination, Peel Tower, on the hill above. Holcombe is an essay in stone Pennine architecture and includes the excellent Shoulder of Mutton pub.

A little after the pub cross carefully over the main road and take the first right into Cross Lane. During WWI a German zeppelin crossed the North Sea and flew towards Manchester. The zeppelin ditched bombs over Holcombe. There was one fatality: a surprised cow.

Just as Carr Lane becomes cobbled turn right along a track called Moorbottom Road. A few metres down, take another track to the right and zig-zag up to Peel Tower.

When you reach the austere tower you are 330m (1,100ft) above sea level. The 36m (120ft) tower was built in 1852 to mark the achievements of local man Sir Robert Peel, ex-prime minister who repealed the Corn Laws and the man who created the modern police force, hence the name Bobbies, short for Robert.

The tower is usually closed but if the flag is flying you can climb the 148 steps to the top. Call Bury Tourist Information on 0161 253 5111 if you want to check ahead. From the tower on clear days you can not only see central Manchester dominated by Beetham Tower (page 134/5) but also into Wales and the Lake District.

Retrace your steps to the train station. There's a lovely cricket ground and cute football ground should you wish to take in sport. The Grants Arms in Market Square is named after the Grant Brothers, major cotton manufacturers of the town in the 19th century, who Charles Dickens immortalised as the Cheeryble brothers in *Nicholas Nickleby*. They had the cunning tactic of partly paying workers' wages in tokens which could only be rescinded in the Grants Arms thus guaranteeing custom.

By the way the name Ramsbottom has nothing to do with sheep, but derives from the ramson plant, wild garlic. In other-words Ramsbottom means 'Valley of the Wild Garlic'.

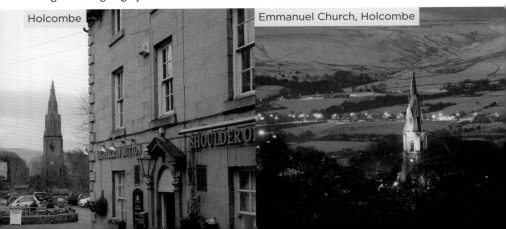

Holcombe

Emmanuel Church, Holcombe

Liverpool

If you spend time in Manchester make sure you take a day trip west to Liverpool - less than an hour by train from Manchester. The rivalry between the two cities can be over-stated and mostly reduced down to rivalry between Manchester United and Liverpool Football Club. Even this is a recent distortion, the rivalry stems not from football but from commercial (see p225) and ideological differences in the 19th century.

One of the more profound disagreements was over slavery. For instance, during the American Civil War, Manchester supported Abraham Lincoln's Union while Liverpool, through its trading links, supported the Confederacy and even had a Confederate consulate. This is something the city has regretted ever since.

The wealth of 18th century and 19th century Liverpool is visible on the city streets. It has one of the grandest collections of showpiece architecture outside capital cities in Western Europe. Its academic, scientific and industrial claims to being a pioneer may seriously lag behind those of Manchester, 50km (35mile) to the east but physically it's a stunner.

On a first visit take in the greatest neo-classical 19th century building in the country, St George's Hall, the three buildings of the Pier Head – the Liver, the Cunard and the Port of Liverpool buildings (known locally as the Three Graces) - the Anglican Cathedral, the Walker Art Gallery and Albert Dock. Always take a trip on the Mersey Ferry. After that it has to be the Tate North and the Maritime Museum.

Also try the Museum of Liverpool to gaze on the best architectural model in the UK of Sir Edwin Lutyens' Roman Catholic Metropolitan Cathedral of Christ the King proposed in the 1930s and never delivered due to lack of funds. The much smaller, but still very big, concrete and modernist, sixties alternative by Sir Frank Hibberd is worth a visit too.

Equally worth a visit are the cultural attractions of the Everyman Theatre, Bluecoats and the Liverpool Philharmonic. The weekend bar and nightlife in Mathew Street and around the Ropewalks is as lively as it's possible to get anywhere. Sefton Park provides a breather if you require, and remember at some point a Liverpudlian (or Scouser as they like to be known) will tell you they're the funniest breed of people

Liverpool

in the world. They're not, but smile and humour them, they'll love you for it and might even buy you a drink. Liverpool ladies are famous for their distinctive and flamboyant style.

Oh, and then there's the small matter of the Beatles who you won't fail to notice came from Liverpool. There's the Beatles' Museum at Albert Dock, the Cavern Club and the monuments down Mathew Street, even the Hard Days Night Hotel. And the Magical Mystery Tour. If you're going to do one Beatles' activity do the tour, the guides are superb.

Chester

Chester is a classic tourist town and lies an hour away by train from Oxford Road Station. It has it all, a full circuit of walls, a large medieval former abbey now the cathedral, the River Dee for boat excursions, a superb gardens and the remarkable medieval feature of The Rows: a unique covered walkway with shops on two levels.

It was founded by the Romans in the 1st century as Deva, a legionary fort for the Twentieth Legion, strategically placed to control North Wales and North West England from a site with sea access via the River Dee. Aside from surviving parts of

Roman walls, there's an amphitheatre to view as well from that earliest period.

The lovely St John's church close to the amphitheatre recalls the Norman period of architecture almost a thousand years ago and is reputedly the church where the English King Edgar worshipped in 973 after being rowed down the river by six tributary kings from other parts of Britain.

The city was commercially important, and much bigger than Manchester or Liverpool, until the 17th century, when the River Dee silted up. It then gradually slipped into senility until during the industrial revolution it became an important rail hub and gained a significant manufacturing base.

Much of the area in and around Chester is owned by the Duke of Westminster, one of the UK's richest men with properties scattered across Mayfair in London. His family name is Grosvenor, his family seat is 8km (5 miles) south of Chester. The five star hotel of Chester with the Michelin-starred restaurant is the Grosvenor Hotel and the Grosvenor Museum is superb for those seeking an understanding of the history of the city. Finally Chester Races are one of the great social events of the year in the North West.

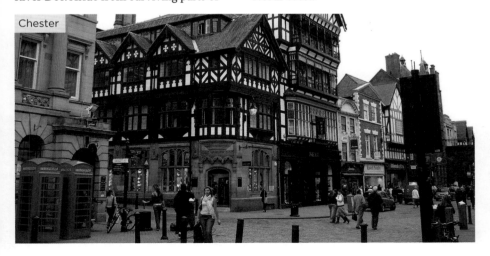

Chester

Further afield

At every point of the compass Manchester is surrounded by glorious scenery and interest.

To the east less than 25km (15 miles) away is the highest point of the Peak District National Park, Kinder Scout. The limestone villages in the south of the Peak District such as Tidewell are exquisite as are the valleys such as Dove Dale. North, an hour away, is the Yorkshire Dales National Park with more castles, waterfalls, wild hilltops and pretty villages such as Grassington. North and west is The Lake District National Park containing some of the best and most heroic mountain scenery in the UK. From Manchester Piccadilly to Windermere station in the Lake District can take as little as 1 hour, 33 minutes.

Closer to Manchester is the lovely city of Lancaster with its castle and further south again is the seaside resort of Blackpool. This place is a snob's nightmare, but for any overseas visitor who wants to make a fun study of an essential part of the British psyche, it is irresistible. There's the Tower, the ballroom, an excellently refurbished promenade and Blackpool Pleasure Beach with the towering rollercoaster The Big One a mighty 65m (213ft).

East of Blackpool are the hills and dales of the Trough of Bowland, an area the Queen once stated was her favourite in the UK. Just south is the spectacular Stoneyhurst College with its unforgettable gatehouse of the 1590s. Due west of Manchester, is the seaside resort of Southport with handsome Lord Street. Further down the coast is the remarkable sand dune landscape of Formby and Crosby: the latter featuring Antony Gormley's award winning *Another Place* sculptures.

West of Cheshire, and into Wales, lie some of the mightiest castles in Europe such as Conwy, the lovely seaside resort of Llandudno, the soaring mountains of Snowdonia.

There are a number of lovely areas much closer to home. In Saddleworth, east of Oldham, are classic Pennine stone villages. Delph and Dobcross are particularly pretty. The most dramatic area of Saddleworth includes high hills, cliffs and reservoirs at Dovestones on the A635. Due south of the city, off the B5087, and through the village of Alderley Edge, lies the wooded Edge itself. With its legend of a wizard guarding the sleeping King Arthur and his knights, its woods and rocky landscape make for literally a magical place. Two acclaimed children's novels are set here, *The Weirdstone of Brisingamen* and *The Moon of Gomrath* by Alan Garner.

One of the most interesting country parks is Rivington and Lever Park, northwest of Bolton off the A673. These are the former gardens and estate of the Bolton entrepreneur William Hesketh Lever, Lord Leverhulme – his name is still commemorated in the company Unilever – raising up to Rivington Pike.

Ullswater, Lake District

Food&Drink

in association with www.manchesterconfidential.com

The Vault in Jamie's Italian

Variety is the spice of life

MANCHESTER'S never had it so good when it comes to food and drink. You can sample almost forty styles of cuisine in the city at all prices from £80 tasting menus in The French to gut-stuffing curries in This'n'That for less than £5.

The appeal of eating out, taking in good bars and pubs and even seeking out the best tea and coffee shops has grown and grown. In this section we look at many aspects of the city's food and drink range from restaurants, through bars and pubs to tea and coffee shops.

If there is a cloud on the horizon then the city knows exactly when it'll arrive. In autumn every year Michelin announces which restaurants have gained stars and invariably rains on Manchester's parade. Gastronomes moan, the media run features, but most locals shrug their shoulders and get on with the business of eating. And drinking. Lots of drinking.

After all the range, variety and quality of the Manchester food offer is astonishing. A visit to any comparably sized European city reveals this in about ten minutes. Delight is round every corner if you've got eyes to see and a mouth to fill.

This section sets out to show you where to find the best food and drink, mainly in the city centre. It's delivered in association with ManchesterConfidential.co.uk, the city magazine majoring in food and drink.

Vegetarian

For a city that was at the heart of mass Western vegetarianism in the 19th century (p74) it might appear there are few proper vegetarian outlets around. This isn't the case. The main contact for veggies is the Vegetarian Society in Altrincham which runs cookery schools and residential courses. For restaurants try **1847** (*58 Mosley Street, M2 3LQ, 0161 236 1811*) in the city centre and **Greens** (*43 Lapwing Lane, M20 2NT, 0161 434 4259*) in West Didsbury, both offering dishes that aspire to more than hearty soups, stews and an over-reliance on goat's cheese. **Earth Café** in the Buddhist Centre (*20 Turner Street, Northern Quarter, Manchester M4 1DZ, 0161 834 1996*) provides pleasant less formal food. For stocking up the vegan **Unicorn Grocery** (*89 Albany Road, M21 0BN, 0161 861 0010*) is exceptional but requires a journey to the suburb of Chorlton. Closer to town a little way down Oxford Road is **Eighth Day** (*111 Oxford Road, M1 7DU, 0161 273 4878*) with a veggie shop and café. Remember also Indian, Pakistani, south Asian and Chinese restaurants offer a wide choice of purely vegetarian dishes although you may want to ensure they cook them free of meaty cross-contamination.

Fine dining

The French *(Midland Hotel, Petersfield, M60 2DS, 0161 236 3333)* The city's restaurant *grande dame* with a 1903 oval room that's hosted prime ministers, monarchs, stars and countless lovers of each other or of food. Re-invented under Simon Rogan, presently the most celebrated UK chef, with Adam Reid as head chef. Raw materials are often sourced from Rogan's Cumbrian farm. Two options of exquisite tasting menus (£59 or £89), dishes such as swede dumplings, duck yolk sauce, onion, nasturtium or guinea fowl, bacon fat potatoes, turnips, hen of the woods and rosemary.

Manchester House *(Bridge Street, Spinningfields, M3 3BZ, 0161 835 2557)* A busy and exciting restaurant, the kitchen positioned in the dining area. Aiden Byrne is the chef. The food matches The French but the atmosphere is positively relaxed. The mains are usually priced between £20 and £40 but look out for the excellent lunchtime deals. Dishes might include Squab pigeon with cherries, pistachio and violet mustard or sea bass, avocado and sesame purée, soft shell crab, chicken satay or the entertaining belted Galloway beef, mushrooms, sticks and stones.

63 Degrees *(High Street, City Centre, M4 1PN, 0161 832 5438)* The Moreau family uprooted themselves from France to settle in Manchester to deliver this sweet Northern Quarter French dining room with a glorious menu. Dishes such as sea bass tartare with Imperial Oscietre caviar, whole Lobster with tarragon butter and crepe soufflé with salted caramel will charm. Main courses range from £14 to £35, good value £18 lunch menu. The service is personal and often from the family.

Australasia *(Deansgate, Spinningfields, M3 3AP, 0161 831 0288)* Hard to believe this is a basement restaurant given the lighting scheme which lulls you into believing natural light must come from somewhere. This is a see and be seen, dress up and show off venue, with a good bar. Pan-Asian dishes from the Aussie Dave Spanner include razor sliced octopus with passionfruit and yuzu gel or Spiced duck breast with cherries, citrus jus and sweet potato purée. Mains range from £13 to £48. Good lunchtime deals from £11 to £22.

...fine dining continued

Michael Caines at Abode *(Piccadilly, City Centre, M1 2DB, 0161 247 7744)* Elegant, basement venue with a reputation for exceptional food. Celeb chef Michael Caines helps design the menus while executive chef Robert Cox does the day-to-day cooking. Expect to pay for main courses £18 to £30. Lunch menus of two or three courses are less than £20. Dishes include roasted Lake District beef sirloin with horseradish and shallot confit, roasted shallots, asparagus, red wine sauce or chocolate orange confit mousse, orange sorbet, dark chocolate ice cream.

Second Floor Restaurant *(Harvey Nichols, New Cathedral Street, Central Retail District, M1 1 AD, 0161 828 8898)* A pin-sharp venue in the famous department store with good views across Exchange Square and a menu designed to please both shoppers and evening guests. Lunch menus around £25 for three courses. Mains off the a la carte cost between £16 and £25. Dishes might include stone bass, roast butternut squash, cep, truffle gnocchi or Manchester tart, coconut ice cream, banana jelly. Brasserie next door for more informal eating and drinking.

James Martin *(235 Casino, Great Northern, Petersfield, M3 4LP, 0161 828 0345)* Celeb chef James Martin's restaurant in Manchester235 has a superb chef and it's not James Martin, it's Douglas Crampton. In the sturdy brick and iron surroundings of an old railway warehouse Crampton produces delightful food such as deep fried soft boiled organic Goosnargh hen's egg with watercress and asparagus or ox cheek with smoked mash puree, tongue, bone marrow fritter and a parsley and shallot salad. Mains are priced between £13.50 to £19.

Mr Cooper's House and Garden (Midland Hotel, Petersfield, M60 2DS, 0161 236 3333) Another Simon Rogan vehicle a notch down from The French: most people won't notice. Gareth Jones is head chef. The house and garden design is odd inspired by carriage maker Mr Cooper's 19th century house and garden on this site. Dishes include smoked eel torte, lovage and pork belly or lamb rump, spiced lentils and minted chargrilled courgettes. Lunch menus £15 for two courses, £19 for three, a la carte mains from £16 to £23

General dining in alphabetical order

Almost Famous/Luck, Lust, Liquor and Burn *(High Street, Northern Quarter, M4 1HP, 0161 832 8644)* Two super cool venues in the same building from the pioneering company led by eccentric Beau Myers. Almost Famous broke burger mania in Manchester and provides filibusters such as the Animal Burger: 'triple peppered cheeseburger, fried onions in magic mustard mayo, beef monster munch, lettuce, chipotle ketchup and jalapenos onions.' LLLB is the Mexican sister of AF majoring in burritos and nachos with the standout dish the street tacos. Tortillas are served on an American licence plate. Mains: under £10.

Cicchetti *(House of Fraser, King Street West, Central Retail District, M3 2GQ, 0161 839 2233)* Sharply designed restaurant providing delicious food based on the Venetian 'small plates' idea of cicchetti delivered with verve and an appreciation of latest Italian food fashions. Never fails with exceptional seafood and pasta dishes plus more complex plates such as paillard of black pig from Etna cooked on lava stone with aubergine and mint. Good for celebrity spotting as is the sister restaurant over the road, San Carlo. Excellent drinks including Italian craft beers. Prices: £4-£10.

El Rincon de Rafa *(M3 4BQ)*, **Evuna** *(M3 4EW)*, **Iberica** *(M3 3HF)*. You could be in Madrid with El Rincon de Rafa with its double height room fizzing with Iberian energy and its classic tapas. The host is Rafa, an adopted Mancunian and ex-pro footballer, who was on the substitutes' bench when United won the 1968 European Cup. Evuna, nearby, is all moody wood, good food and exceptional Spanish wines. Evuna has a Northern Quarter base *(M4 1LQ)*. Iberica is a London based chain with a menu devised by two star Michelin chef Nacho Manzano.

Gorilla *(Whitworth Street West, Oxford Road area, M1 5WW, 0161 407 0301)* Restaurant inside a railway arch, 700 capacity gig venue behind, with unaccountably lovely world food. Here's an over-heard conversation. "How is the food?" "I think this chicken with its moist flesh, its superb thyme and garlic skin, rich with rock salt and elevated with side pots of excellent aioli and chimmi churri is a thing worthy of high praise." "Wow. Do you talk like that all the time?" Mains: £9-£17, £24 steak.

...general dining continued

Grill on the Alley (*5 Ridgefield, Central Retail District, M2 6EG, 0161 833 3465*) If you want oysters in Manchester this place is your best bet but it's also good for dover sole, steak, burgers and so forth. The top tip here is get yourself a range of starters as these carry the more exquisite flavours. If you've won the lottery grab yourself a £55 Wagyu steak. Grill on the Alley, and its sister Grill on New York Street, provide popular and smoothly comfortable places attracting a well-dressed crowd plus people who love oysters. Mains: £11-£30 (excluding the Wagyu).

Jamie's Italian, Room/Rosso/Browns (*In and around upper King Street in the Central Retail District*) These four restaurants provide spectacular dining spaces – see pages 110-111. Jamie's Italian is all about power-house imperial architecture - the fish specials are the dishes to try. The green marble of Browns restaurant is equally powerful but the food has a British accent. Rosso, another Italian restaurant, provides decent food under an ornate dome, while Room provides the best cooking of the four in an astonishing former gentlemen's club.

The Northern Quarter Restaurant and Bar aka TNQ (*108 High St, Northern Quarter, M4 1HQ, 0161 832 7115*) Chef Anthony Fielding is building up a real reputation here for good reasonably priced food in attractive surroundings. The terrace over the road is great for summer dining. The modern British menu is exemplary but people might want to rush along to try dishes such as lamb sweetbreads with broad beans, peas and gentle salsa verde or suckling pig with onion and sage confit, pancetta potatoes and Bury black pudding jus. Mains: £9-£24.

Sam's Chop House (*Back Pool Fold, Central Retail District, M4 1PJ, 0161 834 3210*) With over a hundred year's pedigree this British food stalwart is still going strong in an atmospheric half-basement complete with a full-size statue of LS Lowry, the Greater Manchester artist and one-time regular. Indulge yourself here with excellent beers, wines and spirits plus steak and kidney puddings, cabbage and bacon, fish and chips, ribeye steak, lemon meringue possets and Eccles cakes plus a glorious Sam's smoked haddock Scotch egg. Mains: £12-£20.

Salvi's Cucina *(John Dalton Street, Central Retail District, M2 6FW, 0161 222 8021)* This place is the product of Maurizio Salvi's passionate belief in his native region of Campania. In some respects when we think of classic Italian food - its freshness, its lightness, its quicksilver character - it's this region we're thinking of, pizzas, seafood, zest, ciao bella. The key to Salvi's Cucina is the way all that southern Italian Mezzogiornoness is packaged and parcelled, delivering to the table the best pasta and pizza dishes in town. Good wine list too. Mains: £8-£15.

Solita *(37 Turner Street, Northern Quarter, M4 1DW, 0161 839 2200)* Solita is famed for its 'dirty' food; usually fried, intoxicatingly calory-packed and not good for your health. This is all part of the Anglicised Americana food style in fashion across the UK most of which is horrible, fortunately Solita displays enough imagination to rise above the crowd. Typically exuberant is the Mac Daddy consisting of burger, bacon, pickle and cheese wedged between two bits of fried mac'n'cheese (instead of the usual bun). Take a defibrillator. Mains: £8.90-£25.

Superstore *(Smithfield Building, Tib Street, Northern Quarter, M4 1NB. 0161 834 3303)* An instant hit in 2014 with warm brick, an open kitchen, well laid out and comfortable with superb innovation from chef Matt Bailey. The dining crowd is younger and brainy. Maybe dishes such as roast bone marrow, garlic and thyme with toast help boost the grey matter. Other winning plates include samphire and coriander tempura battered fish and chips but also sweet potato, lentil and spinach korma. Mains: £9-£14.

Outside the city Good eating can be had in the hills, west of Rochdale, with the acclaimed restaurant of the talented and eccentric Andrew Nutter, called **Nutters**. Further east in Oldham there's the elegant yet wholesome **White Hart**. Chocolate addicts are spoilt at **Slattery's** in Whitefield. Further north not far from the exquisite countryside of the Ribble Valley, there's the **Freemasons** at Wiswell and the Michelin-starred **Northcote Manor**. South of the city centre, **The Rose Garden** in West Didsbury is worth seeking out, as is the restaurant of the **Alderley Edge Hotel** in Cheshire.

San Carlo Effect, Living Ventures Experience and the Trendsetters

Several restaurants in the city centre go stellar. They capture a quality people find beguiling and alluring. In Manchester it's called the *San Carlo Effect*.

San Carlo *(42 King Street West, Central Retail District, M3 2WY, 0161 834 6226)* opened in 2004 on a site which had been a serial failure. Its delivery of classic Italian dishes, innovative fish specialities (the best element of the food) and the highest ratio of waiters to customers in world history was a winner from the start even though people could never work out why the waiters were always rushing about so much and banging plates. Then there was the pin sharp interior, the inevitably beautiful reception staff and the sheer verve of the place. The self-made business women and men of the region and their party dressed partners found it irresistible. This was reinforced when celebs and football players discovered San Carlo, the staff took their photos, the photos were mounted and signed, the legend spread and, bang, the city had the San Carlo Effect. In Manchester San Carlo group has several operations including one of the very best in **Cicchetti**, plus others across the country and abroad, all fostered under the careful gaze of Carlo Distefano, his son Marcello and all those rushing waiters. It's a phenomenon.

Living Ventures Group is another roaring Manchester success story, led by Aussie Tim Bacon and Brit Jeremy Roberts. The company has many mainstream food and drink brands aimed at the mass market, Gusto, the New World Trading Company, The Alchemist, Blackhouse Grills but also more refined venues such as the perfectly polished and presented restaurants of **Manchester House** and **Australasia**. As with San Carlo, for certain Mancunians sitting down to dinner in Manchester

Australasia

House and Australasia is a mark of success, a mirror showing how far they've come. For others the excellence of the food in these two restaurants proves how Manchester is maturing and appetites becoming more sophisticated.

For yin there has to be yang. There's another type of food and drink entrepreneur appealing to a very different market. These are people such as Joel Wilkinson of **Trof**, Beau Myers of **Almost Famous**, and Ross Mackenzie and Jobe Ferguson of **Black Dog**, appealing to that group of world aware and usually younger people horribly tagged 'hipsters'. These bar and dance hall dreamers are changing the face of the scene in Manchester majoring in cunning cocktails and craft ales, reinventing the Northern Quarter of the city in the process and in the case of Trof giving new life to some of the more extraordinary spaces in the city such as Albert Hall. In Almost Famous' case their vision of how the humble burger should be delivered led to a flood of copycats. In Black Dog's case, aside from their eponymous Black Dog bars, they opened a venue called the Liar's Club, which is a barometer of your state of mind. If you're in there it's probably 4.30am and you said you'd be home by 2am and you're already in so much trouble you might as well stay till the death. One more drink. One more.

Steak specialists

Smoak

Gaucho *(2a St Mary's Street, Central Retail District, M3 2LB, 0161 833 4333)*, **Scottish Steak Club** *(Macdonald Hotel, London Road, Piccadilly, M1 2PG, 0161 272 3200)*, **Smoak** *(Malmaison Hotel, 1 Gore St, Piccadilly, M1 3AQ, 0161 278 1000)*, **Steak & Lobster** *(Radisson Blu Edwardian Hotel, Petersfields, M2 5GP, 0161 835 8903)*. Gaucho in an impressive former Methodist hall specialises in Argentine steaks and dishes. The Scottish Steak Club has cuts from north of the border but also brings in American steak styles. Smoak includes the drama of an upright glass chiller in full view of the restaurant. The meat hangs for a minimum of four weeks. The 1.4 kilo wing rib is superb but you might need a couple of friends to help you finish it. Steak & Lobster delivers the classic surf and turf combo in well-heeled surroundings. Of course most of the restaurants listed in earlier pages are proud of their steaks as well.

Breakfast Specialists

You don't have to have breakfast in a hotel or even at home, a proper English breakfast is available across the city featuring all or most of these, bacon, eggs, toast, tomatoes, beans, mushrooms, black pudding, sausages. For the real cafe experience try **Koffee Pot** *(21 Hilton St, Northern Quarter, M1 1JJ)*, shabby chic defined, where you rub shoulders with artists, designers, musicians and Mabel waiting for the bus home. **Albert's Chop House** *(Albert Square, M2 5PF, 0161 834 1866)* provides cracking homemade black pudding, great bacon and the morning papers. **Cicchetti** *(House of Fraser, Central Retail Area 98-116 Deansgate, M3 2QC, 0161 839 2233)* is an Italian restaurant that does 'English' breakfasts as well as the locals. **Gorilla** *(54-56 Whitworth Street West, Oxford Road area, M1 5WW. 0161 407 0301)* features The Royal Breakfast with double everything. **Home Sweet Home** *(49-51 Edge Street, Northern Quarter, M4 1HW, 0161 244 9424)* helps the digestion with home baked sourdough. **Superstore** *(Smithfield Building, Northern Quarter, M4 1NB, 0161 834 3303)* provides another two-by-two Noah's Ark of a breakfast. **Terrace** *(43 Thomas Street, Northern Quarter, M4 1NA, 0161 819 2345)* delivers a low-lit easy-going full spread. As for hotels, perhaps try **The Great John Street Hotel** *(Great John Street, Castlefield, M3 4FD, 0161 831 3211)*. You can even treat yourself to a glass of bubbly but it's perhaps best to leave that until after 12 noon.

Breakfast

Chinese, Japanese, Thai, and Korean food

Manchester has a broad spread of Far Eastern foods. Many of these are found in Chinatown (p122) but there are other worthwhile places across the city.

The most famous Chinese restaurant is **Yang Sing** *(Princess Street, Chinatown, M1 4JY 0161 236 2200)* and the biggest too. Opened in 1977 by the Yeung brothers, Harry Yeung, the older brother and principal chef is still around while the next generation, Bonnie, Yinhen and Yinting, are all involved. There is a truly epic dim sum menu but mains of crispy suckling duck with jellyfish show the flair in the kitchen. Meanwhile **Red Chilli** *(70-72 Portland Street, Chinatown, M1 4GU, 0161 273 1288)* is a basement restaurant with Beijing and Sichuan dishes including an unusual selection of cold starters such as Red Hot chilli pork stomach shreds and poached tofu with sesame oil and spring onion. Exotic dishes such as the Husband and Wife Lung Slices are worth trying.

The eye wateringly hot food of Chairman Mao's home region, Hunan, is represented by the aptly titled **Hunan Restaurant** *(1st Floor, 19-21 George Street, Chinatown, M1 4HE, 0161 236 8889)* where dishes include kelp with garlic and soy sauce and the spicy velvet crab Hunan style. Away from Chinatown **Wings** *(Lincoln Square, M2 5LN, 0161 834 9000)* provides clever dishes, with the fish dishes delicate, light and finessed and the meat dishes big and robust. The walls are covered with plates signed by Wings' celebrity guests.

For Japanese try **Yuzu** *(39 Faulkner Street, Chinatown, M1 4EE, 0161 236 4159)*. This has been acclaimed as one of the UK's finest Japanese restaurants, presenting a traditional, almost austere, experience, backed-up by wonderful food. Staples of the menu include sashimi, easy-to-pincer sticky rice, cucumber pickles, finely shredded white daikon radish and miso soup. **Umezushi** *(Mirabel Street, City Centre, M3 1PJ, 0871 811 8877)* in a hard to find railway arch close to Victoria Station is a usually a match for Yuzu and has a more relaxed atmosphere. Recent arrival **Sakana** *(23 Peter Street, M2 5QR, 0161 884 1292)* is the luxury Japanese and Pan-Asian restaurant with a fine dining menu and real talent in the kitchen.

Thai restaurants **Phetphailin** *(46 George Street, Chinatown, City, M1 4HF, 0161 228 6500)* and **Try Thai** *(52-54 Faulkner Street City, M14 FH, 0161 228 1822)* have their fans but the darling of 2014 was **Siam Smiles** *(48 George Street, Chinatown, M1 4 4HF, 0161 237 1555)* part supermarket part restaurant with popular dishes such as Kuai Tiew Yen Ta Fo, a vivid pink bowl of flat noodles, tofu and fish balls in soup, garnished with coriander and morning glory. A good Manchester-based Pan-Asian chain is **Tampopo** in Albert Square *(M2 5PF, 0161 819 1966)* and Exchange Square.

For Korean food it's worth taking a stroll up to **Baekdu** *(Shudehill, Northern Quarter, M4 4AN, 0161 834 2227)*, a canteen-style venue but with an excellent sharing hotpot of swimming crab, cod, squid, green shell mussels, prawn, radish, leek, tofu and small octopus. Otherwise try the oldest Korean restaurant in the UK, **Koreana** *(40a King Street West, M3 2WY, 0161 832 4330)*.

Eastern

South Asian food

Given the size of the Pakistani and Bangladeshi communities in Greater Manchester it's no surprise that the number and range of South Asian restaurants in the region should be so high – there are several Indian restaurants as well.

The trio of **Zouk** *(The Quadrangle, Chester Street, M1 5QS, 0161 233 1090),* **EastzEast** *(Princess Street, M1 7DG, 0161 244 5353)* and **Akbars** *(73-83 Liverpool Rd, Castlefield, M3 4NQ, 0161 834 7222)* and the Northern Quarter curry cafes in and around the city centre are perhaps the easiest way to enjoy south Asian food. The first three above provide smart surroundings, extremely good cooking, a bright and busy ambience, liveried doormen in traditional costumes on weekend nights and several thousand wedding parties seemingly each day. Curiously the owner of Zouk, Amjad Bashir, is a UKIP MEP, the political party committed to curtailing immigration and getting the UK out of Europe.

Ask for your food 'apna' or 'our' style. Or ask for it 'desi' or 'traditional' style. This should ensure you don't get a 1980s style British curry experience. Be especially careful about outmoded south Asian food along the most renowned 'Indian' food-strip in the region, the famous Curry Mile of Rusholme, a couple of miles south of the city on Wilmslow Road.

Some of the restaurants seem stuck in a timewarp here, but it remains an interesting place to visit especially on evenings when it bursts with neon brilliance complete with jewellers' shops filled with the yellowest gold you've ever seen. The best bet here is **Mugli** *(28-32 Wilmslow Road, M14 5TQ, 0161 248 0900)* a restaurant that cares about the total experience with not only fine 'apna' food but also good service and good surroundings.

The A6, Stockport Road, in Longsight and Levenshulme, two or three miles from the city centre in south east Manchester provides equally diverse south Asian cuisines, as does Cheetham Hill road, a mile or two north of Victoria Station. Further out again, both **Lily's Vegetarian Indian Cuisine** *(75-83 Oldham Road, Ashton, OL6 7DF, 0161 339 4774)* and the **Indian Tiffin Room** *(Chapel St, Cheadle, SK8 1BR, 0161 491 2020)* have in the last couple of years gained admirers for the creativity and rich flavours in their dishes.

As for the Northern Quarter curry cafes mentioned earlier they feature on the next page in Eating Cheaply section.

Food at Zouk

Cheap Eats, 'Street food' and Fish and Chips

Street food at the Great Northern Warehouse

Fry-up Firsts?

The small Greater Manchester town of Mossley claims the first proper fish and chip shop. In 1863 John Lees set up in a wooden hut selling battered fish and fried potatoes as an offshoot to a pig's trotter and pea soup operation. The claim is disputed but not by people in Mossley.

If you want to spend no more than £5 then the **Arndale Food Market** *(Manchester Arndale Centre, Market Street. M3 3AH. 0161 234 5000)* is a good place to start with a whole range of world foods. **Panchos Mexican, Zorbas Greek** and **Viet-Shack** are stand outs here, alongside affordable Indian, Chinese, Afro-Caribbean, Brazilian, Pan-European and Pan-Asian options.

The Northern Quarter curry cafes are legendary in the city, and originally served the rag trade in the area. The perennial favourite was one of the first, **This'n'That** *(Soap Street, off Thomas Street, M4 1EW, 0161 832 0708)*, pioneer of the 'rice'n'three' concept (rice with any three combinations of meat and veg). **Cafe Marhaba** *(36 Back Piccadilly, M1 1HP, 0161 228 7377)* is the only N4 café with its own tandoor oven

for crafting exceptional breads. Yagdar and Kabana are two more much loved curry cafes.

The formidably popular **Changos Burrito Bar** *(91-93 Oxford Street, M1 6ET, 0161 228 2182)*, is excellent for Tex-Mex, at lunch time the queues stretch to Acapulco. For pizza slices in the Roman not the Neapolitan manner try **Slice** *(Stevenson Square, Northern Quarter, M1 1DN, 0161 236 9032)*.

The vogue at present across the UK is 'street food' often with groups of providers clumping together to create more informal food markets with food that is cheaper than traditional restaurants if not usually as cheap as some of the providers on this page. These 'street food markets' are great fun, often come armed with live music and take place in unusual non-traditional foodie spaces such as old mills and warehouses. Keep an eye out for activity from Manchester operators Guerrilla Eats and B.Eat Street on this front.

Two good traditional British cafes are **Linda's Pantry** *(23 Ducie Street, M1 2JL, 0161 236 4252)* and **Koffee Pot** *(21 Hilton St, Northern Quarter, M1 1JJ)*. Both do good builder's strength tea with the former specialising in homemade pies and double-cooked chips and the latter providing all the comfort food faves and fry-ups along with occasional specials such as haggis.

Both the cafes above do decent fish and chips but the best take-away fish and chips in the city centre come from **Wrights** *(82 Cross Street, Central Retail District, M2 4LA, 0161 222 6105)* with excellent battered fish, good chips and even black pudding. British cities generally though aren't the best places for traditional fish and chips, smaller, less-cosmopolitan towns tend to major in them better.

MANCHESTER PUBS AND PUB CRAWLS

HUMOURIST Hilaire Belloc decreed in the early 20th century that 'once you have lost your pubs, you will have lost the last of England'.

There's perhaps some truth in this. If a country is defined by qualities which are uniquely their own then pubs reach to the core of Britishness. If a visitor wants to leave behind the tourist sites and hotels for a while and reach under the skin of the nation then a visit to the pub and a chat with the locals is the most accessible and quickest route.

But pubs are in crisis, squeezed by tiny profit margins and changes in society and particularly its male drinking habits. Only in city centres does there seem a future for the urban pubs and in Manchester there are many such classics. These are set out in the pub crawls on the following pages.

So what makes a good pub? Is it that atmosphere of age, the frisson of time passing? Is it beautiful fittings and fixtures? Is it talkative locals and a friendly landlord or landlady? Is it finely kept real ales and good food?

It's actually all of these. The really good pub should tempt you in for a quick half and make you feel so comfortable you stay all night.

Short of time?

If you are short of time and want to enjoy the classic pub then try The Briton's Protection, The Marble Arch, The City Arms, Mr Thomas's and The Kings Arms. The best pubs for food are The Wharf, The Oxnoble, Dukes 92, Mr Thomas's, The Marble Arch. These are described on the following pages.

Southern city centre pub crawl

Detail of Peveril Peak tilework

Start at **Peveril of the Peak** *(127 Great Bridgewater Street, M1 5JQ, 0161 236 6364)*. This is a late Georgian property which gained (in the 1890s) an emerald external tiling scheme with Art Nouveau lettering. Internally the design is period but maverick, the weirdness climaxing in the triangular, squashed bar area with the legendary period table football – the oldest pub table in continuous use in the UK, dating from 1955 (pic p183). There are pool and music nights too. The name comes from the original owner's stagecoach which made him enough money so he could open the pub in the 1820s.

A short walk west on Great Bridgewater Street is **The Briton's Protection** *(50 Great Bridgewater Street, M1 5LE, 0161 236 5895)*. A multi-roomed unmissable classic full of elegant wood, tile and plaster – it dates from at least 1811. The straight-from-the-street bar area is particularly hand-some - note the ceiling. But also try the cosy snug behind and, if sunny and warm, venture into one of the most oasis-like pub gardens in the city. There are local ales, more than 200 whiskies (mostly single malt) and bourbons, gigs, meetings and much else. The name comes from the pub being a recruiting office in the past.

Leave the Briton's, turn left, cross over Lower Mosley Street and continue under the Metrolink bridge, under Beetham Tower, over Deansgate and down

Briton's Protection

fresh baked pies from 12.00-Close

Liverpool Road to **The White Lion** *(43 Liverpool Road, M3 4NQ, 0161 832 7373)*. This dates back to 1778. There's lots of ale on offer, a bargain menu and a good outdoor drinking area adjacent to the reconstructed foundations of the Roman fort. City fans beware it is emphatically a Red pub.

A short walk further down Liverpool Road is **The Oxnoble** *(71 Liverpool Road, M3 4NQ, 0161 839 7740)*. This good-looking building houses a pub with a good food reputation and an easy-going comfortable atmosphere. The pub was named, uniquely, for a low-grade potato that came up the canals from west Lancashire and was sold in the market (now part of the Museum of Science and Industry opposite). Good ales and wines but food is the emphasis here.

Turn left at The Oxnoble and follow Duke Street down under the railway bridges and left to the Rochdale Canal. Over the canal is **Dukes 92** *(19-20 Castle Street, M3 4LZ, 0161 839 8646)*. This is a modern pub with the name arising from the building's former use as stables for the Duke of Bridgewater's canal, and its location adjacent to the 92nd lock of the Rochdale Canal. Outside is a huge sun-trap terrace. Food is a feature either in the Grill as bar food, or with full restaurant service in Albert Shed.

Retrace your steps over Rochdale Canal and take the white footbridge over the Bridgewater Canal to straight ahead **The Wharf** *(6 Slate Wharf, M15 4ST, 0161 220 2960)*. This is an epic new boozer, an airy, light-filled feast of bric-a-brac on three floors, with a fine outdoor drinking terrace on the banks of the canal and good food, wine and beer.

Cross the timber bridge in front of The Wharf and follow the canal path towards Beetham Tower. Cross the black bridge and take the stairs on the left up to Castle Street and turn right to **Knott Bar** *(374 Deansgate, M3 4LY, 0161 839 9229)*. Called a bar, but definitely a pub, this place

has fabulous ales, a good old fashioned jukebox, real charm, atmosphere and character, plus robust, gut-busting food. It's a railway arch and the trains rumbling above add to the atmosphere.

Turn right out of Knott Bar and then immediately left up Deansgate to **The Deansgate** pub *(321 Deansgate. M3 4LQ, 0161 839 5215)* on the other side of the road. This occupies a handsome 1920s' exterior right and contains quaint multi-roomed interior. There's a big function area on the first floor, and some of the oddest outdoor terraces in the city. The pub was formerly the Crown and has one of the oldest licences in Manchester dating from the 18th century.

Inside the White Lion

The Wharf

Northern Quarter pub crawl

The Castle

The Crown and Kettle detail of the ceiling

The Marble Arch

Start at **The Castle Hotel** *(66 Oldham Street, M4 1LE, 0161 237 9485)*. Behind the crazy skewed Art Nouveau lettering on the façade, you'll find an elaborate mahogany bar smack bang in front of you. Immediately behind the bar is the snug and behind that down a corridor is a beautiful performance room with a glorious timber skylight. Food is basic but to use that most over-used word in the pub food lexicon - wholesome.

Turn right out of Knott Bar and then immediately left up Deansgate to **The Deansgate** pub *(321 Deansgate. M3 4LQ, 0161 839 5215)* on the other side of the road. This occupies a handsome 1920s' exterior and contains a traditional multi-roomed interior. Huge Gothic timber pendants hang down from a ceiling alive with crazy quatrefoil (fourleaf) tracery. Lots of cracking beers. There's a good story about the three entrances. In 1950 when a drunken journalist from the Daily Express next door tried to get in the landlord threw him out, he tried in the next entrance and then the next with the same result. Finally he asked the Landlord, "Do you own all the pubs round here?"

Turn right out of the Great Ancoats Street door of the Crown and Kettle, cross over the junction, taking Swan Street. Turn right at Rochdale Road and walk to the junction with Gould Street and **The Marble Arch** *(73 Rochdale Road M4 4HY, 0161 832 5914)*.This is from 1889, has an elaborate entrance and an interior alive with tile and mosaic. It's home-base for the wonderful micro-brewery Marble Beers and offers excellent food and a lovely atmosphere.

Retrace your steps down Rochdale Road to the first traffic lights. Set back on the right is **The Angel** *(6 Angel Street, M4 4BR, 0161 833 4786)*. This is one of Manchester city centre's best locals. There's food, live music, real fires and although the ghost has been exorcised, it's a very spirited pub and a real favourite. The pub is on three levels, restaurants above the bar area, and has been a boozer for a couple of hundred years. Like all good pubs it attracts a mixed age clientele.

Return to Rochdale Road and turn right. Rochdale Road after a short distance becomes Shude Hill. Just before the tram lines you'll see on the left hand side another 'local', the late 1700s' **The Hare and Hounds** *(46 Shudehill, M4 4AA, 0161 832 4737)*. Outside the pub has a handsome tiled façade. There's a lounge, a basic but comfy vault with TV and darts, and a long lobby doubling as the live entertainment space – if there's no older Mancunians on the karaoke it's only a

The Hare and Hounds

matter of time before the singing begins. There's good period detail and delicacies such as homemade pickled eggs.

On the other side of the tram lines is **The Lower Turks Head** *(36 Shudehill, M4 1EZ, 07814 184384)*. This place claims to date from 1745 which maybe the case, but it definitely features another marvellous 1920s' tiled facade. Inside if you dream of traditional boozers there's room after room of intimate spaces, low-lit to encourage wit, flirtatiousness, rhetoric, ease of mind. The next door shop has been converted by The Lower Turks Head to create the Scuttlers bar named after the notorious 19th century Manchester youth gangs. There's decent food as well.

The Lower Turks Head

Central Manchester and over the river

Start at **The Circus Tavern** *(86 Portland Street, M1 4GX, 0161 236 5818)* dating from before 1800. The most peculiar feature is a bar so small (perhaps the smallest in the UK) it fits the bar person and no-one else. The name comes from an equestrian circus that was founded nearby by Mr Hardy. In 1797 his circus went on tour to Liverpool and then Dublin. The boat sank and performers and horses died. Mr Hardy survived because he was catching a later boat.

Turn left out of the Circus and left down Nicholas Street, over the tram lines on Mosley Street, and then left on Cooper Street where you'll see three pubs with the most distinctive being **The City Arms** *(48 Kennedy Street, M2 4BQ, 0161 236 4610)*. This is a busy little conversation breeder with one of the city's best ranges of beer. Predictably popular with office workers and with Town Hall staff – the Council Leader is often in here - the City Arms, cuddles and coddles every type of citizen. There's lunchtime food, a bizarre outdoor smoking 'well', a selection of books, darts, and some period details.

Turn left out of The City Arms, passing the homely local of The Vines pub, and walk down Kennedy Street. At the junction turn right then immediately left via another

Mr Thomas's

homely local, The Town Hall Tavern, on Tib Lane. At the junction with Cross Street turn right, cross King Street and over the road you'll see the adorable facade of **Mr Thomas's Chop House** *(52 Cross St, M2 7AR, 0161 832 2245)*. This present building dates from 1901 and has one of the best period interiors with immaculate green tiled walls and brown tiled arches. There's superb food, a cracking winelist and a lovely rear terrace next to St Ann's Church.

Turn right out of Mr Thomas's Chop House and continue into Albert Square, past the new pub called Duttons, turn right down pedestrianised Brazennose Street into Lincoln Square. To the left you'll see **The Rising Sun** *(Queen Street, M2 5HX, 0161 834 1193)*. This has a huge range of beers and dates from sometime very early in the 19th century and is a 'cut-through' pub. In other words it connects two streets in the centre of a city block. Stories abound for the reasons behind this, for instance if the police came in on one side you could run out the other, or if your lady was hunting you down you could escape double quick. Now they're useful for quick get-aways if a hen or stag party staggers in.

The Circus

"The smallest bar ~in europe~ The biggest welcome in the world!"

Turn left out of the Rising Sun, cross Deansgate, and take the pedestrianised street called The Avenue on the left of the Armani shop down to **The Oast House** *(The Avenue Courtyard, M3 3AY, 0161 829 3830)*. This is a clever Disneyfication of pubs, modern with good beers, quirky food, live music and a huge outdoor drinking area. An oast house is a southern English building used for drying hops, the ingredient which flavours beer.

Turn right out of the Oast House and then right again to Bridge Street and turn left over the bridge into Salford. On the right by the riverside here is the Mark Addy pub (p92) with another fine drinking terrace. Otherwise continue straight on, under the railway arches at Salford Central to the traffic lights, cross straight over into Bloom Street and to **The Kings Arms** *(1 Bloom St, M3 6AN, 0161 839 8726)*. This grand building hosts the UK's oldest angling club, was the backdrop for Channel 4 student sitcom *Fresh Meat*, and has a theatre space and live music. It also has great beers, reasonable food, an oval lounge and the weirdest squashed up royal coat of arms on the facade. That lion looks in pain.

Pained lion on the Kings Arms

If you want to linger this side of the river, seek out **The New Oxford** *(11 Bexley Square, M3 6DB, 0161 832 7082)* and **The Eagle** *(18 Collier Street, M3 7DW, 0161 819 5002)*. The former is a city local with a couple of handsome rooms and a renowned beer selection. The Eagle is more boho located close to Blueprint recording studios. There's a lovely bar, three small rooms and a fine performance space hosting a regular programme of live music.

The Oast House

TEA, COFFEE, CAKE AND AFTERNOON TEA

For true tea fanatics two venues run by Gary McClarnan are must visits, **Teacup Kitchen** *(53-55 Thomas Street, Northern Quarter, M4 1NA)*, and **Propertea** *(10 Cateaton Street, M3 1SN)*, co-run with TV personality Yvette Cooper. Both are very pretty and both have so many varieties of tea it brews your brain. Perhaps the best homemade cake is available in these two as well. **Richmond Tea Rooms** *(15 Richmond Street, M1 3HZ, 0161 237 9667)* in the Village is another winner. This is Lewis Carroll's *Alice In Wonderland* re-imagined, chintz, china and the 'Best Independent Coffee Shop' at the Manchester Food and Drink Awards 2014.

For java demons there's plenty of choice away from bitter Starbucks' brews. **Caffeine & Co** (Old Granada HQ, Atherton Street, M60 9EA), produces smooth coffee from Square Mile roasters. The strange isolation of **Grindsmith** *(Greengate Square, M3 5AS, 07796 546489)* over the river from the Cathedral is appealing, located in a sweet eco-friendly pod, aka a shed. **Pot Kettle Black** *(Unit 14 Barton Arcade, M3 2BW)*, provides superb coffee and is housed in the splendid surroundings of the Barton Arcade and owned by two

strapping St Helens' rugby league players - Jon Wilkin and Mark Flanagan. **Takk** (6 Tariff Street, Northern Quarter, M1 2FF) defines trendy indie, based on Icelandic coffeehouses and permanently filled with Mac-warriors. **North Tea Power** *(36 Tib St, M4 1LA)* is similar, brimming as it is with freelancers and creatives that look like they all own dot-com start-ups.

For afternoon tea operators such as Propertea above oblige. Or you can glam up, put on a posh frock and heels and take it with Prosecco in one of the hotels, although it's cheaper with just tea. Most of the hotels do an afternoon tea with the loftiest at **Cloud 23** *(Deansgate Hilton, M3 4LQ, 0161 870 1600)*, 23 floors up and starting at £23. **Harvey Nichols** *(New Cathedral Street, M1 1AD, 0161 828 8888)* is £23.95 per person with champers and £17.95 without. One of the loveliest places to quietly sneak an afternoon tea is at the **Great John Street Hotel** *(M3 4FD, 0161 831 3211)*, £27.50 per person with champers and £21.50 without. The **Sculpture Hall Cafe** *(0161 831 3211)* in Manchester Town Hall provides afternoon teas from £12.95 per person. This is a lovely place to relax and chat throughout the day.

Propertea

BARS

Stand long enough in an empty unit in Manchester and a bar will slowly form around you. There has been a revolution in the depth and range of drinking dens in the city centre over the last decade and it shows no sign of slowing. This can get confusing so we've split the most popular bars into rough categories below so you don't end up feeling out of place. Bars that major in live music are featured in the Entertainment section.

Show-off and dress up bars

If you like to dress up, show off and spend, spend, spend then maybe try these places. **Cloud 23** *(Deansgate Hilton, M3 4LQ, 0161 870 1600)* on the 23rd Floor of the Deansgate Hilton in Beetham Tower provides grand views across the whole region. If possible book seats on the side with the northern view to a get a dramatic, almost aerial, experience of the city centre. Light bites and very good cocktails here but you pay for the view. Another place with views, this time on the 12th floor is the bar of Manchester House restaurant, called **Lounge on 12** *(Tower 12, 18-22 Bridge Street, Spinningfields,*

M3 3BZ, 0161 835 2557) from Manchester company Living Ventures. Superb 'mixologists' here, not bad beers and great spirits, inside a sharply designed see-and-be-seen bar. Nearby, the bar of **Australasia** *(1 The Avenue, Spinningfields, M3 3AP, 0161 831 0288)*, also owned by Living Ventures, is fine for giving a sharp suit or a glam dress an airing, as is the attached Grand Pacific.

Cloud23

Lounge on 12

Room Bar and Restaurant *(81 King Street, M2 4AH, 0161 839 2005)* has a splendid bar in a splendid 1870s' building (see Walk Two, p110) with extravagant decor. Harvey Nichols Second Floor Brasserie *(1 New Cathedral Street, M1 1AD, 0161 828 8888)* has a fine bar area for smartly dressed sorts who like to preen. Good food here and good cocktails too. Three of San Carlo group's city centre venues, San Carlo *(42 King Street West, M3 2WY, 0161 834 6226)*, Cicchetti and Fumo, all drag the upwardly mobile in with their generous bars and air of luxury.

Indie and Hipster bars

It's a horrible word 'hipster', so over-used it's almost lost all meaning, but it does sum things up accurately. These indie bars are usually filled with people who fulfil the arty, beardy stereotype, although the distinction is blurring a little as more mainstream punters invade the home territory – in other words the Northern Quarter of the city centre. Either way expect lots of drink variety, lots of distressed interior design, artshows, djs and occasionally can't-be-bothered service.

Apotheca *(17 Thomas Street, Northern Quarter, M4 1FS, 0161 834 9411)* is all low level lighting, dark leather interior and heavy velvet curtains with more than 50 cocktails on offer. There are DJs and a cinema screen downstairs. Big Hands *(296A Oxford Road, 0161 272 7309, M13 9NS)* is out in University land and comes with a dingy indie appeal. Lots of Manchester musos nip in so expect DJs and live music. Black Dog NQ *(Church Street, Northern Quarter, City. 0161 839 0664, M4 1PW)* is a 'New York style speak-easy diner'; a perfect location for city slickers to kick back and relax, with a pool table lounge and dance floor. Common *(Edge Street, Northern Quarter, M4 1HW, 0161 832 9243.)* displays a constantly mutating mix of street art and cartoonish doodles on its walls hinting at the canny, funny, and unintimidating character of the place which comes with DJs and quiz nights. Deaf Institute *(135 Grosvenor Street, City, M1 7HE, 0161 276 9350)* is part of the Manchester Trof empire of bars with three floors, a roof terrace, food and a calendar bursting at the seams with regular nights catering for the full spectrum of musical tastes from soul and swing to rap, reggae and rock. Kosmonaut *(10 Tariff Street, Northern Quarter, M1 2FF)*

Black Dog

Elixir

Cocktails and Wine

Elixir Tonics & Treats *(123 Deansgate, M3 2BY, 0161 222 8588)* has created one of the best cocktail lists around over two comfortable floors. They feature crazy things such as the Mermaid's Teardrop, made of vodka, kwai feh, coconut and ocean syrup with a teardrop ice bomb and chocolate sea-glass shell. More mainstream are the two Alchemists in Manchester. The original **Alchemist** *(3 Hardman Street, Spinningfields, 0161 817 2950, M3 3HF)* sports tarnished wooden cabinets filled with test-tubes and skulls. Cocktails are brewed like potions using bunsen burners and finished with syringes full of exotica.

Tiki bars bring the warm flavours of Hawaii and the Caribbean. Try **Hula** *(11 Stevenson Square, Northern Quarter, M1 1DB, 0161 228 7421)*, **Keko Meku** *(100 High Street, M4 1HPO)* and the beautiful upstairs bar of **Cane and Grain** *(49-51 Thomas Street, Northern Quarter, M4 1NA, 0161 839 7033)* - the latter also does a mean vodka martini. **Revolucion de Cuba** *(11 Peter Street, M2 5QR, 0161 826 8266)* as the name might suggest, has a fine expertise in rum. For gin seek out the gin

has table tennis, food, a fine cocktail list, DJs and events galore. **Odd Bar** *(Thomas Street, Northern Quarter, M4 1ER, 0161 833 0070)*, and sister bar and restaurant **Blue Pig** *(69 High Street, Northern Quarter, M4 1FS, 0161 832 0630)* are part of one of the older indie mini-chains. Both are great for drinks, with the former more about the mood, and the latter more about the food. Both have plenty of personality not least from owner Cleo Farman who's frequently about. **Terrace** *(43 Thomas Street, Northern Quarter, M4 1NA, 0161 819 2345)* is so trendy it's hard to find and ignores flim-flam such as signboards. Still its moody ambience is rewarding as are the good ales, cocktails, decent food and event nights.

Cane and Grain

Jon and Sara of Salut Wines

parlour at **Gorilla** (*54-56 Whitworth Street West, M1 5WW, 0161 407 0301*). **Almost Famous and Luck, Lust, Liquor and Burn**, occupying the same Northern Quarter building (*102 High Street, M4 1HP*), have owners who were cocktail pioneers in Manchester so don't be shy about nipping to the bar areas of these largely foodie places.

The Liquor Store (*40 Blackfriars Street, City, M3 2EG. 0161 834 6239*). Hidden underneath an office building the owners deliver scrupulously concocted cocktails, straightforward bar snacks, sleek design and impressive customer service.

There's a new fashion for enomatic machines. These are wine dispensers operated by pre-paid card that allow people to enjoy wine by the glass and thus experience plenty of variety. **Salut** (*11

Port Street Beerhouse

Cooper Street, M2 2FW, 0161 236 2340*) is the best for this, where there are 42 wines available at different prices. Of course you can still buy one of over 300 bottled varieties. Tiny **Hanging Ditch Wine Merchants** (*42 Victoria Street, M3 1ST, 0161 832 8222*) has a very discerning selection of wines and about 8 stools at a counter from which to drink them. The terrace outside is a different matter though, it's an expansive sun trap with a strangely stirring view of Salford.

Beer Bars

Beer is the new old thing. With a product again fashionable, specialist beer bars have cropped up to join an established list of Steady Eddies. **Cask** (*29 Liverpool Road, M3 4NQ*) elevates the palate with a fine range of beers, a jukebox and a tiny beer garden. **Brewdog** (*35 Peter Street, M2 5BG*) provides own brand beers of fierce, bordering on the ridiculous, strength with a fierce, often bordering on the ridiculous, bitter taste. There's pinball, board games and good pizzas. Locally brewed Marble beers and guests feature at **57 Thomas Street** (*Northern Quarter, M4 1NA*), in a tiny former shop unit with board games.

Pie and Ale *(Unit 1 & 2, The Hive, Lever Street, Northern Quarter, M1 1FN)*, part of the Bakerie complex delivers on the promise of its title in a curious space, while **Port Street Beerhouse** *(39-41 Port Street, Northern Quarter, M1 2EQ, 0161 237 9949)* is perhaps the daddy of them all. Spread over an entire building with a beer garden in the back this is a treasure trove of blended barley, hops and yeast, brimming over with craft beers, real ales, and unique brews - UK, US and from round the world. The bar regularly hosts beer festivals.

Curiosities

Fitzgerald *(Little Lever Street, Stevenson Square, Northern Quarter, M1 1DB)* is a devil to find as it lies essentially down a back alley. This is one place that has taken the '20s American speak-easy concept (hence the name) and run with it. There's period furniture on dark wooden flooring, nude flappers on the wall and very fine drinks. **Gas Lamp** *(50 Bridge Street, M3 3BW, 0161 478 1224)* lurks in the former kitchens of a street children's mission. It's composed of tiles throughout in a clinical yellow wash-down shade that should make the bar the most alarming to be inside in central Manchester. Yet strangely it all works. Good spirit selection. **The Lawn Club** *(Byrom Street, M3 3HG, 07857 964334)* is the most permanent pop-up known to man which not only provides a lovely drinking experience, summer or winter, on the Spinningfields' lawns, but also just about the best food in any of these bars. **The Temple** *(100 Great Bridgewater Street, M1 5JW)* occupies a former gents toilet and is so tiny it's full with twelve people, yet it somehow puts on DJs and somehow is a pleasant place to drink. **Twenty Twenty Two** *(20 Dale Street, M1 1EZ, 0161 237 9360)* is where arts, music, drinks and table tennis seamlessly meld. Finally there are **The Liars Club** *(19A Back Bridge St, M3 2PB, 0161 834 5111)* and **The**

The Lawn Club

Press Club *(St Johns House, 2-10 Queen Street, M2 5JB, 0161 834 8562)* where people who don't want to go home find a home. The former is lively, cool and fun, describing itself as 'a tiki dive bar with over 300 rums'; the latter is old (founded 1870), mad, sticky, serves endless Red Stripe, and could be fun but you're never sure until you've reassessed the night many days later.

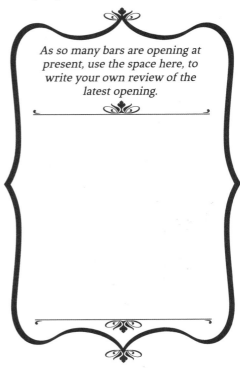

As so many bars are opening at present, use the space here, to write your own review of the latest opening.

Chorlton and The Didsburys

Fletcher Moss Gardens

This guidebook is mainly concerned with the central areas of Manchester but there are three classic leafy suburbs full of independent businesses in the south of the city. They are all conveniently linked by a direct Metrolink line (the tramline) from the city centre and make for interesting excursions.

Chorlton-cum-Hardy comes first on the Metrolink tram. The politics of the place can be gauged by the fact one of the newsagents apparently sells more Guardian newspapers - the leftfield national newspaper - than any other small retailer nationally. There's also the country's largest vegan grocery, the excellent Unicorn. Fine bars are everywhere such as Electrik, Beagle and Dulcimer. Beech Road and Chorlton Green are quaint with good food, drink or both at Parlour, San Juan and The Beech pub plus decent clothes shops such as McQueen and Nood. Elsewhere you can find a notable butchers,

Frosts, a notable fishmongers, Out of the Blue, and a superb bakery, Barbakan. A short walk south of the Green is a country park area by the banks of the River Mersey. Chorlton Water Park and Sale Water Park are close by.

Three stops on from Chorlton is West Didsbury, with on Burton Road, a number of interesting businesses including wine merchants, Reserve, fashion shop Steranko, restaurants such as The Rose Garden and bars such as Volta and Folk. On Lapwing Lane there's the Metropolitan pub and restaurant, veggie restaurant Greens and award-winning, The Lime Tree. Further along Lapwing Lane and over Palatine Road is the Northern, the main lawn tennis club in the city, and wine and ales specialist Wine & Wallop.

Another couple of stops along the line is cute Didsbury with perhaps the finest patisserie in the city, Alex Moreau's Bisous Bisous, the best cheese shop in the city, The Cheese Hamlet, a good butchers in Axons and the utterly charming Art of Tea with its excellent second hand bookshop. Way down the far end of 'the Village', as the locals call it, are Fletcher Moss and Parsonage Gardens, mini-botanical gardens, the former boasting a fine rockery with pools. If gardens are your things seek out the Marie Louise Gardens in Didsbury too.

Mille-feuille at Bisous Bisous

Sport

Some visitors, given the fame of the football clubs, define the city by sport. As the rest of this book shows Manchester is far more than that, but it's still comforting for locals, despite the red and blue rivalry, to have such prestigious names carrying the name of their city. Football's merely the tip of the iceberg though, there is so much more sport to watch or participate in. For instance, Lancashire Cricket Club hosts international matches and there are top flight rugby league and union clubs, while the National Cycling centre has proved a goldmine for Olympic medals in recent years.

The oldest continuously used table football machine from the 1950s at Peveril of the Peak pub

Football

Manchester United

Sir Matt Busby Way, Old Trafford, M16 0RA, 0161 868 8000

An attacking style of football and exciting players have all helped create the legend of United: a legend which began with tragedy and the Munich Air Disaster. On 6 February 1958 nine players of the 'Busby Babes' team, died as their plane crashed on take-off. That was followed by lovely football in the rebuilt team of the 1960s from Charlton, Best and Law. More recently the teams of Sir Alex Ferguson have fuelled the mythology, especially through the 1999 campaign when United won a unique Treble of League, FA Cup and Champions League. If you don't get a ticket for a game a good way of experiencing United's potency is by visiting the Museum and Tour. Tickets at time of press for this are £18 for adults and £12 for children, although there are deals and family tickets. The museum provides an overview of the club's story with exceptional sections on both the Munich Disaster and the Treble season. The tour is the best part of the experience.

The Chronology

1878 Newton Heath Lancashire and Yorkshire Railway Football and Cricket Club announced.

1892 Promotion to the First Division of the Football League.

1902 The name Manchester United is adopted.

1908 United are crowned First Division champions for the first time, they also win the Charity Shield.

1909 The team beats Bristol City 1-0 to win the FA Cup.

1910 The club move to Old Trafford and lose the first game 3-4 to Liverpool.

1911 First Division title won again.

1931 The club is relegated again.

1941 Old Trafford bombed during a Nazi attack on Trafford Park.

1945 Company Sergeant Major Matthew Busby becomes manager.

1948 United set the record (still existing) for the highest ever league attendance of 83,260 against Arsenal, the match was played at Manchester City's Maine Road stadium because of bomb damage to Old Trafford.

1948 United win the FA Cup against Blackpool.

1951 Age of the 'Busby Babes' begins and the First Division title is won.

1952 Title won again, Charity Shield won.

1956 United win the First Division Title, enter the European Cup and reach the semi-finals.

1958 The Munich Disaster. 11 members of the United playing and coaching staff killed among 23 deaths.

1963 With the famous team of Bobby Charlton, Denis Law and George Best now united the team win the FA Cup 3-1 against Leicester.

1965 First Division won and also in 1967.

1968 United become the first English team to win the European Cup 4-1 at Wembley against Benfica.

1969 Matt Busby steps down.

1973 George Best leaves the club.

1974 United relegated to the Second Division, helped on their way by a Denis Law backheel playing for Manchester City.

1975 United promoted back to the First Division with Tommy Docherty in charge.

1976 United lose FA Cup final to Southampton but the following year United beat Liverpool 2-1 in the FA Cup final.

1979 The famous three minute FA Cup final - United lose 3-2 to Arsenal.

1981 Ron Atkinson is appointed manager.

1983 Bryan Robson becomes the most expensive British player (£1.5m). United beat Brighton, after a replay, in the FA Cup final.

1985 United beat Everton 1-0 in the FA Cup final.

1986 Alex Ferguson becomes manager.

1990 FA Cup final triumph against Crystal Palace saves Ferguson's job.

1991 United win the Cup Winner's Cup against Barcelona, 2-1.

1992 United beat Nottingham Forest in the League Cup final. Peter Schmeichel arrives.

1993 After 26 years United win the title – the inaugural Premier League title, galvanised by the arrival of Frenchman Eric Cantona.

1994 United win the Double, the Premier League and FA Cup. Sir Matt Busby dies.

1996 Another Double, this time beating Liverpool 1-0 in the FA Cup. This was the famous team of 'kids', as Ferguson's youth policy blossomed with the arrival in the regular first team of the Neville brothers, David Beckham, Paul Scholes and Nicky Butt to join Ryan Giggs.

1997 The Premiership won again, Cantona leaves.

1999 The team win the Treble - Premier League, FA Cup and Champions League - in the most dramatic season of the club's history, culminating in two stoppage time goals to steal the Champions League from Bayern Munich's hands.

2000 United win the World Cup Trophy in Japan and retain the Premiership.

2001 With a third title in a row the club land a treble of titles.

2002 £30m Rio Ferdinand becomes the most expensive British player.

2003 United grab the Premier League title. Cristiano Ronaldo is signed from Sporting Lisbon. 2004 United beat Millwall 4-0 in the FA Cup final.

2005 Wayne Rooney signs. United lose on penalties to Arsenal in the FA Cup final. George Best dies in hospital, aged 59, after multiple organ failure. The charismatic winger fought a long battle with alcoholism and finally died on 12 November. The Glazer family from America buy the club. United become a club £790m in debt. Fans set up FC United in protest. Green and yellow scarves become a regular sight at Old Trafford, the colours of the original Newton Heath.

2006 United win the League Cup.

2007 United regain the Premier League.

2008 United win both the Premier League and the Champions League with Ronaldo scoring 42 goals in all competitions. Off the pitch the club commemorate the 50th anniversary of the Munich Air disaster.

2009 The club equal Liverpool's 18 league titles fulfilling Ferguson's 1986 promise to 'knock them off their perch.' They win the League Cup and the FIFA Club World Cup but lose the Champions League final 2-0 to Barcelona. Cristiano Ronaldo leaves for Real Madrid for a world record £80 million fee.

2011 Sir Alex Ferguson becomes Manchester United's longest serving manager. A 29 match unbeaten run sends the club to their 19th title. A third Champions League final in four years ends in another defeat to Barcelona, 3-1.

2013 Robin Van Persie fires United to an emphatic 11 point Premier League retrieval. Sir Alex Ferguson announces his retirement. After almost 27 years and 25 trophies Ferguson has been the most successful manager in English football. Everton boss David Moyes is announced as Ferguson's successor.

2014 Moyes is sacked 9 months into a 6 year contract after United finish 7th in the League and fail to qualify for European competition for the first time in 25 years. Ryan Giggs is appointed temporary player-manager for the final four games of the season. Louis Van Gaal is announced for the permanent position and Giggs becomes his assistant.

2014 Van Gaal breaks English transfer record fee of £59.7 million for winger Angel Di Maria.

Manchester City

Etihad Stadium, Ashton New Road, M11 3FF, 0161 444 1894

City fans are still dazzled. Just a few years ago the club seemed permanently destined for second best in Manchester. Now they're winning titles, playing beautiful football, and if it's not quite happened yet in Europe, with phenomenally rich owners Abu Dhabi United set to stay for the long-term, Champions League success doesn't seem too far away. At the time of press for the first time in decades City is the dominant team in Manchester.

However the legend of City still needs nurturing so for many games at the Etihad there are plenty of tickets available on general sale. The stadium expansion from 48,000 to over 62,000 will inevitably release more tickets as well. If you want to visit the club other than on match days there's always the Stadium and Club Tour, £16 for adults, £10 for children. This gets beneath the skin of the Etihad stadium and includes time in the museum dedicated to the club's heritage plus a look at what the future might hold.

The Chronology

1880 Manchester City enter the world as a church club, St Mark's of West Gorton, subsequently they become Gorton playing at the charmingly named Pink Bank Lane.

1887 The name Ardwick FC is adopted.

1892 Ardwick enter Division Two.

1893 The club goes bankrupt but re-emerges as Manchester City.

1899 City promoted to Division One.

1904 The club wins the FA Cup 1-0 against Bolton.

1905 Billy Meredith, who would also play for United, is suspended for allegedly attempting to bribe an Aston Villa player. 17 players and two directors suspended from club.

1923 The club moves to Maine Road, Moss Side.

1926 City meet Bolton again in the FA Cup final but lose 1-0 and are also relegated.

1929 City promoted to the First Division.

1933 City lose again in the FA Cup final to Everton 3-0. Against Everton the players had worn numbered shirts for the first time in a final, oddly numbered between 1-22 across both teams.

1934 City reach FA Cup final again and this time beat Portsmouth 2-1.

1937 Under Wilf Wild the club wins its first Division One championship.

1938 City relegated - after scoring more goals than any other team including champions Arsenal.

1947 Promoted to the First Division again.

1955 City lose the FA Cup final 3-1 to Newcastle United.

1956 City win FA Cup final against Birmingham City 3-1 with City's Goalkeeper and ex-prisoner of war, Bert Trautmann, playing the last 15 minutes with a broken neck.

1968 Another First Division championship arrives in what is considered the golden age of Manchester City with players in the next few seasons including Mike Doyle, Colin Bell, Francis Lee, Tony Book and Tony Coleman.

1969 City win the FA Cup final 1-0 against Leicester.

1970 A European Cup Winners Cup win at Maine Road comes courtesy of a 2-1 win against Gornik Zabrize of Poland.

1976 City beat Newcastle 3-1 in the League Cup final. It is the last major honour the club will win for 35 years.

1981 City defeated by Tottenham Hotspur in a replayed FA Cup final.

1983 Relegated to Division Two.

1985 Return to Division One.

1987 Back down again.

1989 Up again.

1996 Down again. The season includes the shortest appointment in City's team management history when Steve Coppell, appointed in October, quits after 32 days citing health problems.

1998 The unthinkable happens and City slip into the third tier of English football for the first time in their history. On the first day of the new season in the Second Division City's attendance was on a par with all the other clubs playing the same division that day.

1999 With Joe Royle at the helm City win an incredible play-off at Wembley against Gillingham, coming back from two goals down in the dying minutes to win promotion.

2000 Another tense final game of the season sees City back in the Premier League.

2001 And then they go straight back down.

2002 Kevin Keegan takes charge and City gain promotion again.

2003 City leave Maine Road and move back to the 48,000 City of Manchester Stadium, the former home of the Commonwealth Games.

2005 Stuart Pearce takes over as temporary manager from a weary Kevin Keegan.

2007 At the start of the new season controversial Thaksin Shinawatra (ex-Premier of Thailand later found guilty of corruption) takes over the club and appoints ex-England manager Sven-Goran Eriksson.

2008 Mark Hughes becomes Manchester City manager. On 23 September the Abu Dhabi United group takeover. The group are a financial powerhouse. City now have access to more money than any other in the land. To show their intent the British transfer fee record is broken to bring Robinho from Real Madrid for £32.4m.

2009 Roberto Mancini appointed as manager. The club sign Carlos Tevez from United. The club causes anger amongst Reds by installing a huge banner in the city centre depicting Tevez and reading; 'Welcome to Manchester',

a reference to the fact Old Trafford is technically outside the city's boundary.

2010 The club spends £126m on new players during the summer, in a bid to gain a top four finish and a debut in the Champions League.

2011 Manchester City win their first trophy in 35 years as Yaya Toure inspires with the winning goal in the semi-final (against Manchester United) and the final where City beat Stoke City 1-0. They finish third in the Premier League and qualify for the Champions League.

2012 City win a first Premier League trophy in dramatic fashion beating United on goal difference. At 2-1 down into stoppage time their fans fear it's another story of 'bottling' it. Edin Dzeko and Sergio Aguero both score, gaining a 3-2 win against QPR, in 'Fergie time' as people quipped.

2013 City lose to underdogs Wigan Athletic 1-0 in the FA Cup final. Mancini resigns Manuel Pellegrini takes over.

2014 City regain the title and a ground expansion to more than 62,000 begins. The huge Etihad Campus takes shape next to the main stadium worth more than £200m with its own 7,000 capacity reserve ground, 16 pitches, an accommodation block and a sixth-form College for the local community.

Crowds gather at Old Trafford

Other football

There is Championship football at Bolton Wanderers *(01204 673 673)* and Wigan Athletic *(01942 774 000)*. League One and League Two football is represented by Rochdale *(01706 644 648)*, Oldham Athletic *(0161 624 4972)* and Bury (0161 764 4881). You can play football at **Soccer in the City** *(M3 4JW, 0161 834 3295)*. It can be just as rewarding to watch football in the lower tiers as it can at United or City. Manchester also has an unusual and very fledgling club, **FC United** *(0161 273 8950)*. They are based in Moston and play in the Northern Premier League and were formed in protest at the takeover of Manchester United by the Glazers in 2005.

Cricket

The big name in the region is **Lancashire County Cricket Club** *(Talbot Road, Old Trafford, 0161 282 4000)*, County Champions as recently as the 2011 season. They have been champions outright nine times and shared the title four times. The club was founded in 1864 and merged with Manchester Cricket Club in 1880. In one form or another it has played on the present site since 1857. Notable players have included AC McClaren who made 424 against Somerset in 1895, the county's highest ever individual score, Brian Statham who took 1,816 wickets including 252 for England, West Indian captain, Clive Lloyd, and powerful all-rounder Andrew 'Freddie' Flintoff, now a TV personality as well. Current bowling mainstay of the England team is James Anderson, another Lancashire player.

Tickets are always available for county matches, for internationals when Lancashire hosts England, tickets can be hard to come by, nigh impossible if Australia are the opposition. The ground has a capacity of 15,000 for county games and 26,000 for internationals. Watching cricket in some of the villages and suburbs around Manchester can be delightful, especially with a pint of beer on a summer's day. For fixtures and venues contact **Lancashire Cricket Board** *(0161 282 4029)*.

Rugby League and Union

In 1895 the Northern Union split away from the Rugby Union over the question of professionalism and League came into being. The working class northern teams couldn't afford to take time off to play and needed their players to be paid. Over time the two codes divided further, for example, League reducing the number of players to 13 on each side and Union sticking with 15. Fortunately in Manchester both codes can be sampled at the same location, the AJ Bell Stadium *(Stadium Way, Eccles, M30 7WH)* by watching either Salford Reds (League) or Sale Sharks (Union). Ring *0161 820 2610* for tickets to the former and

0844 499 4994, for tickets to the latter. Not far away are Rugby League giants Wigan Warriors and St Helens.

Other sports

Athletics can occasionally be viewed at the Athletics Arena at the Commonwealth Games' Sportscity complex at the Etihad Stadium. This is one of the Sale Harriers Athletics Club locations. Contact the club for further information if you want to join in. **Basketball** is a growing sport with competitive matches of local team Manchester Magic taking place at the John Amaechi Basketball Centre *(Wilbraham Road, Manchester, M16 8GW, 0161 881 0090)*. Climbing walls can be found across the region but **Manchester Climbing Centre** *(Bennett Street, Ardwick, M12 5ND, 0161 230 7006)* is the most spectacular with 76 climbing lines in a large former church. The **National Cycling Centre** *(Stuart Street, M11 4DQ, 0161 223 2244)*,

Heaton Park Golf

which contains the adjacent BMX Centre, is superb both for watching competitions or sampling the main track or the BMX course yourself.

Dog-racing can be enjoyed at Belle Vue *(Kirkmanshulme Lane, Gorton, M18 7BA, 0870 840 7557)* every Friday and Saturday night. **Golf** courses surround the city with the links courses of the Open, such as Royal Birkdale, not too far away. In Manchester and convenient for the tram, there's a public course a Heaton Park Golf Centre *(Middleton Road, Prestwich, M25 2SW, 0161 654 9899)*. There's hockey at Belle Vue too *(Belle Vue Leisure Centre, Kirksmanhulme Lane, Longsight 0161 953 2470)* and ice hockey with Manchester Phoenix *(Altrincham Ice Dome, Altrincham, 0161 926 8782)*. **Public ice skating** is found at the same venue or everywhere on public squares at Christmas. The Manchester region is the home of English **lacrosse**. Should you wish to watch a game or take part contact the English Lacrosse Association (0843 658 5006).

For **speedway** racing try Belle Vue Aces *(0161 223 8000)* and for **karting** the nearest to the city centre is at Daytona *(Trafford Park, 0845 644 5505)*. Public **swimming** is at Manchester Aquatics Centre *(Booth Street East, off Oxford Road, 0161 275 9490)*, and open water swimming at Salford Quays (contact the USWIM organisation). Lawn **tennis** can be enjoyed at The Northern in Didsbury *(0161 445 3093)* and at the Regional Tennis Centre at Sportscity *(0161 220 3840)* close to the Etihad stadium. Also at Sportscity is the **National Squash Centre** (0161 220 3800) which features a mobile show court on a hovercraft. For **skiing** try Chill Factore *(Trafford Quays Leisure Village, M41 7JA, 0843 596 2233)* with its 180m slope and lots of other snow and ice experiences. Adjacent to Chill Factore is **Air Kiks** *(0845 331 65490)* for indoor skydiving in a wind tunnel. A very wide range of **watersports** can be enjoyed at the Helly Hansen Centre at Salford Quays *(M50 3SQ, 0161 877 7252)*.

Chil Factore

Entertainment

Take That in concert at the Etihad Stadium

Theatre and Comedy

"I know not of any way so effectual to eradicate that dark, odious and ridiculous enthusiasm as by giving to the people cheerful rational amusement, which may operate against their methodistical melancholy," said the Earl of Carlisle in 1775 as construction of new theatre was being debated in Manchester. Given the rise of non-conformity in the city he saw theatre as a way to lighten hearts and minds. People seemed to agree with him and over the following half century Manchester rose to be the capital of the North when it came to theatre, music and shows. A position it maintains today.

The main city centre theatre is the **Royal Exchange** (p21). This theatre in the round puts on a mixed programme of classics and new work throughout the year and also has free music event, Special FX, early Friday evening in the spectacular former trading hall. For West End musicals and shows, occasional one-offs, and pantomimes with celebrities **the Palace Theatre** (*Oxford Street, M1 6FT, 0844 871 7660 and p126*) and **the Opera House** (*Quay Street, M3 3HP, 0844 871 7660 and p91*) provide beautiful and elaborate early 20th century interiors. A new theatre space is opening at **HOME** (*First Street, M15 4FN*) a multi-function arts venue, in the First Street development, in the south of the city centre. This includes a 500-seat theatre; a 150-seat flexible studio space; a 500m2, 4m high gallery space; five cinema screens; digital production and broadcast facilities; a café bar and restaurants. It will continue the work of the former Library Theatre in delivering progressive theatre. The major theatre space outside the city centre is **the Lowry** (*Pier 6, M50 3AZ 0843 208 6000*) at the Quays, p142, and a major receiving house for top end drama and music. There are two main spaces, the Lyric and the Quays. At the University there's the **Contact Theatre** (*Oxford Road, M15 6JA, 0161 274 0600*) specialising in producing work and providing opportunities for young people. In the other towns of

A Royal Exchange production
PHOTO: JONATHAN KEENAN

Greater Manchester high quality theatre is put on at the Bolton Octagon, the Oldham Coliseum and Bury Met. Also look out for informal theatre spaces in venues such as **Victoria Baths** (p57). **The Kings Arms** (p157) pub in Salford has a theatre group, and there are small independent theatres such as the **New Playhouse** (231-233 Deansgate, M3 4EN).

Manchester and Lancashire have been the home of famous and infamous comedians for as long as theatre has flourished in the city. Peter Kay, John Thomson, Steve Coogan, Caroline Aherne, Victoria Wood and Mike Harding come from the city as did the controversial Bernard Manning. There are two main locations in which to see comedy, **The Frog and Bucket** (102 Oldham Street, M4 1LJ, 0161 236 9805) started life in 1993 and the heart of the Manchester comedy scene. **The Comedy Store** (Arches 3-4, Deansgate Locks, M1 5LH, 0870 593 2932) is the London operator hosting big names and emerging talent. Celebrity comedians tend to perform at big venues such as the Phones4U Arena,

the Lowry or The Bridgewater Hall. Keep an eye out for pub nights too such as XS Malarkey at **Pub/Zoo** (126 Grosvenor Street, M1 7HL, 0161 273 1471).

Television and Film

Manchester is home to *Coronation Street*, the longest running TV soap opera from 1960. The area is also home, or provided a location, to movies and TV series such as Richardson's *A Taste of Honey*, Lean's *Hobson's Choice*, Finney's *Charlie Bubbles*, Beatty's *Reds*, Spielberg's *Empire of the Sun*, Sheridan's *In the Name of the Father*, Ritchie's *Sherlock Holmes*, Johnson's *Captain America*, Lloyd's *The Iron Lady* amongst many films. Classic TV dramas produced in the city, mostly through the former Granada TV, have included *Sherlock Holmes*, *Brideshead Revisited*, *House of Cards*, *Cracker*, *Prime Suspect*, *The Royle Family*, *Clocking Off*, *Queer as Folk*, *Pride and Prejudice* and *Life on Mars*. Popular TV shows such as *Blue*

Inside the Rover's Return on the Coronation Street tour

Peter, Match of the Day and the Jeremy Kyle show are produced in the city. These are filmed at **MediaCityUK** (p140), perhaps Europe's largest centre for broadcasting hosting the BBC and ITV.

There are three main city centre cinemas: **AMC Cinema** (Great Northern, 235 Deansgate, M3 4EN, 0161 817 3000), **Odeon** (The Printworks, 27 Withy Grove, M4 2BS, 0871 224 4007) and **HOME** (First Street, M15 4FN). The second of these has an IMAX screen, the last is the arthouse cinema for the region.

Coronation Street: The Tour (Atherton Street, Castlefield, M3 4FD, 0844 277 0700) With ITV moving out of the city centre for MediaCityUK and a new set for Coronation Street constructed, the former set of the soap has re-opened on a temporary basis as a tour before being demolished as part of a mixed use development. So, for a limited time only, fans are able to walk the famous street and also to study the stage sets in Stage One. The tours (starting at £16.50, but there are deals available online) are guided with free time at the end.

Classical Music

Not only is the city a centre for performances but of musical education. **Chetham's School of Music** (p33) provides education for 8-18 year olds and the **Royal Northern College of Music** (124 Oxford Road, M13 9RD, 0161 907 5200 and see p56) takes care of undergraduate and postgraduate studies. **The Hallé, the BBC Philharmonic** and the **Manchester Camerata** are the three main orchestras and there are several venues to watch these perform with the principal one being the **Bridgewater Hall** (p44-45). Others include the aforementioned and splendidly refurbished Royal Northern College of Music and the purpose-built hall at **MediaCityUK** (p140) for the BBC Philharmonic. The Hallé has secured a beautiful rehearsal space at **St Peter's** (p59) in Ancoats. Expect to find Classical music cropping up in the Cathedral, St Ann's Church and The Albert Hall. The Halle's Thursday series, running from September to May, is an unbroken tradition going back to 1861. Look out for their Opus One series too. Visiting opera and ballet tends to arrive at the Opera House, Palace and The Lowry.

St Peter's, the Halle rehearsal space

Popular Music

For a while in the 1980s and early 1990s it seemed as though Manchester ruled the musical world. From the punk explosion of 1976 groups from Greater Manchester included **The Buzzcocks, The Fall, Joy Division, New Order, James, Simply Red, 808 State, Durutti Column, Lisa Stansfield, The Smiths, The Stone Roses, Happy Mondays, Oasis, Verve** and the first coming of **Take That**. This was part of a legacy stretching way back. Prominent Manchester bands in the 1960s and 1970s included **The Hollies, Herman's Hermits** and **10cc**.

Why there was such remarkable creativity in Manchester leading to - with The Stone Roses and Happy Mondays - a whole scene called Madchester involving fashion, attitude and, of course, the music, has been endlessly debated. Maybe the bloody-minded truculence of Manchester's musical pioneers is part of this. Anthony Wilson (p236), Alan Erasmus and Rob Gretton with the chaotic, but heart warmingly indie Factory Records seem part of this with Wilson saying: 'Factory Records are not actually a company. We are an experiment in human nature.' Manchester band members such as Mark E Smith of the Fall, Morrissey (p236) of the Smiths, Ian Brown of The Stone Roses, the Gallagher brothers of Oasis, all conform to the opinionated, mouthy, Manc muso stereotype. Peter Saville, graphic designer with Factory, captured this perfectly in a 2004 interview: "There is a wilful elitism about Manchester which is very condensed compared to other cities, one which elsewhere becomes diversified and weakened. There's something historically, geographically, socially about the climate, the people, that prepares you for something. We didn't think we were the best, we knew we were."

In the present digital, fractured and globalised world localised scenes such as Madchester seem unlikely. Manchester in recent years with bands such as **Elbow, Hurts, Money** still proves it can provide the tunes, while the remarkable reunion shows of The Stone Roses in Heaton Park in 2012 reveals the potency of the past: all 225,000 tickets for the three shows sold out in 68 minutes. The back together Take That carry on selling out stadiums as well.

Manchester loves dancing and clubs as well. From the beat and northern soul clubs of the 1960s such as Twisted Wheel through The Hacienda (p129) to today's Warehouse Party nights there's always been plenty going on. Of course times change, so you'll find lots of dancing in the bars in our food and drink section, p177. The most celebrated recent club nights have tended to revolve around the eclectic mix of music at **the Warehouse Project**, an itinerant musical project that moves each year into an appropriate ex-industrial space. Tickets are like gold dust but try 0161 835 3500.

Live Music Venues and Clubs

Many of these venues mix live music with club nights so check out their individual websites, many have regular club nights such as Tribal Sessions at Sankey's. The bigger venues are the **Phones4U Arena** *(Victoria Station, Hunts Bank, Manchester M3 1AR, 0161 950 5000)*, **Manchester Apollo** *(Stockport Road, Ardwick Green, Manchester M12 6AP, 0161 273 6921)*, **The Academy** *(Oxford Road, M13 9PR, 0161 275 2930)*, **Sound Control** *(1 New Wakefield Street, Manchester M1 5NP, 0161 236 0340)*, **The Ritz** *(Whitworth Street West, M1 5NQ, 0161 236 3234)* and **Gorilla** *(54-56 Whitworth Street West, Manchester M1 5WW, 0161 407 0301)*. **Albert Hall** *(22 Peter Street, M2 5QR, 0844 858 8521 and p87)* is an achingly beautiful former Methodist meeting hall,

that should be experienced). Medium and smaller venues can be great fun. **Antwerp Mansion** *(Rusholme Grove, off the Curry Mile, Wilmslow Road, M14 5AG, 07939 173063)* is a truly eccentric run-down Victorian mansion turned into a music, art and photography hotspot. **Islington Mill** *(1 James Street, Salford, M3 5HW, 0161 278 6404)* has artists studios in a labyrinthine former cotton mill with live and club spaces too. **The Castle** *(66 Oldham Street, M4 1LE, 0161 237 9485)*, **The Eagle** *(18 Collier St, Salford M3 7DW, 0161 819 5002)* and **Gullivers** *(109 Oldham Street, M4 1LW, 0161 819 2970)* are three associated pubs buzzing with live music. **Joshua Brooks** *(106 Princess Street, M1 6NE)* is popular with students. Meanwhile the indefatigable **Night and Day** *(26 Oldham Street, M1 1JN, 0161 236 1822)* has been boosting the scene for years and is a real

rock'n'roll central. **Ruby Lounge** *(28-34 High Street, M4 1QB, 0161 834 1392)* and **The Roadhouse** *(8 Newton Street, M1 2AN, 0161 237 9789)* are similar stalwarts. **Sankeys** *(Radium Street, Ancoats, M4 6AY)* is a very well-known club in a former mill. Two real oddities but excellent nonetheless are the church venues, **St Phillip's** *(2 Wilton Place, Salford, M3 6FR, 0161 834 2041)* and **Sacred Trinity** *(Chapel Street, Salford M3 5DW, 0161 839 1180)*.

For jazz and world music there are two main venues. **Matt & Phred's** *(64 Tib Street, M4 1LW, 0161 831 7002)* is for jazz but also watch out for the annual Manchester jazz festival in each summer. For World Music try **Band of the Wall** *(25 Swan Street, M4 5JZ, 0161 834 1786)* although the music and performances are not confined to any one genre.

Antwerp Mansion and the action starts

Accommodation

Great John Street Terrace

Manchester's hotels are doing fine according to official reports. In 2014 the city had its highest occupancy rates at 78% occupancy rates. The average room rate was £75 per night. The big problem for the city is the lack of good B&B's close to the city centre and it could do with more central pub accommodation as well. Meanwhile Manchester is poor for convenient camp and caravan sites. With prices always enquire about discounts when booking. Haggling might not be pretty but it could save you a whole heap of money. The best resource for booking is the official www.visitmanchester.com website and its 'stay' section. The prices below are Visit Manchester's at the time of publication. All hotels are city centre and all of them apart from the very basic offer conference and event spaces.

Five Star equivalent

Lowry Hotel *50 Dearmans Place, Chapel Wharf, M3 5LH, 0161 827 4000, 165 rooms, from £118.* The Lowry is a five-star hotel with elegant rooms, marble en-suite bathrooms, River Room restaurant, an excellent terrace bar and the Lowry Spa, with six large treatment rooms and separate relaxation lounges for men and women. Very close to all central amenities.

Radisson Blu Edwardian *Free Trade Hall, Peter Street, M2 5GP, 0161 835 9929, 263 rooms, from £79. Walk one p88.* A Manchester conversion that retains features of this important city building's original charm whilst incorporating new construction and state of the art technological detail. There are two restaurants and a spectacular health spa. Centrally located for all amenities.

Boutique hotels

Great John Street Hotel, *Great John Street, M3 4FD, 0870 220 2277, 30 duplex suits, from £235.* This former schoolhouse bang in the city centre has a cocktail and champagne bar, gym and rooftop garden. There's even a hot tub up on the roof for pure al fresco indulgence. The hotel is adjacent to the former Coronation Street set in the Castlefield area of the city centre. The design throughout reflects the proprietors love of the contemporary.

Velvet Hotel, *2 Canal Street, M1 3HE, 0161 236 9003, 19 rooms, from £119.* Sumptuous bar, restaurant, and hotel on Canal Street in the Village and a stone's throw from Piccadilly train station

Four Star or equivalent

ABode Manchester, *107 Piccadilly, M1 2DB, 0161 247 7744, 61 rooms, from £77.* The hotel sits inside a sparkling conversion of an 1899 textile warehouse complete with some sumptuous tilework. The basement restaurant hosts a Michael Caines restaurant, the two Michelin starred chef from Gidleigh Park in Devon.

Arora Hotel, *18-24 Princess Street, M1 4LY, 0161 236 8999, 141 rooms, from £69.* Contemporary in design yet still maintaining the character of its Grade II. There's a restaurant and bar, a gym and a good location opposite Manchester Art Gallery.

Crowne Plaza, *Manchester, 70 Shudehill, M4 4AF, 0161 828 8600, 228 rooms, from £75.* Set in the Northern Quarter, Crowne Plaza is less than a five-minute walk from major city centre attractions such as Manchester Arena, Printworks, the Arndale Centre. Includes Glasshouse bar and restaurant and gym.

Hilton, *Manchester Deansgate, 303 Deansgate, M3 4LQ, 0161 870 1600, 279 rooms, from £139. Walk three, p135.* Situated within Beetham Tower, Hilton Deansgate also includes Cloud 23, a bar on the 23 floor with 360 degree views. There's a spa, sauna and gym and Podium Restaurant. It's a hotel where football teams love to stay.

DoubleTree *by Hilton, One, Piccadilly Place, 1 Auburn Street, M1 2HY, 0161 242 1000, from £65.* Good location opposite Piccadilly Station with a chic and cool

design livened by contemporary art. There's a sky lounge and a good restaurant.

Macdonald, *Manchester Hotel and Spa, London Road, Piccadilly, M1 2PG, 0161 272 3200, 338 rooms, from £68.* Former Telecoms office cleverly converted into a hotel with perhaps the longest corridors anywhere but also good steak in the Scottish Steak House and full spa facilities.

Macdonald Townhouse Hotel, *101 Portland Street, M1 6DF, 0161 236 5122, 85 rooms, from £68.* Set in a former cotton warehouse, this hotel a good blend of style, space, and comfort. Conveniently located for the Manchester shopping district, theatre, exhibitions, and the city's nightlife. Includes 101 Brasserie restaurant.

The Malmaison, *London Road, Piccadilly, M1 1LZ, 0161 278 1000, from £79.* A funky alternative convenient for Piccadilly Station. The rooms have a bold design and are filled with clever touches. Smoak restaurant is one of the very best providers of steak in the city. There's an on-site spa as well.

The Midland, *Peter Street, M60 2DS, 0161 236 3333, 312 Rooms, from £94.* The grand old lady of Mancunian hospitality from 1903 – see p85. The main atrium provides the best people-watching space in the city. The two dining areas of The French and Mr Cooper's House and Garden, led by celeb chef Simon Rogan, have pushed the hotel to the top of Manchester food and drink tree. Pool, spa and beauty treatments available.

Novotel, *21 Dickinson Street, M1 4LX, 0161 619 9003, 164 rooms from £65.* Modern, crisp design, on the doorstep of Chinatown, the Gay Village and the Oxford Road entertainment corridor.

Hotel Football *99 Sir Matt Busby Way, M16 0SZ, 133 rooms, from £80.* Close to MUFC's Old Trafford stadium and owned by former players, Ryan Giggs and Gary Neville. There's a Café Football restaurant and a rooftop five-a-side pitch.

Palace Hotel, *Oxford Road, M60 7HA, 0161 288 1111, 275 rooms, from £69.* Grade II listed, Palace Hotel is a showcase for the artistry of tilework from the 1890s. The building was the old Refuge Assurance headquarters and it shows in the splendor of the main banking hall. There are two bars and a restaurant.

Victoria and Albert, *Manchester Marriott, Water Street, M3 4JQ, 0161 832 1188, 151 rooms, from £71.* Exposed beams and brick, quaint rooms, bar and restaurant inside a riverside 19th century bonded warehouse. Convenient for Castlefield, Spinningfields and the Museum of Science and Industry.

Aparthotels

Blue Rainbow ApartHotels, *High Street, M4 1QB, 0800 779 7779, 19 apartments, from £99.* Convenient one and two bedroom apartments in the Northern Quarter and useful for the main leisure amenities of the city. There are more Blue Rainbow apartments on the south side of the city centre close to Castlefield (same phone contact as above).

The Place Apartment Hotel, *Ducie Street, Piccadilly, 0161 778 7500, 108 apartments, from £117.* Very impressive loft apartments in former railway warehouse.

SACO Serviced Apartments, *5 Piccadilly Place, M1 3FS, 0161 870 1909, from £85.* One and two bedroom apartments in a modern building close to Piccadilly Station.

Three Star equivalent

Be careful with Holiday Inns, Travelodges and Premier Inns as they might hint they are in the centre but most aren't, the ones listed below are.

Holiday Inn Express, *Oxford Road, 2 Oxford Road, M1 5QA, 08432083005, from £69.*

Premier Inn, *Bishopsgate, 7-11 Lower Mosley Street, M2 3DW, 0870 238 3315* and *72 Dale Street, M1 2HR, 0871 527 9390, from £29.*

Travelodge, *22 Great Ancoats Street, M4 5AZ, 0871 984 6282* and at Townbury House, *Blackfriars Street, M3 5AL, 0871 984 6159, from £42.*

City Centre Pub accommodation

The Crown and Anchor, *41 Hilton Street, Manchester, M1 2EE, 0161 228 1142, several rooms, from £30.* 19th century Northern Quarter pub with startling refurbishment.

The Ox, *71 Liverpool Road, Castlefield, 0161 839 7740, 10 rooms, from £49.95.* Pub accommodation with good food. The en-suite rooms are simple but attend to all the needs of the budget-conscious weekend breaker. Good location in the historic Castlefield area.

Youth Hostels and Backpacker Hostels

YHA, *Manchester, Potato Wharf, Castlefield, 0161 839 9960, 144 beds in dormitories, from £26.* Cheap and cheerful with self-catering kitchen and canal-side restaurant.

Hatters, *50 Newton Street, M1 2EA, 0161 236 9500, 23 rooms, from £15.* Classic backpackers hostel in former cotton warehouse in the Northern Quarter with communal self-catering kitchen and lounge. Close to the main shopping areas and Piccadilly Station. Also Hilton Chambers, *Hilton Street, 0161 236 4414, from £15,* associated business round the corner from Hatters.

GAY MANCHESTER

The Gay Village is principally a social space filled with bars and meeting places. The big celebration is at August Bank Holiday with Manchester Pride and the colourful Mardi Gras procession through the streets. On certain evenings when the place seems populated more by hen parties than locals the Village mood can change and not for the better, but if you know where to go there are cultured retreats. A more serious side is offered by the charities in the area such as the **Lesbian and Gay Foundation** *(5 Richmond Street, M1 3HF, 0845 330 3030)*. This provides information for lesbian, gay, bisexual, transsexual and transvestite communities on sexual health, well being, groups and events.

The history of how the Gay Village developed is set out on page 120. Manchester certainly has a place in the struggle for equal rights. For instance it was in Manchester in 1894 where Edward Carpenter published *Homogenic Love and*

Manchester Pride

its place in a free society which sought to explain and validate homosexual relationships. 'It's difficult to realise the great strain,' Carpenter wrote, 'under which these persons grow up who find their deepest and strongest instincts under the ban of society around them'.

Venue round-up

For excellent drinks, tapas and a lively but good looking venue try the **Molly House** *(26 Richmond Street, M1 3NB, 0161 237 9329)*. Two bars side by side also offer something far removed from the hurly-burly of some of the drinks promotion venues. **Velvet** *(2 Canal Street, M1 3HE, 0161 236 9003)* not only delivers a lush interior for drinks and food but includes a boutique hotel. **Taurus** *(1 Canal Street, M1 3HE, 0161 236 5707)* is almost the Canal Street social club with an easy-going atmosphere for food and drink. **Sackville Lounge** *(46 Sackville Street, M1 3WF, 0161 940 4444)* merges mid-range dining with cosiness. **Via** *(28/30 Canal Street, M1 3EZ, 0161 236 6523)* has a crazy interior full of recycled architectural pieces and gets very popular at the weekend. **Gay** *(63 Richmond Street, M1 3EZ, 0161 228 6200)* seems to having a party every night, is an energetic place, with pop music, dancing and a friendly atmosphere as standard. **Vanilla** *(39-41 Richmond Street, M1 3WB, 0161 637 6258)* is one for the girls and for male friends who know how to behave. **The New Union** *(101 Princess Street, M1 6DD, 0161 950 0101)* has a regular cabaret which is the oldest in the Village and defines rough and ready. The biggest nightclub you couldn't confuse with a bar is is **Cruz 101** *(101 Princess Street, M1 6DD, 0161 950 0101)*. For a complete change of tone the Alice-in-Wonderland themed **Richmond Tea Rooms** *(15 Richmond Street, M1 3HZ, 0161 237 9667)*, is great for cakes, coffees, light meals and quirkiness.

Shopping

Empire Exchange, Newton Street

SHOPPING

There are three main shopping areas in central Manchester.

The shops west of Cross Street and north of John Dalton Street - **Deansgate, King Street, New Cathedral Street and St Ann's Square** - provide a mix of mid-market to high-end shops. This area, especially around King Street and St Ann's Street, is also the place to go jewellery hunting along with the Craft Centre in the Northern Quarter. **Manchester Arndale and Market Street** provide all the household names. The Arndale is the city centre's main shopping mall with fashion shops such as Next plus Waterstones Booksellers, the Apple Store, electronic goods stores, a couple of toy shops and a small market. The main sports clothing shops are split between Manchester Arndale and Market Street. The latter also boasts Boots for pharmacy products, HMV for music and Primark for bargains. **The Northern Quarter** was the old markets area and is defined by smaller shop units, so expect independent and vintage shops, record shops galore, bric-a-brac outlets plus Afflecks Palace and Manchester Craft and Design Centre. Away from these three main areas, Chinatown provides a large concentration of shops specialising in food and drink but there's also gift and electronic goods available.

Department stores and designer

The big department stores names are **Harvey Nichols** (*M1 1AD, 0161 828 8888*), **Selfridges** (*M3 1BD, 0800 123 400*) and **House of Fraser** (*M3 2QG, 0844 800 3744*). The first of these is the place to spend a fortune with all the top designer names in fashion and beauty. Matthew

Harvey Nichols Fashion Show

Williamson, the celebrated Manchester designer, is also represented here. House of Fraser was formerly Kendal, Milne and Faulkner, see p96, and one of the oldest department stores anywhere. In a purpose built department store of the 1930s it retains an air of old-fashioned tradition.

The biggest fashion store dedicated solely to dressing up is in Spinningfields. **Flannels** *(M3 3FL, 0844 332 5787)* is where you're likely to trip over Premier League footballers and their ladies. Most of the big brand designers are there including Jimmy Choo, Alexander McQueen, Stella McCartney, Paul Smith and Versace. Round the corner from Flannels is **Mulberry** *(M3 3FL, 0161 839 3333)* and close by is **Armani** *(M3 3AE, 0161 220 2980)* with a fifteen minute walk away at the top end of King Street the store for designer **Vivienne Westwood** *(M2 2BG, 0161 835 2121)*.

Two minutes from Vivienne Westwood is lingerie specialist **Agent Provocateur** *(M2 4AH, 0161 833 3735)* and down the road **Diesel** *(M1 1JN, 0161 236 5797)* and **Tommy Hilfiger** *(M2 7AZ, 0161 831 7364)* with dedicated stores. **Hermes** *(M2 6AA, 0161 834 5331)*, on the pedestrianised section

of King Street, is for lovers of scarves and accessories. New Cathedral Street is a fashion heavyweight with **Reiss** *(M1 1AD, 0161 831 7994)*, **Ted Baker** *(M1 1AD; 0161 834 8332)* and **Hugo Boss** *(M1 1AD, 0161 834 4047)*.

Second-hand and vintage is all the rage at present. Try **Elite Dress Agency** *(M3 2PW, 0161 832 3670)* on King Street West for hand-me-down designer names otherwise it's up to the Northern Quarter for **Blue Rinse** *(M1 1JG, 0161 834 7877)* **Junk** *(M1 1JW, 0161 238 8517)*, **Pop Boutique** *(M1 1JN, 0161 236 5797)* and **Retro Rehab** *(M1 1JR, 0161 839 2050)* amongst others.

There are a number of good clothes retailers for men. **Edwards** *(M3 2BW, 0161 834 1339)*, the oldest store in Manchester from 1830, and **Jeffery West** *(M3 2BB, 0161 835 9284)* will sort people out for shoes. For handmade suits and shirts try **Frank Rostron** *(M2 4FN, 0161 236 5379)*, **Docherty, Evans & Stott** *(M3 3BN, 0161 835 3245)*, or **James Darby** *(M4 1ER, 07846 614353)*. For 'crafted menswear with an urban edge' seek out **Oi Polloi** *(M4 1LQ, 0161 831 7870)*.

Frank Rostron

Antiques, Music, Oddities, Food and More

Manchester does a good line in crazed bric-a-brac shops. In the Northern Quarter a good exponent of this is **Oklahoma** *(M4 1ES, 0161 834 1136)* while in Chinatown **T.LA Art** and **Craft** *(M1 4EJ, 0161 236 2333)* carries a crazy array of kitsch and even fireworks. **Empire Exchange** *(M1 1HW, 0161 236 4445)* on Newton Street is weirder than both with its stock accurately summed up by the picture on p201.

Manchester city centre doesn't do antique shops but there are two excellent places within a couple or so miles of the city centre. The excellent **In-Situ** *(M15 4EX, 0161 839 5525)*, is a kilometre or so outside the city centre on Chester Road, and a little further out, this time on Stockport Road, is the equally splendid **Levenshulme Antiques Village** *(M19 3NP, 0161 225 7025)*.

Music is very important to the city. For Manchester's oldest, independent, record shop head for **Piccadilly Records** *(M1 1JR, 0161 839 8008)* on Oldham Street in the Northern Quarter. Over the road is **Vinyl Exchange** which does exactly what it says in its title. On the same side of Oldham Road is **Magma** *(M1 1JN, 0161 236 8777)* which sells a fine selection of design, art and style books plus rare magazines. **Paramount Books** *(M4 2AF, 0161 834 9509)* on Shude Hill provides second-hand books. Back to music and if you wish to purchase an instrument then try the charming **Johnny Roadhouse** *(M1 7DU, 0161 273 1111)* on Oxford Road, notable for its folk instruments of all different shapes and sizes. Meanwhile **Forsyths Music** *(M3 2GR, 0161 834 3281)* on Deansgate is among the top five oldest retailers of the city dating from 1857, the piano room is very grand.

A real centre for destination shopping is **Manchester Craft and Design Centre** *(M4 5JD, 0161 832 4274)*, a former fish market, converted into two floors of workshops and retail units. If people want distinctive

Piccadilly Records

jewellery, textiles, accessories and art-works, this is the place. There are over 30 designers at work in the centre.

If art materials, paints, glue and rolls of paper are your thing then try crafts specialist **Fred Aldous** *(M1 1LW, 0161 832 7895)* on Lever Street. Another oldie from 1886 it stocks more than 25,000 products. Sharing the same block is camera central for enthusiasts **The Real Camera Company** *(M1 1JA, 0161 907 3236)*. This has used cameras and helpful staff. On Turner Street not far away is the boutique florists **Frog** *(M4 1DN, 0161 833 3463)* competing with **Northern Flower** *(M4 1LG, 0161 832 7731)* on Tib Street, for lovers of floral artworks.

Between the two on tiny John Street is Manchester's best chocolate specialists, **Bon Bon** *(M4 1EQ, 0161 839 4416)*. Round the corner is **Teacup** *(M4 1NA, 0161 832 3233)* for cakes and bakes. Other good food and drink shops include the **Harvey Nichols deli** *(M1 1AD, 0161 828 8888)* at the Exchange Square store, **Hanging Ditch Wine Merchants** *(M3 1ST, 0161 832 8222)*,

Salut Wines *(M2 2FW, 0161 236 2340)*, **The Whisky Shop** *(M2 7EA, 0161 832 6110)*, **Spirited Wines** *(M3 2BB, 0161 834 7328)* and **Astons** *(M2 7EA, 0161 832 7895)* for rare spirits. **Hang Won Hong** *(M1 4HF, 0161 228 6182)* in Chinatown is a superb grocery.

Afflecks Palace and Arcade

Afflecks *(52 Church Street, M4 1PW, 0161 839 0718)* is an indoor urban bazaar from the 1980s with hundreds of independent traders across the interconnected sites of Afflecks Palace and Afflecks Arcade. Expect a bright colourful, fun retail experience with new fashion, start-up designers, vintage wear, glamour wear, art for sale, second-hand bikes, bits of old robots, fancy dress, poster shops, a condom shop, music, leather goods, accessories, tattooists, tarot and food. The audience is mainly younger but anybody at any age can enjoy a stroll around. Outside on the Tib Street walls are Mark Kennedy's mosaics depicting famous people associated with the city.

Afflecks Palace

INDEPENDENT GALLERIES OF MANCHESTER

Manchester has a thriving art scene beyond the main public galleries. The two most spectacular independent galleries here are Rogue Studios and Islington Mill in former cotton mills. Always ring ahead or email to ensure access.

ARTZU Gallery *(Old Granada Studios, Quay Street, City centre, M3 4PR, 0161 827 1717)* Freshly moved to their new premises, ARTZU is a commercial gallery that is always worth a look. They support established, local, new and international artists working in sculpture, painting and sculpture. **Bureau** *(Ground Floor, 3 Hardman Square, Spinningfields, City centre, M3 3EB)* Located on the ground floor of one of the Spinningfield banking buildings, the exhibitions spread out across the length of the lobby. Varied and diverse, and constanting rotating. **Castlefield Gallery** *(2 Hewitt Street, City centre, M15 4GB, 0161 832 8034)* One of the more venerable galleries, now part of the national Arts Council Portfolio, their exhibitions cover everything from film to painting, design work, the Koestler Foundation, group shows and single retrospectives.

Centre for Chinese Contemporary Art *(Market Buildings, Thomas Street, Northern Quarter, City centre, M4 1EU, 0161 832 7271)* Open since 1986 this gallery reflects the city's Chinese links and community and exhibits works from British of Chinese origin and touring Chinese artists. **Islington Mill** *(Islington Mill, James Street, Salford, M3 5HW, 0161 278 6404)* A former spinning mill with a packed schedule of bands, gallery shows, djs, talks, after parties, residencies and workshops. There is something intriguing on just about every other night, all through the year. **Mirabel Studios** *(14-20 Mirabel Street, City centre, M3 1PJ).* Five years old Mirabel studios houses a host of artists from the region's art schools. They have two galleries – Paper (which showcases works on paper) and PS Mirabel, which is their project space.

Rogue Artists' Studios & Project Space *(66-72 Chapeltown Street, Piccadilly, City centre, M1 2WH, 0161 273 7492)* Rogue Studios' Open Studio is one of the highlights of the Manchester art-year. Over 100 studios are thrown open for three days in September, showcasing a bewildering number of artists' work in just about every medium. They also have two independent galleries in-house including Caustic Coastal. **Untitled Gallery** *(Friends' Meeting House, 6 Mount Street (Bootle Street Entrance), City centre, M2 5NS, 0161 833 3087)* Tucked away underneath the Friends' Meeting House, Untitled is a discrete and occasionally fascinating venue. Minimalist, experimental, surprising.

Work from Manchester artist David Gledhill

CONCILIO ET LABORE

Manchester Coat of Arms

Granted in 1842, the three bands in the shield are derived from the arms of the former Lords of the Manor of Manchester, the Gresleys. At the top there's a ship in full sail, symbolising international trade and enterprise. The coat of arms is crowned by a globe covered with Manchester's symbolic beast, bees. This is because the city's industry, its scientific achievements, and its political credo of Free Trade, had global influence. The supporters, an antelope and a lion, come from the arms of King Henry IV, Duke of Lancaster - Manchester is traditionally in Lancashire. The lion is an obvious symbol of authority, bravery and strength. The antelope, complete with a chain to mark Manchester's industry, is a symbol of harmony, and polity (negotiation is better than conflict). This matches the city motto; Concilio et Labore meaning 'Through council and hard work' or 'By working together we can achieve great things'.

CITY CHRONOLOGY

79 Manchester, 'Mamucium', founded by the Romans.

411 Romans leave Manchester area.

920 Manchester mentioned in the Anglo-Saxon Chronicle when Edward the Elder occupies the town.

1227 An annual fair begins in Acres Field, now St Ann's Square.

1282 Market charter granted to Manchester.

1322 A fulling mill reported, indicating a textile industry already in place.

1375 According to tradition a group of Flemish weavers set up in the town.

1421 St Mary's Church becomes Collegiate - one with a college of priests and elevated status.

1515 Manchester Grammar School is founded by Hugh Oldham, Bishop of Exeter.

1605 Outbreak of plague in Manchester. And again in 1645.

1642 Civil War. Parliamentarian Manchester repels the Royalists.

1712 St Ann's Church is consecrated.

1729 First Cotton Exchange, later the Royal Exchange, is built.

1745 Bonnie Prince Charlie passes through Manchester.

1751 John Wesley, founder of Methodism, preaches at Manchester.

1752 Manchester Infirmary, (later Manchester Royal Infirmary) founded.

1761 Opening of the Bridgewater Canal.

1772 Manchester's first bank opened.

1772 Literary and Philosophical society opens.

1783 First steam mill in the city.

1788 First petition to ban slavery in the British Empire sent from Manchester to Parliament.

1804 Rochdale Canal opens – first trans-Pennine industrial link.

1806 Portico Library, Mosley Street, opens.

1809 New Exchange opened on Market Street.

1817 Manchester Gas Works built on Water Street.

1819 Peterloo Massacre

1820 Manchester Chamber of Commerce founded. Manchester Guardian founded.

1823 Royal Manchester Institution formed - now Manchester City Art Gallery.

1826 Manchester branch of the Bank of England opened.

1830 Liverpool and Manchester Railway opened.

1832 Reform Act gives Manchester two members of Parliament and a third for Salford.

1838 Anti-Corn Law League is founded by Manchester industrialists. The town gains an elected Council.

1842-44 Friedrich Engels settles in Manchester and writes 'The Condition of the English Working Class'.

1846 John Owens leaves money to found Owen's College, now Manchester University.

1847 Collegiate Church becomes Manchester Cathedral.

1853 Manchester formally declared a city.

1857 Art Treasures Exhibition comes to Old Trafford.

1858 First Hallé concerts are held.

1862 Famine in Lancashire and Manchester due to interruption of raw cotton supply during the American Civil War.

1867 Fenian murder of Sergeant Brett on Hyde Road. Three Irishmen are publicly hanged in Manchester and become known in Ireland as the 'Manchester Martyrs.'

1877 New (present) Town Hall in Albert Square opens.

1894 Manchester Ship Canal opens. Thirlmere aqueduct opens, providing Manchester with clean water from the Lake District.

1938 Ringway Airport (now Manchester International Airport) opens.

1940 Christmas Blitz - serious damage on central Manchester, Salford and Stretford.

1948 World's first electronic stored programme computer developed in Manchester.

1952 Smokeless zones introduced.

1956 Granada Television established.

1958 Munich Air Disaster kills 23 including 9 of Manchester' United's Busby Babes.

1960 First episode of Coronation Street is aired.

1962 The Manchester Guardian decamps to London.

1962 Co-operative Insurance Society building opens - the tallest office block in Europe at the time.

1968 Royal Exchange ceases trading.

1974 Greater Manchester Council (GMC) created with Manchester as official centre of 2.5m people. GMC dissolved 1984.

1976 Royal Exchange Theatre opens in former Cotton Exchange.

1977 The Arndale Centre opens - Europe's biggest city centre shopping mall.

1982 Hacienda nightclub opens, closed 1996

1986 G-Mex Centre opens for conferences and conventions.

1992 Metrolink opens - trams return to the streets.

1996 IRA bomb wrecks city centre. The Bridgewater Hall opens.

1998 The Trafford Centre opens - 6 miles west of city, threatening traditional centres.

1999 Manchester United wins the first Treble in English Club football.

2000 Manchester International Convention Centre opens. The Lowry (arts complex) opens at The Quays.

2002 The Commonwealth Games comes to Manchester. Imperial War Museum North opens.

2003 The European Cup Final is held at Old Trafford.

2005 Labour Party Conference held in Manchester the first of many important conferences.

2007 First Manchester International Festival, a festival of 'premieres and original work'.

2007 Tony Blair hands over leadership of the Labour Party and the Prime Minister role to Gordon Brown.

2008 Manchester City bought by Abu Dhabi United.

2010 Ed Miliband elected as leader of the Labour Party beating his older brother David Miliband.

2011 Multi-million pound Etihad Campus announced, Manchester City training facility in East Manchester.

2011 Several thousand relocated BBC staff start working from MediaCityUK.

2012 Manchester City win their first league title for the first time in 44 years. They'd won the FA Cup in 2011.

2013 ITV Granada move to MediaCityUK.

2013 Plans for a high speed link (HS2) announced between Manchester, Birmingham and London. In 2014 HS3 – a high speed link between Manchester and Leeds is announced.

2014 Central Library reopens after four years closed for refurbishment.

2014 £1bn deal announced between Manchester City Council and Abu Dhabi United to build 6,000 homes in East Manchester.

2014 Plans for 13 acre Granada site in the city centre announced.

2014 The biggest political change in Greater Manchester in several generations announced as the ten borough councils reach agreement with Conservative-led coalition Government for devolution and an Elected Mayor for the metropolitan area.

Murder and Sir Lancelot

Lindow Man was sacrificed almost 2,000 years ago. He'd been bludgeoned, garrotted and his throat cut. His persecutors threw his body into a bog or pool which now forms part of the Lindow Moss area of Wilmslow, just south of the city. Celtic ritual murder such as this wasn't unusual. Water carried religious significance for the Iron Age peoples in Northern Europe and it was common practice to make offerings of weapons, clothes, food and even each other, to the deities they imagined lived in water.

Ancient Celtic murder, Lindow Man

Lindow Man takes us back to a pre-Roman Britain, but otherwise there have only been flints, axeheads and pottery discovered in the area. What survives physically is found in the uplands, a hillfort in Mossley, a tiny stone circle above Bolton, but in prehistoric times Manchester was nothing as active as the ritual landscape of Wiltshire with its Stonehenge.

Close to Manchester United's Old Trafford stadium is the A56, Chester Road, a Roman road. When the Roman surveyors planned that straight route in the years after 79AD they would have been cutting a road through a wilderness of scrub oak and birch where wolves, boar and bear roamed. A landscape under which rich coal seams lay waiting for the cataclysm of industry to happen 1,700 years later. There's more on the Roman occupation on page 136.

After the Romans, eventually the Saxons arrived but we know almost as little about them as we do about the area's prehistory. The Dark Ages really were the dark ages. The key physical development was the movement of the settlement at Manchester a mile down the Roman Road to the area of, what is now, the Cathedral. The rocky outcrop here, where the Rivers Irwell and Irk joined was, in the lawless Dark Ages, easier to defend.

The Saxons also signed their names across the region. Greater Manchester is full of tons, hams, fords, hulmes. There is one physical remnant of the Saxon period. Straggling through the south of the city is the old boundary division of Nico Ditch.

There is King Arthur as well. This is *from the Annals of Manchester and Salford* by William Axon from 1878. He quotes the seventeenth century writer Hollinworth. 'It is sayd that a Sir Tarquine, a stout enemie of King Arthur, kept this castle, and neere to the ford in Medlock, hung a bason on a tree, on which bason whosoever did strike, Sir Tarquine, or some of his company, would come and fight with him, and that Sir Launcelot du Lake (below centre), a knight of King Arthur's Round Table, did beate upon the bason, fought with Tarquine, killed him, possessed himselfe of the castle, and loosed the prisoners.'

But at this time Manchester, as with all Lancashire, suffered from its location. The south of the county was an inhospitable place of marsh and bog, isolated between the sea and the hills of the Pennines. When the Domesday Book was compiled, after the Norman Conquest in 1066, Lancashire and Manchester warranted a mere one-and-a-half pages out of 1,700, and that as an appendix to Cheshire.

The Siege of Manchester 1642

During the Civil War Manchester was one of very few towns in Lancashire to support Parliament against King Charles I. It bears the dubious distinction of claiming the first casualty of the war. In a skirmish on Market Street Richard Percival, linen weaver, was shot dead.

On 26 September, 1642, Lord Strange, in command of several thousand Royalists, attacked the town along Deansgate and across Salford Bridge (the Town Hall Mural on this page depicts this assault). When Strange demanded the town give up its store of gunpowder and its weapons, he received the reply that he would get 'nothing, not even a rusty dagger'. The defenders were led by Robert Bradshaw and William Radcliffe under advice from Colonel Rosworm, a German mercenary who'd been hired by the Parliamentarians for £30. The Royalists then offered him £150 but he refused as 'honesty is worth more than gold'.

It rained every day during the siege. As assault after assault broke on the barricades Rosworm had erected, the make-shift soldiers gathered by Strange began to lose heart. On 29 September the popular Captain Standish was killed by a lucky sniper's shot from the church (now Cathedral) tower. The final attack came on 30 September. At the battle's height two barns caught fire, the smoke of which caused confusion. It was raining move heavily than ever. As the smoke cleared it became clear the assault had failed. Strange lifted the siege, still in the rain, on 1 October. 'You came with fire, but God gave us water', the Parliamentarians wrote.

The Royalists lost 200 men, the defenders a mere four plus 'a strange boy' who was 'gazing about him'. Manchester became the headquarters of Parliament in the North West and after the victory gained its first Member of Parliament. The new representative was one of the local gentry: Sir Charles Worsley from Platt Hall in Fallowfield.

After the war Colonel Rosworm would claim Manchester still owed him money. Meanwhile Lord Strange lost his head for a massacre at Bolton, a few miles north of Manchester. Then in 1661 the coronation of Charles II was extravagantly celebrated and the conduit was said to run with claret. Despite this Manchester was punished for supporting Parliament and lost its MP. Such is the fickle nature of human endeavour. By the way it had stopped raining on 2 October the day after Strange had lifted the siege.

Ford Madox Brown's mural in the Town Hall of the siege of Manchester

The '45 Rebellion

The steady 18th century rise to industrial preminence was interrupted in 1745 during the Stuart rebellion. Charles Edward Stuart, the so-called Bonnie Prince Charlie, landed in Scotland to try and wrest the throne from George II of the Hanoverian dynasty. He marched south gathering volunteers. Manchester, as with most British towns and cities, was divided over the cause.

The advance party arrived on 28 November 1745 and consisted of 'two men in Highland dress, and a woman behind with a drum on her knee'. The rest of the army and the prince soon followed. People appreciated having the celebrity of the Prince amongst them and there were 'gatherings and illuminations' but there was less enthusiasm for his cause than he'd supposed. Only 300 volunteers joined him. They advanced as far as Derby and then faced with an overwhelming force of British army retreated.

As they returned through Manchester they demanded £5,000 and took a hostage to ensure payment. The party had turned sour. In 1746 the Stuart cause would be extinguished permanently at the Battle of Culloden. The Manchester men were captured at Carlisle, the officers tried for treason in London and hanged, drawn and quartered.

One of the executed was James Dawson, the fiancé of Katherine Norton. The pair became a song. Nine traitors were to die on the same day as Dawson. Miss Norton followed the hurdles on which the condemned were dragged from prison to gallows at Kennington. She watched as her lover was half hanged, stripped naked, his stomach opened, his heart ripped out and his head cut off. As one report goes, 'she got near enough to see all the dreadful preparations without betraying any extravagant emotions; but when all was over, she cried, 'My dear, I follow thee! I follow thee! Sweet Jesus, receive both our souls together!'

Norton's death by broken heart was marked by the nationally popular 'The Ballad of Jemmy Dawson' with lines such as, 'And ravish'd was that constant heart, She did to every heart prefer; For though it could its king forget, 'Twas true and loyal still to her.'

The heads of two of the officers, Deacon and Syddall, were returned to Manchester and impaled on the roof of the Manchester Exchange as a warning to other Stuart sympathisers.

The confusion over allegiance was summed up by Manchester writer John Byrom whose house still survives converted to the Old Wellington Inn, close to Manchester Cathedral.

God bless the King, I mean our faith's defender!

God bless (no harm in blessing) the Pretender!

But who Pretender is, or who is King,

God bless us all, that's quite another thing!

Bonnie Prince Charlie

The Peterloo Massacre 1819

This crucial event in the struggle for democracy took place on 16 August 1819. The site lies under the Convention Quarter of the city centre. The meeting was part of a larger movement campaigning for a national extension of the vote to all adults at a time of deepening poverty. It also called for representation in Parliament with a redistribution of MPs to new industrial towns such as Manchester.

To have little direct influence on the government was a cause of growing anger. Thousands, in particular, of handloom weavers were caught in a downward spiral of wages and a rise in the price of bread. Representation for them was a matter of life and death.

Words typical of the mood were incorporated in the Declaration to be sent to London by the protesters: 'Governments, not immediately derived from and strictly accountable to the People, are usurpations and ought to be resisted and destroyed '. Yet, despite this, the leader of the meeting Henry Hunt asked people to come 'armed

with no other weapon but that of a self approving conscience; determined not to be irritated or excited.' He didn't want the magistrates to have an excuse for violence.

It didn't work. Shortly before 1pm, the chair of the magistrates, William Hulton, decided the 'town was in great danger', read the riot act and sent the deeply unpopular deputy constable, Joseph Nadin, to arrest Hunt. Nadin said it was impossible so the troops were called in.

Unfortunately it was the volunteer Manchester and Salford Yeomanry who reacted first. Moving into a crowd of around more than 60,000 the Yeomanry became separated from each other, panicked and started to lash out with their sabres. Finally the regular soldiers, the 15th Hussars, led by Lieutenant Colonel Guy L'Estrange, arrived and within 15 minutes the field was clear. Fifteen people died on the day and more than 600 were injured. One man survived because he'd put his lunch, a large lump of Lancashire cheese, under his hat and when the sabre fell it stuck in the cheese. The event was nicknamed Peterloo through its location at St Peter's Field in Manchester and because participants on both sides had fought at the Battle of Waterloo four years earlier.

The immediate effect was further government repression but the long-term influence was one of disenchantment with the existing electoral system, a key step towards modern democracy had been taken.

Shortly after the event, Percy Bysshe Shelley wrote the *Masque of Anarchy* about the massacre with the famous final lines: *'Rise, like lions after slumber, In unvanquishable number! Shake your chains to earth like dew, Which in sleep had fallen on you: Ye are many—they are few!'*

George Cruikshank's version of Peterloo

MANCHESTER 1750

THIS map and description of Manchester, by John Berry, 1750, shows the quiet before the industrial storm. The town already has a reputation for textiles, but the processes are still water or beast powered. The full mechanisation of industry, its power to transform production, to rip raw materials from the landscape, to fill the sky with smoke is just over the horizon.

So while Manchester is an interesting town in 1750 it is still a step away from greatness and notoriety. Yet fortunes are being made, look at the pictures and you can see houses of the wealthy scattered through the town.

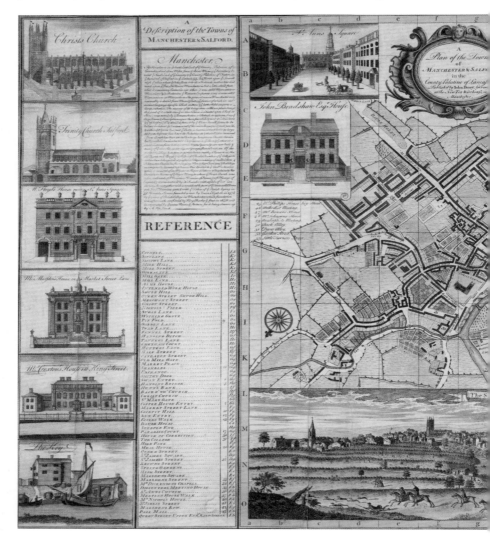

Evidently the gap between super rich and poor was closer in 1750. From the packed impoverished streets around the Cathedral and Withy Grove to the houses of the rich was a five minute walk. Friedrich Engels would note in the early 19th century, how the well-to-do were moving further from the city centre to avoid the poverty and smoke of the new industrial megalopolis.

The classes had yet to split in 1750.

From the buildings in the view below only the three churches are still around today - Manchester Cathedral in the centre - and the towers of all three have been altered. In fact the only constant are the hills in the background, even the original line of the river would be altered as the Industrial Revolution made its impact felt.

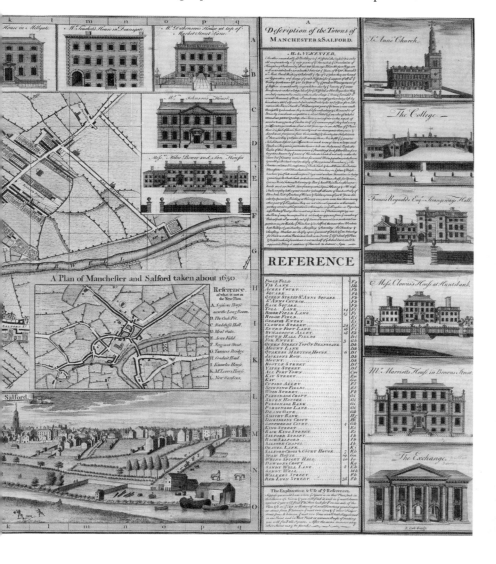

The Liverpool and Manchester Railway

When Prime Minister, the Duke of Wellington, opened the Liverpool and Manchester Railway in September 1830 he ushered in a transport revolution. Despite the earlier line at Stockton and Darlington in the North East of England it was this one which proved rail travel had a future as it almost immediately made money. With an emphasis on passenger travel it also made travel more democratic – for the first time poorer people could journey regularly for a reasonable price. The oldest station in the world survives in the Museum of Science and Industry.

Station on the right, the 1830 warehouse on the left, the oldest surviving railway buildings in the world

It all got off to an inauspicious start with an angry crowd at Manchester protesting about the price of food and about the lack of representation in Manchester. There was tragedy too when William Huskisson, a Liverpool MP, was run down and killed by a train.

The railways made travel easier but also the separation of the classes more pronounced as the purely commuter towns of south Manchester such as Wilmslow, Alderley Edge, Sale and Cheadle Hulme spread over farm fields. This led to a debate about those who owed their wealth to the city abandoning it. 'If God made the country and Man made the town.. the Devil made the suburbs,' thundered local progressive Charles Rowley in 1899.

Manchester man George Bradshaw (1801-1853) understood the effect of the railways more than most. As the impact of the railway system became more obvious

The line crossing Chat Moss

and its organisation more complicated Bradshaw came up with a national railway map and then the famous *Bradshaw's Railway Companion* in 1839. This was the first national railway timetable, a revelation at the time, 'seldom has the gigantic intellect of man been employed upon a work of greater utility,' wrote one commentator.

Unsurprisingly this and subsequent guides were deeply unpopular with the railway companies who found themselves tied to running services on time. Bradshaw has a part to play in the metronomic nature of modern life, the schedules and due dates. In 1844 *Bradshaw's Continental Guide* appeared. This made foreign leisure travel much easier. French author Jules Verne was one of many famous writers who mentioned the works. In *Around the World in Eighty Days* Phileas Fogg sets out from Charing Cross station and, 'Under his arm might have been observed a red-bound copy of *Bradshaw's Continental Rail and Steam Transport and General Guide....* Recently former Conservative Cabinet minister Michael Portillo has based a popular TV series around the guides, *Great Railway Journeys*.

The Manchester School: 'The Myth we live by'

John Bright and his ally Richard Cobden, were in the 1830s and 1840s, the architects of the Manchester School – the only political and economic philosophy named after a UK city. The definition of the Manchester School goes like this. Take away government interference in the economy, let business and trade look after itself and free enterprise will flourish. Thus by encouraging entrepreneurship and rewarding hard work everyone will benefit. Regulate the economy and society will become mired, clogged by a lack of enterprise and limited ambitions.

For Manchester businessmen the delivery method would be free trade, where states removed all tariff barriers to the flow of goods and services between nations. The impetus behind the idea came from the Anti-Corn Law League led from Manchester, which opposed Britain's Corn Laws. These by taxing imported corn, impeded business, kept the necessities of life for the poor (in this case bread) expensive and along with other tariffs caused strife between nations which in turn got in the way of wealth creation for all society from top to bottom. Manchester's Free Trade Hall (now Radisson Blu Edwardian Hotel) marks the victory of the League in 1846, which then moved on to the battle for free trade.

The Manchester School is entwined with liberalism. The influence of the philosophy was important through much of the mid and late 19th century as free trade was increasingly adopted by nations. It withered in the 20th century as governments raised tariff barriers and protectionism re-established itself. But the idea still had legs. Christened neo-liberalism, the Manchester School appeared again in the 1980s with Margaret Thatcher and Ronald Reagan. The underlying morality of the original idea had been lost though and it twisted into globalisation, its symbol the movie *Wall Street*.

Opposite orthodoxies have found common ground in condemning the Manchester School. For the left it was a product of cold careless capitalism and therefore wrong. For conservatives and aristocrats it was unpatriotic and threatened the established relationship between the propertied and the poor and the concept of the nation state. Both Bright (who was a Quaker) and Cobden were anti-war and anti-imperialist, opposing the Crimean War in 1854 at the price of their reputations.

In their version of the doctrine, free trade would ensure world peace, no less. Inevitably this would result in higher living standards for everybody with the ultimate goal of ending conflicts between individuals, groups and nations. In this way and with these freedoms the human spirit would be raised up. Cobden speaking in Manchester in 1846 said, '(With free trade) I believe that the motive for large and mighty empires, for gigantic armies and great navies, for those materials that are used for the destruction of rewards of Labour, will die away'.

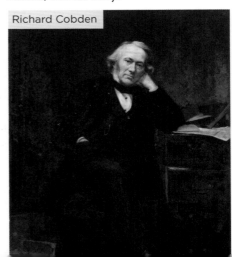

Richard Cobden

The Perfect Industrial City – Nineteenth Century Manchester

Where the actual touch-paper of industrialisation was lit has been the subject of much debate, but its first urban product was Manchester. The growth of the city, in terms of those times, was astonishing. By 1801 the population had climbed to 90,000 and by 1861 it was 355,000. As usual this was a misleading figure. If the wider urban area is taken into account the city was half a million in population, packed into an area not much larger than today's city centre. By 1901, there were more than two million people in the area of present day Greater Manchester.

The whole place was a bustling melting pot of people and businesses: for instance in 1849, along just 300 metres of Oxford Road there were 70 types of occupation from the nation's biggest locomotive works to watchmakers, surgeons and tea dealers. In 1844, Benjamin Disraeli had called Manchester 'the most wonderful city of modern times'. The wonder lay in the way the city had changed economically and socially and had become the model for the new capitalism and its positive and negative effects. Manchester had crashed into international consciousness, it was in historian Asa Briggs' words, 'the shock city of the age'.

The growth in the wealth, fame and prestige corresponded to a similar growth in pride and confidence. As the century progressed art galleries and museums were founded, new libraries opened, parks were laid, and theatres were established. The Collegiate Church was raised to Cathedral status in 1847. Soon after, in 1851, Manchester gained a new university: only the fifth in Britain. In 1853 Manchester obtained the overdue Royal Charter which gave it formal city status.

Cotton might have made Manchester famous but it certainly wasn't the only employer. Other fields of manufacture grew at the same time: iron founding, boiler making, heavy and precision engineering became key players in the local economy. Similarly, Manchester came second only to London in the number and variety of its banks and insurance houses. The city also became the centre for regional retailing.

The former Royal Exchange

Poverty at The Flat Iron Market, Salford

Often this energy was harnessed to political ends. Throughout the century the city was at the forefront of radical political thought. The Peterloo Massacre had profound influence on the fight for democracy. In the years after Peterloo the Anti-Corn Law League was formed, centred in Manchester, which became the Free Trade movement. The city became the capital of Chartism, another route to spreading the vote.

Manchester inherited from such events a reputation for liberalism and radicalism that exists to the present day. The *Manchester Guardian,* now simply *The Guardian*, embodied these principles when it first went to print in 1821. Mass Western vegetarianism began in Salford in 1809, the Co-operative Movement began in Rochdale in 1844 and the Trades Union Congress first met in the city in 1868. A year later, the Reform Bill of 1867 enfranchised much of the male population but excluded females.

In response, Mancunian Lydia Becker formed the National Society for Woman's Suffrage to fight, through constitutional means, for the vote. Later the Manchester family of the Pankhursts would turn the movement radical, the Suffragettes were born. In 1832, the Reform Act had, at last, given Manchester two MPs but it wasn't until 1838 that the town gained an up-to-date administration. This blossomed to such an extent that by the end of the century Manchester was an expansionist city state running education, parks, water, gas, the police and much else. It even pro-vided a large part of the money to build the Ship Canal.

In science and engineering too, Manchester was prominent in many areas. Figures such as John Dalton, J.P Joule, William Fairbairn, Eaton Hodgkinson, Joseph Whitworth and James Nasmyth were globally famous - see the Significant City on pages 74-77.

There was a price for all the dynamism. Visitors were amazed by the contradictions between the wealth where the rich lived, and the poor areas where the factories and the dwellings of the workers lay side by side. The French political philosopher, de Tocqueville remarked, 'everything in the exterior appearance attests the individual powers of Man: nothing the directing powers of society.' The most famous commentator was the German socialist Frederick Engels with his 1844 book describing Manchester, *The Condition of the Working Class in England*.

Generally though, the forces at work in this industrial maelstrom were not understood or were ignored. The drive for increased production and profit ensured that the city grew randomly with little regulation. As a consequence, the poor were largely at the mercy of their masters and any economic vagaries. People frequently led dreadful lives, overworked from an early age, living in insanitary and cramped conditions. The lack of regulation meant pollution destroyed the quality of the air, the water and the earth. The unpredictable nature of the cotton industry, with its frequent periods of booms and bust, simply exacerbated the problem.

Conditions were slow to improve. Real national regulation of industry and industrial practice came in 1833 with the first partially effective Factory Act and there were some local initiatives with the private development of factories and hospitals. Generally however, Manchester's unregulated expansion provided a grim model for future urban development.

MANCHESTER 1889

THIS remarkable bird's eye view of Manchester comes from the imagination of H Brewer. It shows the city in its full industrial splendour. Magnificent and towering buildings grace the city. The Cathedral, The Town Hall, The Royal Exchange are the most prominent – church, commerce, and city.

Manchester was proud of its position in the world and proud of the distance it had travelled from the tiny 18th century town.

As radical politician John Bright had said in 1877, "The population is extraordinary in its number, extraordinary for its interests and industries, for the amount of its wealth, for the power it exercises on other nations." Manchester controlled around 80% of the finished cotton trade and was a major manufacturer of heavy engineering and chemicals.

But a price had been paid for this position. The river, in the foreground, for

instance, is described by a contemporary, as an open-sewer. 'Whole wagon-loads of poisons from dye-houses and bleach-yards are thrown into it; steam boilers discharge their steaming contents, and drains and sewers their fetid impurities.'

Crowded round the central area lie the insanitary rookeries of the poor.

Back in 1844 future prime minister Benjamin Disraeli had written about this new world in his novel *Coningsby*.

'From early morn to the late twilight, our Coningsby for several days devoted himself to the comprehension of Manchester. It was to him a new world, pregnant with new ideas, and suggestive of new trains of thought and feeling. In this unprecedented partnership between capital and science, working on a spot which Nature had indicated as the fitting theatre of their exploits, he beheld a great source of the wealth of nations which had been reserved for these times, and he perceived that this wealth was rapidly developing classes whose power was imperfectly recognised in the constitutional scheme, and whose duties in the social system seemed altogether omitted.'

COTTONOPOLIS

How did the city become Cottonopolis?

A repeated part truth is that it has a wet, humid climate ideal for spinning yarn. More importantly south-east Lancashire has steep streams which could provide power for the mills and give soft water for the washing and bleaching of cotton, there is a coalfield to fire steam engines, salt supplies for developing chemicals and easy access to the west coast for importing the raw material and exporting the finished product. Crucially Lancashire's industrial organisation was fluid. Manchester was unhampered by guilds and trade restrictions. Entrepreneurs were encouraged.

Beginnings

Traditionally textile manufacture began in 1363 with the arrival of Flemish weavers. By the reign of Elizabeth I wool and linen production was important, followed by manufacture of fustians, a mix of linen and cotton. But it was with the manufacture of pure cottons in the mid 18th century when Manchester became significant.
The process of production was run on the 'domestic system'. Merchants 'putting out'

Manchester Town Hall is topped by a 1.8m (6ft) double symbol of a golden 'cotton boll' but also the sun because the city's trade, particularly cotton, featured across the globe wherever the sun shone

The raw material, a cotton boll

raw cotton to spinners, weavers, cutters and bleachers who worked from home. Technological advance gradually swept this away and the Factory System took over. Kay invented the Fly Shuttle in 1733 and between 1760 and 1790, Hargreaves invented the Spinning Jenny, Arkwright, the Water Frame and Crompton, the Spinning Mule. Meanwhile good turnpike roads were improving communications, cheap coal arrived with the Bridgewater Canal in 1761 and the first steam mill fired up in 1783. Cotton was being imported at a rate of 1000 tonnes a year by 1751, and stood at 45.2 thousand tonnes by 1816.

Heyday

The mighty engine of manufacturing and servicing the cotton industry seemed unstoppable. Production would peak in 1912-14 with up to 8bn linear yards of finished cotton produced, the nearest

Mill workers

Ancoats and industry

rival was Japan with 56m linear yards. As Britain expanded its industrial base the significance nationally of the cotton trade to overseas earnings fell from 50% in 1830 to 25% by WWI – but that was still a huge contribution. The character of Manchester changed during the period, not least as the buildings blackened under the endless smoke and soot. It also changed as the cotton mills employed less in the city as the century wore on. By 1840 only 18% of the work force worked in cotton manufacture, but Manchester became the commercial centre of the industry, its clearing house. The dominant building was the stately warehouse for the display of finished cotton goods or the ornate bank and office providing loans and credit for the production of cotton. Above all Manchester was the town of the Royal Exchange. Production became concentrated in the outer towns, spinning nearby in Bolton, Oldham and Stockport, weaving in towns to the north such as Preston, Burnley, and Blackburn. The trade in cotton amounted to 50% of British exports in the 1830s, and stood at 80% of global cotton piece goods in the 1880s.

Decline

Reliance on a distant raw material made the trade vulnerable. The American Civil War showed this, when the supply from the Confederate States had been blockaded by the Union North. Sourcing raw cotton

from India and Egypt and the growth of trade with the British Empire maintained the industry until after WWI. But business declined as production rose in countries close to the raw material and with cheaper labour or with more up-to-date methods. To shore up the industry, there was a rise in tariffs for cotton imports plus schemes to reduce excess production. It was too late, a reluctance to develop new business practices and to invest in new machines, for example move from spinning mules to ring spinners, killed the Manchester and UK trade. It was 'the most terrible retreat in the history of industry'.

Ancoats mills, symphonies in brick

Manchester Art Treasures Exhibition 1857

Following on from the success of the Great Exhibition in London in 1851, and subsequent exhibitions in Dublin and Paris, all focussing largely on industry and science, Mancunians proposed an Art Treasures Exhibition. The idea was dreamt up in February 1856, money raised in March, royal approval granted in May, building at Old Trafford began in late summer and by February 1857 a building the size of a couple of football pitches with its own railway sidings was ready to receive more than 16,000 artworks.

In May 1857 the Exhibition opened and during the next 142 days 1.3m people visited including Queen Victoria and Prince Albert, the King of Belgium, the Queen of the Netherlands, Louis Napoleon, Benjamin Disraeli, William Ewart Gladstone, Lord Palmerston, the 2nd Duke of Wellington, Charles Dickens, Alfred Lord Tennyson, Florence Nightingale, Elizabeth Gaskell, John Ruskin, Nathaniel Hawthorne, and Maria Mitchell. Over the entrance to the Exhibition were words from poet John Keats, 'A thing of beauty is a joy forever'.

The Exhibition didn't last forever. By the end of the year in 1857 it had been demol-ished, its 650 tons of cast iron, 600 tons of wrought iron, 65,000 square feet of glass and 1.5 million bricks recycled.

The organisers and sponsors of the Exhibition, who all had to come from Manchester postal addresses, made a small profit of £304 which was used for charitable purposes. From inception to demolition had taken less than two years for what is still, arguably, the largest temporary assembly of artworks ever achieved.

There are some permanent reminders of the event. German musician Charles Hallé had assembled a group of musicians to entertain the guests. The response encouraged him to set up the Hallé Orchestra in the city. Meanwhile a work by Michelangelo, now at the National Gallery gained the name, the *Manchester Madonna*, after display at the Exhibition.

The Exhibition was also responsible for popularising the works of British 'Pre-Raphaelite' artists, and the new curatorial idea of displaying art in schools or periods rather than randomly scattered together.

Art Treasures Exhibition, below, The Manchester Madonna, right

Manchester Ship Canal

In 1882 Daniel Adamson, an eminent Manchester engineer, organised a campaign for the construction of a canal to allow ocean-going traffic to sail inland as far as the city. In 1885 Parliament approved the Ship Canal Act, despite strong opposition from Liverpool Docks and the railway companies. It was these bodies which had fuelled the impulse for the canal through the tariffs they imposed on Manchester products. It had cost 19s 3d to send a ton of finished cotton from Manchester to Calcutta in 1856, of which 12s 6d was incurred getting it out of Liverpool.

Manchester Ship Canal was the largest single engineering project undertaken in 19th century Britain. It took more than 16,000 navvies six years to excavate the 56km, eight metre deep canal. Opened by Queen Victoria in 1894, the trade the canal generated together with the large industrial area of Trafford Park, which grew along the south bank, helped bolster Manchester industry for decades. At one point Manchester was the third largest port in the UK by tonnage despite its distance from the sea.

The Making of Eastham Dock by Benjamin Leader Williams, Tatton Hall

Manchester Ship Canal as it was

The headwaters became redundant as container vessels grew too large. The last commercial visit to the headwaters was in 1982 although large ships still arrive at the grain works and scrap yard a couple of kilometres further down the canal.

Manchester Ship Canal company was during construction publicly funded with Manchester taxpayers' money. After acquiring a majority share holding as the canal declined in the 1970s and 1980s a private company, now called Peel Group, bought the remaining shares. They have developed schemes on the vast property holding of the Ship Canal such as MediaCityUK, The Trafford Centre and the AJ Bell Salford Stadium.

Epic engineering mostly designed by Sir Edward Leader Williams remains from the original construction such as Barton Aqueduct which swings 800 tons of water in the Bridgewater Canal over Manchester Ship Canal to allow passage of ships. The bridges and locks such as Irlam High Line Bridge are equally impressive.

Recreation where once there were ships

Epic engineering, Irlam High Level bridge

The Blitz and Social Engineering

Piccadilly bombed

On the 8 August 1940, almost a year after war with Nazi Germany had been declared Manchester was bombed with a bundle of leaflets titled absurdly, 'Hitler's last appeal to reason'. The bundle failed to open and landed on a policeman's helmet. He was unharmed. The worst nights of the bombing campaign, 'the blitz', were December 22/23 and 23/24, 1940, when more than 300 bomber planes attacked the city and almost 1,000 people were killed and 2,500 injured in Manchester, Salford and Stretford. Over 100,000 homes in the area were damaged along with the Cathedral, the Royal Exchange and the

Free Trade Hall. At one point, the fire, fanned by the wind, was so fierce buildings were demolished to prevent its spread. The old market place of Manchester was destroyed as were the celebrated Assize Courts. They would never be rebuilt. *The Tree of Remembrance* in Piccadilly Gardens by Wolfgang and Heron marks the bombing of Manchester.

The 1945 Manchester Plan, drafted as the war ended, was one of the most ambitious proposed redevelopments. This would have destroyed far more than the Luftwaffe's bombing of Manchester with most of the older buildings swept away in favour of grid-iron streets and the separation of pedestrians and vehicles at different levels. Manchester's celebrated Town Hall would have been demolished.

Lack of money let the city centre off the hook, the inner suburbs fared less well. Through misapplied Modernist ideas and through untested theories dreamt up by middle class designers, municipal housing in the UK plunged into catastrophe. Manchester residents, in particular, paid for its councillors' enthusiasm for the new ideas with concrete hell. Hulme Crescents, Fort Ardwick and other schemes blighted the city. Critic Nikolaus Pevsner writing in 1969 had asked whether these would 'be the slums of fifty years hence.' They were slums within ten years. Worse was the social engineering whereby poorer central populations were shifted to council estates many miles from the city with little consultation. These became sink estates turning inward as the region's industrial base declined and unemployment rose. So while the national economy improved through the fifties and sixties in Britain, the city of Manchester's population if not the region's plummeted. In 1931 the population of the city was almost 800,000 by 1971 it was quarter of a million fewer, as people fled the new slums for the suburbs.

The Town Hall replaced

The IRA bomb and the Commonwealth Games

In the 1980s the city's Labour administration led by Graham Stringer realised Manchester had struck rock-bottom. Encouraged by Conservative cabinet minister Michael Heseltine it began working with private enterprise to deliver a better future. At the same time Manchester's two bids for the Olympic Games might have been unsuccessful but they boosted morale. The city's pop musical resurgence and agencies such as the Central Manchester Development Corporation, reinforced the upswing in mood.

Then at 11.17am on Saturday 15 June 1996 the IRA exploded the largest bomb ever exploded in anger in the UK. The 1,500kg of explosive was in a van parked on Corporation Street and placed 80,000 lives at risk. The emergency services, given 45 minutes warning, cleared the streets and nobody was murdered although several hundred were injured. The damage estimates from the huge explosion, which ripped out the prime retail area of the city, amounted to £700m. The atrocity was turned into an opportunity. Within a few weeks and months a Lord Mayor's fund had raised money to help those affected and a decision had been taken to rebuild the city centre better than before. A myth was born as well. This was that the bomb began Manchester's resurgence when in fact it was already underway.

It took the Commonwealth Games in 2002 to really show Manchester was thinking big again. It also proved Britain could handle multi-sports events and directly led to a successful bid for the 2012 London Olympics. The Games attracted 1m visitors with 4,000 athletes in attendance. For some reason the latter had 150,000 condoms distributed among them at the Games Village. Call that training? The physical legacy of stadia was more permanent. The 2002 message was clear. Manchester was again a focus of UK attention. The global influence of 150 years was never coming back and the indices of health and well-being of the inner populations remained and remain stubbornly low, but the city had restored its can do attitude and was facing the new century with renewed confidence and optimism.

Manchester Today is discussed in more detail on pages 8-11.

Fire Service picture of bomb damage

2002 Closing ceremony

Manchester Day 2014

People

The Philanthropist – Sir Humphrey Chetham (1580-1653)

Chetham (pictured right) was born at Crumpsall Hall and with his brother made a fortune as a money-lender and linen merchant. His wealth made him a target for Charles I who offered him a knighthood as long as he paid a compulsory fee. Chetham refused and was fined, but he was made High Sheriff of Lancashire and had to levy the unpopular ship-money which went straight to the King not Parliament. Despite this, during the English Civil War his Royal associations were forgiven and he became Parliament's General Treasurer for the county. Already Chetham had proved himself a philanthropist and had 'taken up and maintained' 22 poor boys of the district. After this death he went further.

He left money to buy the semi-derelict Warden's College to house 40 poor boys of 'honest, industrious, parents' and provide Manchester with a free public library. The library remains, the school has become a school of music and Manchester retains some of the finest medieval secular buildings in the North of England.

The Church Builder - Ann Bland (1664-1734)

Ann Bland, as the only child of Sir Edward Mosley, inherited the Mosley estates. She married Sir John Bland, a drinker and a gambler as she found to her cost, yet she was 'a strong woman of great character and managed to hang on to her own fortune'. She also supported the Hanoverian succession (William of Orange, Queen Anne and then George I) and therefore wouldn't worship at the Stuart Collegiate Church (now the Cathedral). Instead she built St Ann's Church, laying out St Ann's Square in the process. The coincidence of her name, the Queen's name at the time and

St Ann's Church

the saint's name was no accident, she wanted to be remembered. Ann Bland also introduced the 'harmonising assembly' as one account put it, was an art collector, imported a doll from Paris every year with the latest fashions and frequently wore orange as a political gesture and as a snub to her rival Madame Drake who would wear Stuart tartan (and also smoked a pipe and refused to drink tea preferring beer). Ann Bland is buried in St James' Church, Didsbury.

The Diarist - Edmund Harrold (late 1600s-1721)

Harrold was a Manchester peruke maker or wigmaker, and a dealer in books through which he made extra money. Best of all he was a diarist and between 1 June 1712 and 24 June 1716 his diary has survived giving us a gloriously human insight into Manchester life three centuries ago. In the diary (pictured above) held at Chetham's library he describes death, recreation, drinking and reading. A religious man he desperately wanted to give up drink but failed time and time again, tempted to 'ramble' as he called a pub crawl, at every opportunity. For example: 'This morn I had my old melancholy pain seized on me with a longing desire for drink. So I went & paid my rent yn I sold J.G. a lock of hair pro

Loss 5s 6d; yn I spent 2d with Hall etc; yn 4d with Mr Allen Tourney; yn fought with S.B. at Janewins about a hat; yn went to ye [Hanging] Ditch a Rambl, - Keys, Dragon & Castle, and Lyon till near 12 clk, till I was Ill drunken; cost me 4s from 6-12. I made myself a great foole'. But it isn't all grim. Other entries include: 'Came at ten, went to bed, did wife new fashion, yn fell asleep' or 'Spent 4d, came at quarter past ten, did wife old fashion' or 'Did wife after a scolding bout: now we are friends'. Never sleep on a fight they tell couples - but what was 'old' and 'new' fashion remains a mystery.

The Cook - Elizabeth Raffald (1733-1781)

Good eating has a good pedigree in Manchester. In 1769 local superwoman Elizabeth Raffald (below) published *The Experienced English Housekeeper*, which ran to 13 editions and was pirated 21 times. It was the first mass popular cookbook in English with full recipes and menu recommendations. The suggested second course of a grand dinner consisted of 'roast hare, transparent pudding covered with a silver web, snowballs, moonshine, rocky island and burned cream, mince pies, creerant with hot pippins, crawfish in a savoury jelly, snipes in ditto, pickled smelts, marbled veal, collared pig and potted lamprey, vegetables, stewed cardoons, pompadour cream, macaroni, stewed mushrooms and dessert'. During her time in Manchester, Elizabeth ran a shop, a domestic servants' employment agency, an inside and outside catering business and two pubs. She also wrote the first Manchester Street Directory, the first best-selling English cookbook, *The Experienced English Housekeeper*, and in her last years assisted Dr White with his book on midwifery. And for the final twist: in the 18 years Elizabeth Raffald lived in Manchester, it is said she had 16 children. It's said she died of exhaustion.

The Editor - John Edward Taylor (1791-1844)

Born in Somerset in 1791, Taylor moved to Manchester as a young man and became a journalist on the liberal *Manchester Gazette*. At the Peterloo Massacre in 1819, Taylor discovered the only reporter present from a national newspaper had been arrested and imprisoned and so began interviewing eyewitnesses. His report of the tragedy appeared in *The Times* two days later. The launch of his own newspaper came about in an unlikely fashion. Tried for libel in Lancaster in 1819, Taylor took the extraordinary step of justifying rather than denying his statements. The jury was divided 11 to one, but the dissenter stood firm and eventually persuaded the other jurors to change their minds. A group of likeminded Mancunians were so impressed

with this success they financed Taylor's own paper, the *Manchester Guardian*. The prospectus promised it would enforce the principles of civil and religious liberty. Taylor remained the editor until his death. The *Manchester Guardian* became the *Guardian* in the 1960s when it moved to London.

The MP - Joseph Brotherton (1783-1857)

A cotton manufacturer and Salford's first MP from 1832, Brotherton campaigned against child labour and for improved working conditions in factories. He was a man who also wanted a better quality of life for working people promoting with great energy the creation of public parks, museums and libraries. He was a pro-Parliamentary reform, anti-war, champion of anti-slavery in first the British Empire and then in the USA, and he considered the death penalty barbaric, campaigning vigorously for its abolition. He also argued eloquently the case for free non-denominational education without the chains of religious dogma. He was by conscience a vegetarian, a member of Salford's small but significant Bible Christian Church. His wife Martha wrote the first widely used vegetarian cookbook from 1812. Matthew Noble's statue in Salford touchingly shows him with a flower in his lapel. Brotherton wore a fresh flower every day as a symbol of his belief in the potential of his fellow Man, the beauty of Nature and a reminder that life passes swiftly.

Joseph Brotherton in Bronze

The Thinker - John Dalton (1766-1844)

Of all the dead people featured on these pages you can still see part of John Dalton. His eyes were preserved after death and currently reside in the Museum of Science and Industry. Dalton had after all been the first to describe colour blindness so this seemed apt. Dalton was from Eaglesfield in Cumbria from an impoverished background but spotted early as gifted. He settled in Faulkner Street, Manchester, presently Chinatown, taught maths privately, but also developed through his study of gas his acclaimed atomic theory. As one authority has written: 'By finding a way to 'weigh atoms', John Dalton's research not only changed the face of chemistry but also initiated its progression into a modern science'. A bachelor, gruff in his lectures, his recreation was an annual trip to his native Lake District or a walk every Thursday to the Dog and Partridge in Old Trafford, almost 3 miles south west, for a game of bowls. He recorded the weather every day and studied meteorology so the choice was no coincidence. Prevailing winds blew the fumes of smoky Manchester to the north east. He was a national and local hero when he died. A celebrity. 40,000 people viewed his body in the old Town Hall. His cortege was more than 100 carriages strong, factories and shops closed, there were more than 100,000 lining the streets.

Richard Cobden

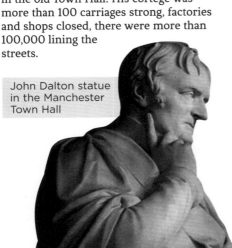
John Dalton statue in the Manchester Town Hall

The Campaigner - Richard Cobden (1804-1865)

Every city needs a Cobden. Born in Sussex, raised in Yorkshire, he came to Manchester to sell and print cotton goods but found politics and the pursuit of injustice far more appealing. This meant he was in financial trouble all his life and had to be maintained by an appreciative group of friends and supporters. The support was handy as he had a wife and five daughters to support. In Manchester he engineered the Charter of Incorporation which gave the city its first modern council, he supported a national system of secular education, campaigned against the Opium Wars, was generally a peace campaigner but perhaps is best known for his association with John Bright MP from Rochdale with whom he led the Anti-Corn Law League to batter down the unjust protectionism of the establishment and land-owning classes. Still with John Bright he then led the Manchester-based Free Trade Movement – see page 217. Famous words of Cobden's include: 'At all events arbitration is more just, rational and humane than resort to the sword' and 'For every credibility gap, there is a gullibility gap'. When he died, John Bright called him 'the manliest and gentlest spirit that ever quit or tenanted a human form'.

Miss Elizabeth Gaskell's house on Plymouth Grove

The Novelist - Elizabeth Gaskell (1810-1865)

Elizabeth Gaskell believed in equal education for men and women, equality of opportunity for all classes and tolerance of others. She utterly rejected the 'seen but not heard' attitude to children. She was orphaned in London at 18 months and brought up in Knutsford by her aunt – an experience underpinning the novel *Cranford*. In 1832 she married William Gaskell, the minister of the Unitarian Cross Street Chapel in Manchester. It was a very happy marriage during which Elizabeth became well-known as a writer, novelist, mother and traveller. She was already a published writer before her novels, but the death of an infant son, threw her into despair. It's said, to take her mind off the pain her husband, William, encouraged her to write her first novel, *Mary Barton*. Elizabeth was clear about her objective from the start. She wanted to show the 'other Manchester', the other Britain, ignored in the salons of polite society, she wanted to understand the effects the new industrial society was having on the urban poor and how that affected relationships between them and the middle classes. For a middle class woman of the mid-nineteenth century to touch on subjects such as crime, poverty and prostitution was courageous, even provocative. In her novels, there's often a returning son, a poignant nod to her dead infant lad, whose death lay behind that first novel. She died

suddenly of a heart attack leaving a devastated husband, four daughters and classic works such as *North and South*, *Ruth* and the *Life of Charlotte Bronte*. Her house, which became the centre of Manchester cultural life, is open to the public.

The Architect - Alfred Waterhouse (1830-1905)

Waterhouse was the perfect Victorian both through his principles but also in the coincidence of his life span which almost exactly matched the duration of Queen Victoria's reign (1837-1901). Born in Liverpool, he studied architecture in Manchester under fellow Quaker Richard Lane. After setting up a practice in 1853, his first big success came in 1859 (he was just 29) when he won the competition for the huge new Assize Courts in Manchester. There was no holding him back after that. In Manchester he built major buildings such as the Town Hall, Strangeways Prison and the main University block, in London he designed the Natural History Museum. The nation is stamped with Waterhouse buildings. His last phase designing hot red terracotta buildings for the Prudential Assurance Society didn't flatter him as the style resulted in the nickname *Slaughterhouse Waterhouse*. He was President of the Royal Society of British Architects from 1888-91, and was a kindly man, married twice, fathering 12 children.

Alfred Waterhouse

The Communist - Friedrich Engels (1820-1895)

Friedrich Engels, a German, lived for almost 22 years in Manchester between 1842 and 1870. He came as an agent for a textile company in which his father had a partnership. Although he loathed the job it allowed him to examine how Manchester had developed. It came to represent for him the perfect capitalist city with all the contradictions and problems that entailed. Touring the city with common-law wife Mary Burns, a working class girl with access to the roughest areas, he compiled material for his famous work *The Condition of the Working Class in England*. This influenced all subsequent thought on industri-

Soviet stamp of Friedrich Engels

alisation, in particular the work of Engels' close friend Karl Marx. The following is an extract: 'Society in England daily and hourly commits what the working-men's organs, with perfect correctness, characterise as social murder, it has placed the workers under conditions in which they can neither retain health nor live long; and so hurries them to the grave'. Marx would visit Engels for weeks on end. In Chetham's Library there's a record of their visit in 1845. It's thought they wrote part of *The Communist Manifesto* in the city.

However Engels was not just a social reformer in a sober suit, in character he was warm and approachable. He loved sport, and used to attend a fox hunt in nearby Cheshire. His character shines through in the list of confessions Jenny Marx, Karl Marx's daughter, extracted from him and her father at Engel's Manchester residence in 1868. Engels is clearly having fun at Marx's sober answers. Engels' last confession is remarkably modern and very funny.

Karl Marx

Your favourite virtue: simplicity
- **in man:** strength
- **in woman:** weakness
Chief characteristic: singleness of purpose
The vice you excuse: gullibility
- **detest:** servility
Aversion: Martin Tupper, Violet powder
Favourite occupation: bookworming
Poet: Dante, Aeschylus, Shakespeare, Göethe
Prose writer: Diderot, Lessing, Hegel, Balzac
Hero: Spartacus, Keppler
Heroine: Gretchen
Flower: Daphne
Colour: Red
Dish: fish
Maxim: Nihil humanum a me alienum puto
(trans) Nothing human is alien to me
Motto: De omnibus dubitandum
(trans) Doubt everything

Friedrich Engels

Your favourite virtue: jollity
Quality in man: to mind his own business
- **in woman:** not to mislay things
Idea of happiness: Château Margaux 1848
- **misery:** to go to a dentist
The vice you excuse: excess of any sort
- **detest:** Cant
Your aversion: affected stuck up women
Favourite occupation: chaffing & being chaffed
Hero: none
Heroine: too many to name one
Poet: Reineke de Vost, Shakespeare, etc.
Prose writer: Goethe, Lessing, Dr Samelson
Flower: Blue Bell
Colour: any one not Aniline
Dish: cold: Salad, **hot:** Irish Stew
Maxim: not to have any
Motto: take it easy

The Inventor – George Garrett (1852-1892)

The remarkable Reverend George William Garrett wasn't a natural clergyman. Born in Moss Side, Manchester, he caught the inventing bug when his father sent him to Owen's College, later Manchester University. After university he persuaded financiers to back his submarine project with £10,000. He had a 33

Emmeline Pankhurst

ton, steam-powered, submarine made at Birkenhead. He set sail for Portsmouth to claim the £60,000 prize the Royal Navy promised if his project worked. The air filtration systems failed and the sub surfaced at Rhyl. Garrett hired a steam yacht hoping to be towed to just off Portsmouth where he'd submerge and re-emerge in triumph. But the yacht broke down, the crew of the submarine went to fix it and the last man out left the hatch open, the submarine sank. A lifeboat came to rescue the crew, rammed the yacht and sank it. The name of the submarine was *Resurgam*, Latin for 'I shall rise again'. It never has. Garrett left the church and in pursuit of his submarine dreams travelled to Sweden, served with the Ottoman Navy, then failed at farming in Florida, became a US Army corporal. He

died of tuberculosis in New York. His father, the vicar of Christ Church, Moss Side, died equally unfortunately; in the pulpit delivering a sermon on the danger of sudden death.

The Suffragette - Emmeline Pankhurst (1858-1928)

Emmeline Goulden's mother and father were both radical in their beliefs, although this hadn't prevented the father surveying his sleeping daughter one night and muttering sadly, "What a pity she wasn't born a lad." Still, Emmeline inherited her parent's radicalism and later married Manchester lawyer, Richard Pankhurst, a committed socialist. Richard died suddenly in 1898. Emmeline, a member of the Independent Labour Party, carried on, becoming the Registrar of Births and Deaths at Rusholme to support herself and four children. In 1903 frustrated by the lack of constitutional progress made by the existing female suffrage movement, which had been led by another remarkable Mancunian Lydia Becker, she set up the Women's Social and Political Union (WSPU) in her home on Nelson Street. After raising the banner of 'Votes for Women' in Manchester in 1905 (page 149) the movement became militant. "That is the whole history of politics," said Pankhurst. "You have to make more noise than anybody else, you have to make yourself more obtrusive than anybody else, you have to fill all the papers more than anybody else, in fact you have to be there all the time and see that they do not snow you under." There is some debate whether the violent tactics put the cause back but, delayed by war, women over 30 got the vote in 1918. Women, over 21, gained the franchise in 1928 – giving them equality with men in this regard. By 1928 Emmeline had done a political U-turn and was standing as a Conservative Party candidate.

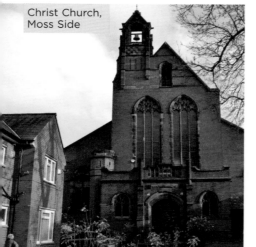

Christ Church, Moss Side

Sir Arthur Lewis

Anthony Burgess

The Economist - Sir Arthur Lewis (1915-1991)

Lewis was the first black Nobel Prize winner in an academic category, indeed the first black winner in any category other than peace. He was from the Caribbean island of Saint Lucia, but studied and taught at the London School of Economics. However it was in Manchester from 1948 to 1957, as the first black professor in the UK, where he made his major contributions to development and growth economics leading to the 1979 Nobel Prize. In essence, he placed 'development in a historical context, stressing the transfer of labour from the traditional agricultural sector to the more productive industrial sector'. In his view development was not an isolated exercise but one in which political, social and cultural influences were crucial. This became known as the 'Lewis Model'. He also believed further education was key to progress. With his prestigious colleague Max Gluckman, Professor of Social Anthropology, he set up two social and educational centres for Manchester's Afro-Caribbean population. After Manchester he led the University College of the West Indies, later working at Princeton in the States. He has a building named after him within the University of Manchester campus.

The Polymath – Anthony Burgess (1917-1993)

One brief biog of deceased Manchester author Anthony Burgess reads 'English author, poet, playwright, composer, linguist, translator and critic'. It might also have added, 'drinker, smoker, periodic curmudgeon, conversationalist and general good egg.' Born in Harpurhey, Manchester, as John Burgess Wilson, he changed his writer's name to Anthony Burgess using his confirmation name and his mother's surname. As for his other parent Burgess claimed he was 'a mostly absent drunk who called himself a father'. He became a novelist while teaching in the then British colony of Burma. He is remembered principally for *A Clockwork Orange*, the bleak but powerful view of a brutal future, adapted into a Stanley Kubrick film in 1971. Other works, such as those in the *Enderby Series* are better novels. For insight into Manchester in the first half of the 20th century, the novel *Any Old Iron* and wonderfully entertaining autobiography, *Big God, Little Wilson*, are recommended. His first wife Lynne, died of cirrhosis. Burgess's second wife, an Italian translator, Liliana Macellari, created the International Anthony Burgess Foundation, financing it through Burgess' estate. Burgess was a *bon viveur* and created his own cocktail called Hangman's Blood: 'Into a pint glass,' he wrote, 'pour double measures of gin, whisky, rum, port, brandy, add a small bottle of stout, top with champagne. It tastes very smooth and induces a somewhat metaphysical elation'.

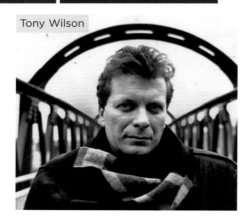

Tony Wilson

The Impresario - Anthony Wilson (1950-2007)

Cultural Manchester adores the legacy and memory of Anthony 'Tony' Wilson. His urbane confidence, fierce wit and sharp humour imbued the city, or at least the people he encountered, with a metro-politan confidence. He was a broadcaster, impresario, writer and the owner of Factory Records, the archetypal post-punk 'indie' label. With bands such as Joy Division, New Order, Happy Mondays and others he was the music critic's darling. When the Hacienda nightclub opened in 1982, the legend of both Factory and Wilson was enhanced. By aiming for excellence Wilson was instrumental in reconstructing the identity of Manchester, during a difficult time of industrial decline. The city would probably not have gained Manchester International Festival without

the example he set. The richness and complexity of his character has led to his portrayal in movies. Manchester actor and comedian Steve Coogan played him in Michael Winterbottom's 2002 film, *24 Hour Party People*, and Craig Parkinson played him in Anton Corbijn's 2007 film *Control*. After his early death to cancer, Phil Griffin, writing on Manchester Confidential, said: 'Tony strode down Deansgate and Quay Street a Made Man. Nobody ever took Manchester this way: took it and made it better.'

The Musicians - Morrissey and Johnny Marr

The impact these two made can be seen regularly on Manchester streets. The music they created in 1980s band The Smiths still drags fans from all over the world to visit the sites associated with the songs. The voice and words of Morrissey (b.1959), the guitar of Marr (b.1963) and that sturdy rhythm section of Andy Rourke and Mike Joyce, combined over five brief years (1982-87) to such good effect that people still can't get the music out of their heads. Morrissey and Marr delivered a sound rich with yearning and wit but also utterly distinctive. There was simply nothing like them during their time together. The part-nership blossomed when Johnny Marr, from Wythenshawe in south Manchester, called on Stephen Patrick Morrissey at his home on Kings Road, Stretford, in the spring of 1982. Marr already had the tunes, Morrissey had the words. The name, the Smiths, was chosen to stand in plain counterpoint to the glamorous New Romantic names popular at the time such as Depeche Mode. It couldn't last, despite albums as strong as the *Queen is Dead* from 1986, the tensions in the band were too strong. Morrissey subsequently embarked on a solo career, courting con-troversy wherever he went, not least with his, 2014 autobiography called *Morrissey*. Marr has guested with a several bands and musicians and is also a music producer.

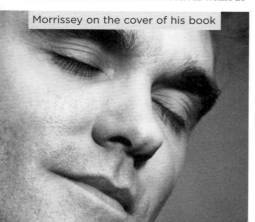

Morrissey on the cover of his book

Ryan Giggs

The Footballer - Ryan Giggs (1973-)

Giggs is Manchester and Salford through and through despite being born in Wales and representing that country at international level. He arrived in Greater Manchester at the age of 6 when his father, Danny Wilson, signed for Swinton rugby league team. When his parents split Ryan Wilson took his mother's surname. The softly spoken Giggs was recognised as a rare talent as a young boy and signed for Manchester United when he was 14. He appeared 672 times for United following his debut at 16, scored 114 times and retired at the end of the 2013/14 season as the most decorated British footballer of all time with amongst other honours, 13 Premier League and 2 Champions' League titles. In the memorable phrase of Sir Alex Ferguson, the overwhelmingly left-footed Giggs left defenders with 'twisted blood'. His most famous goal is perhaps the dribble and fierce shot into the roof of the net in the FA Cup semi-final against Arsenal in Manchester United's greatest ever season, the treble winning 1998/99 campaign. Despite one lurid expose of his personal life in the press, Giggs remains at United as assistant manager. Meanwhile with other ex-players Gary Neville and Paul Scholes, Giggs is investing in his home city with restaurants, hotels and property.

The Broadcaster - Brian Cox (1968-)

Brian Cox is a physicist at the University of Manchester but is better known as the enthusiastic BBC presenter covering astronomy and physics. He grew up a few miles from Manchester city centre in the suburb of Chadderton. At university he combined his studies with his interest in music. He became the keyboard player for the group D:Ream who hit number one in the charts with *Things Can Only Get Better* in 1994. This is appropriate as Cox is a born optimist. In his 2010 TV show *The Wonders of the Solar System* he said: "I think we're living through the greatest age of discovery our civilisation has known. We've voyaged to the farthest reaches of the Solar System. We've photographed strange new worlds, stood in unfamiliar landscapes, tasted alien air." At the Museum of Science and Industry in Manchester in 2011 he underlined the value of knowledge when the £9m cost of a new gallery was criticised. "(It's) a drop in the ocean. Knowledge and its acquisition is priceless. The criticism denies the educational and inspirational potential of these galleries. The investment here can return billions of pounds." Cox is still an active scientist working at the University of Manchester and at the Large Hadron Collider in Switzerland.

Brian Cox

Maxine Peake

Sir Richard Leese

The Actor – Maxine Peake (1974-)

Greater Manchester has given the world a great deal of acting talent with people such as Albert Finney and Ben Kingsley. Maxine Peake, born just outside the city in Bolton, is another in that long line of notable performers and one growing in fame and acclaim as a stage, film and television actress. She is passionate about her city region and also harks back to the old school activist actor with a deep commitment to socialism and heavy involvement in the Working Class Movement Library. Peake has appeared in sitcoms such as *Shameless*, the BBC's legal drama *Silk* and starred in movies such as *The Theory of*

Everything. Her theatre and dramatic work is outstanding. In 2013 she gave a moving and impeccable performance surrounded by candles in the Albert Hall, Manchester, of all 80 plus stanzas of Percy Bysshe Shelley's *Masque of Anarchy*. An associate artist of the Royal Exchange Theatre she took the lead in *Hamlet* in autumn 2014 to, again, great acclaim.

The Politician and the Administrator – Leese and Bernstein

Sir Richard Leese and Sir Howard Bernstein are the double-act of Manchester political and administrative life. Leese is the wily Council Leader and Bernstein is the equally wily Chief Executive. They have ruled Manchester for a very long time, Leese having been in office since 1996, and Bernstein having been in post since 1998. The British system of civic governance, especially where Leese is concerned, has allowed the two men far greater tenure than might be allowed in other democracies. This, and the stable politics of the city of Manchester, has allowed them to pursue long term policies and deliver them – see page 8. They received knighthoods for getting the city back on track after the IRA bomb in 1996, then delivering on the Commonwealth Games, Metrolink extensions and huge physical redevelopment. There have been failures such as their desire to introduce a congestion charge in the city region in 2008 which was defeated in a referendum by 4-1. That aside, the success of these very different men in raising the city's profile has in turn helped boost Greater Manchester's profile to such an extent government has proposed devolving powers and money to the region for the first time in generations. The big question as these men reach retirement is does Manchester have a succession plan good enough to replace talent with talent? Or maybe some say, given they've been in post so long, it's now time for a fresh approach.

Common Architectural Styles

Late Medieval Around the city expect to find half tim-
bered houses, brick buildings and occasional stone structures dating principally from the 1400s and the 1500s.
These are usually of fairly low height, usually houses
of the lower gentry and usually charming, almost as
if they've grown from the ground. The architects have
not been recorded. Almost no humble houses from the
period survive as they were of low quality reflecting
the general poverty of the time. Chetham's is unusual
because it was originally a college of priests rather than
a house. Ordsall Hall; Chetham's; Wythenshawe Hall (pictured); Bramhall Hall.

Georgian The first great building boom of Manchester
largely disappeared under the subsequent Victorian
building boom. Many buildings still survive however,
with classic townhouses and the houses of the nobil-
ity. Most of the buildings attempt harmony, influenced
ultimately by the Italian, Andrea Palladio. Doors with
pediments, generous windows and elegant steps are the
giveaway signs. The Crescent (pictured) in Salford, Platt
Hall, 53 King Street, houses on Lever Street, St John
Street, Heaton Hall. Popular from the second half of 18th
century to the early 19th century.

Neo-Greek As foreign travellers began to travel more
freely around the Mediterranean, the austere purity of the
ancient architecture of Greece became a fashion. Artists
and designers admired its proportions and strength. As
the styled loosened superb buildings showing great creativity were designed, such as the former Bank of England,
King Street by Cockerell sprang up. Portico Library
(Harrison), Manchester Art Gallery (Barry), both Mosley
Street; Friend's Meeting House (Lane), Mount Street.
Popular during the first decades of the 19th century.

Renaissance Seeking a show-off but stately style for
commercial buildings business barons fell in love with
the 'palazzo' style – based on Italian Renaissance
palaces. This followed the construction of Charles
Barry's Athenaeum on Princess Street in 1837. The grand
entrance, the heroic cornice, the regular windows won
the businessmen over completely. Manchester and
Salford Bank (Walters), Mosley Street; The Free Trade
Hall (Walters), Peter Street; Heywood's Bank (Gregan),
St Ann's Street; Princess Street Warehouses (pictured).
Popular from 1830s-1870s.

...common architectural styles continued

Gothic The cold purity of classical styles were 'pagan' according to John Ruskin who lectured in Manchester on several occasions. Gothic was 'christian' it's typical forms, pointed arch, vault, tracery, mimicking God's creations, the trees. Gothic for public buildings and churches dominated the city from the 1850s until 1900. It all began with Alfred Waterhouse's now destroyed Assize Courts and reached its national climax in the Town Hall (Waterhouse), Albert Square. University of Manchester (Waterhouse), Oxford Road (pictured); Police Courts (Worthington), Minshull Street; John Rylands Library (Champneys), Deansgate.

Venetian Gothic Many of Manchester's most notable Gothic buildings were in the sweet almost pretty style of Venetian Gothic with its synthesis of western Gothic and eastern - Byzantine and Muslim – forms. The result is lively facades, beautiful window framings and the jewel-like use of tile or different coloured brick and stone to decorate the buildings. Popular in the second half of the 19th century. Memorial Hall (Worthington), Albert Square; Law Library (Hartas), Kennedy Street (pictured); Reform Club (Salomons), King Street.

Eclectic and Baroque 1890-1914 new steel frame building methods allowed architects to build bigger and faster. The voguish style was Baroque which gave architects greater freedom to produce extravagant structures. The use of tile, terracotta and faience allowed the mass production of decorative work. Eventually, new freedoms led to a hurly-burly of styles called Eclectic. Parrs Bank (Heathcote), York Street (pictured); Midland Hotel (Trubshaw), Peter Street; Bridgewater House (Fairhurst), Whitworth Street; Refuge Assurance (Waterhouse), Oxford Road.

Imperial In the years each side of WWI much commercial architecture became aggressively assertive - Imperial. The preferred material was startlingly white Portland Stone dominating everything around it – until blackened by pollution. The effect was very grand, a disciplined Baroque, as though British architecture was kidding itself that the sun would never set on a British Empire that was effectively dissolved within 40 years. Ship Canal House (Fairhurst), King Street; Midland Bank (Lutyens), King Street (pictured); Arkwright House (Fairhurst), Parsonage Gardens.

Modern New ideas from the continent and America started to hit Manchester in the 1930s with very stream lined modern architecture often with art deco flourishes at Williams' Daily Express Building, Great Ancoats Street, and Kendal's Department Store (Beaumont), Deansgate (pictured). Meanwhile Cooperative buildings such as Redfern House (Johnson and Cropper) brought Dutch Modernism. In the 1950s the International Modern tower arrived particularly with the Albert Bridge House (Banks), Bridge Street), CIS Tower (Hay and Tait), Miller Street, St Andrew's House (Leach Rhodes Walker), Portland Street.

Brutalist A brief period in which architects and sculptors seemed to say we don't care about context, history or geography, we don't care if what we build is attractive; but this ruthless style, with its big concrete members and clumsy collisions is right for the times. Piccadilly Plaza (Covell, Matthews & Partners); Renaissance Hotel (Cruickshank & Seward), Deansgate; Untitled (William Mitchell), Salford University (pictured); UMIST campus (Cruikshank & Seward), south of Granby Row. Popular from the late 1950s to the early 1970s.

Bloody Awful After Brutalism came the reaction. Planners stung by criticism of the 'stained concrete' and 'inhuman' nature of recent work, panicked. The panic manifested itself in chocolate brown and radioactive orange brick buildings so inoffensive they were actively offensive. The big disaster was in Albert Square where opposite the noble Town Hall, the shoddy, brick apologies of Heron House (Leach, Rhodes, Walker) and Commercial Union Assurance (Kingham, Knight Associates), were completed. Popular from the late 1970s and through the 1980s.

Digital/ Eco/ Nobody knows Dominant styles are presently hard to spot. Some Manchester architects such as Simpson still ally themselves to Modernism, others are finding themselves attracted by the opportunities arising from digital technologies and the new disciplines required to be eco-friendly - such as with the headquarters of BDP architects on Ducie Street (pictured). The fashion for statement architecture, The Lowry (Wilford) and the Imperial War Museum North (Libeskind), seems to have waned.

INDEX

Manchester in Literature

Index the city through 19th century novels such as Mrs Banks' *Manchester Man*, Elizabeth Gaskell's *North and South* or Benjamin Disraeli's *Coningsby*. *Hobson's Choice* by Harold Brighouse is a social comedy about a truculent cobbler Henry Hobson. Try Maisie Moscoe's *Almonds and Raisins* for an early 20th century immigrant view. Howard Spring's *Shabby Tiger* is a starker record of the period. Anthony Burgess's novel *Any Old Iron* takes a wry wartime view of the city, while Howard Jacobson's *The Mighty Waltzer* is a post-war love song to youth and table tennis. Emma Jane Unsworth's 2014 novel, *Animals*, looks at ennui, excess and how to navigate modern city life. It's a long way from Mrs Bank's novel.